RELAX

and

REJOICE

for the

HAND ON THE TILLER IS FIRM

By

FATHER M. RAYMOND, O.C.S.O.

DEDICATED
TO
MARY IMMACULATE

THE MOTHER OF THE PEOPLE OF GOD

and

QUEEN OF PEACE

also to

TWO OF HER VERY DEVOTED CHILDREN
MY LOVING AND LOYAL FRIENDS:

Mickey and Jimmie

For All Who Read This Book, I pray:
and as I wrote it I prayed:
"Pour out upon your People,
O Lord God,
THE SPIRIT OF TRUTH AND PEACE,
so that
with their whole hearts they may recognize what is pleasing
to You,
and
in a perfect union of wills, they may
FOLLOW the TRUTH
in
L O V E .   amen.

Publisher
Culligan Book Company
San Bernardino, California

This book can be purchased
at
Publisher's Office
3435 Circle Road
San Bernardino, California
92405

Price $3.50

Nihil Obstat:

JOHN A. BARKER
Censor Deputatus

Imprimatur:

✠ THOMAS J. McDONOUGH
Archbishop of Louisville

May 24, 1968

The *nihil obstat* and *imprimatur* are official declarations
that a book or pamphlet is free of doctrinal or moral error.
No implication is contained therein that those who have
granted the *nihil obstat* and *imprimatur* agree with the
contents, opinions, or statements expressed.

Foreword

Relax!

For everything — yes, everything — is under perfect control — *His!*

Believe that with all your being. For God is not dead. He is not even ill. He is the ever-living God who is the God of all the living. Therefore you can relax fully, know perfect peace of mind, jubilant joy in heart, and live on in love.

That is not pollyannic pap. That is strong meat for strong minds. For it is reality, vibrant with life and more life-giving than the blaze of the sun.

The times are troubled. No one denies that. People are disturbed. Every day brings crises. Many an hour seems to take us to the brink of chaos. Yet, when we have faith in our Faith, we not only know magnificent calm, we communicate it to others.

The "winds of change" are blowing. Fiercely! Were we to give full credence to the press, believe every word from the radio, place complete confidence in television's sophisticated commentators, we could not help concluding that what we are hearing is not the shriek of storm winds, but the angry and menacing howl of hurricanes — and what we see out there, wallowing amid mountainous waves, is the foundering bark of Peter — which will soon sink.

Yet the word to the wise and to all who would have wisdom, is: *Relax!* The reason given is: Everything is under control — perfect control. For it is HIS.

We go further. We suggest that you peer with us through the gloom and gaze steadily upon One who walks the turbulent waters of this world of ours — and realize that what you gaze upon is not a ghost!

Listen — and above the hurricane and the savage hiss of the sea you will hear what we all need to hear these days and these nights of storm: *"Take heart! It is I! . . . Do not be afraid."* (Matt. 14:17)

i

The metaphor is not mine, though the allusion to the Gospel story is. The metaphor is from one who ought to know what he is talking about since he is so fully cognizant of what is actually going on. It was used by Paul VI on May 17, 1967. He told a general audience — and through them, he told the world — that there is a strong hand on the tiller as he calmly said "there can be no surrender of the rudder of our bark — the rudder of the apostolic fisherman."

That metaphor sent me back to the Sea of Tiberias and showed me the similarity between those who were then in the boat that was Peter's and we who are now in his bark. They were out there in that frightening storm by the command of Christ; for it was He who, after the miraculous multiplication of five loaves and two fishes to feed "about five thousand, not counting the women and the children," had ordered them into the boat while He "went up the mountainside alone to pray." They obeyed. They set out bravely and "steered for Caphanaum on the other side of the sea." Night fell. The sea rose; for a "strong wind kept blowing." When they were "far out at sea" and their boat was being "hard hit by the waves," "He came toward them . . . walking upon the sea." Hardy fishermen though they were, and used to struggling with the sea, nevertheless Matthew and Mark tell us that that night "they were perplexed." John goes further and very honestly states that "they were terrified." And we . . . not all of us are "terrified", but many of us are most certainly "perplexed." For the bark of Peter — The Holy Roman Catholic Church — especially since those more than two thousand Catholic Bishops met in Rome to "update" the Catholic Church by that Second Vatican Council, has been finding the sea rather rough, to put it mildly.

Yet there is a sure way to find your "sea legs" and a positively unfailing preventive against "sea-sickness". It lies in listening to the words of Christ and not relying on the voice of some news commentators. It lies in distinguishing clearly between what the Second Vatican Council officially decreed, declared, and constituted, and what the Press of the day claims the council decreed, declared, and constituted. As one reads these "instant theologians" one wonders if they have ever read the sixteen documents that came from the Council as official, or ever realized that there is a difference between a Decree — and there were nine of these, and a Constitution — of which there were four, and a Declaration — three of which were made.

If you would be at ease amid all the restlessness of the times; if you would know tranquility of mind despite the ever-rising perplexities; if you would avoid all serious doubt about the ability of your helmsman or the course he steers; if you would remain utterly calm because completely convinced about the sturdiness of Peter's bark and its never failing sea-worthiness; remember day in and day out that *"Yahweh"* — the name God gave as His own — is properly translated to mean: "I am He who is *always there*," and that Jesus Christ — "God of God, Light of Light, True God of True God" — promised: "I am *with you* at *all* times." That means what it says: *"all* times" — bad times as well as good, amid storm as well as in sunshine, while the "winds of change" blow as well as when there is calm.

You are being told to Stop! Look! and Listen! If you'll heed the advice you'll understand just why Catholics who need to be *concerned* about what is going on in their Church, need never know anything like *consternation*.

Learn from Peter — before he was made Pope. Learn not only how to roll with the roll of Peter's bark, but even how to walk on the turbulent waters of our times. Peter, you know, spoke to Christ that night of storm: "Master, if it is you, tell me to come to you over the water." Jesus said: "Come." Peter actually walked on the waters of a raging sea that night. But, then, he got scared. Matthew tells us that actually "he panicked — and began to sink," because he "saw the fury of the wind." Jesus saved him — but he also rebuked him; and in that rebuke is the lesson we need for our night of storm. "You of little faith. What made you lose your nerve like that?" (Matt. 14:31 Phillips trans.)

Is there any call for us to "lose our nerve"? Indeed there is if we listen to the press. "Vatican Council II burst upon the Roman Catholic scene like a new star . . . Before it closed fourteen months ago, there was scarcely a question that had not been raised about the woof and warp of faith. Its direct and overpowering result: Catholicism has changed more rapidly than in any other period in its 2,000 year history." Thus *Newsweek* for March 20, 1967. One week later *Time* says: "The Second Vatican Council unleashed a passion for change in the Roman Catholic Church that has shown no signs of subsiding. And nowhere has the urge to question and challenge the past taken deeper roots than in The Netherlands, where a branch of the Church once noted for its stodgy conservatism has suddenly become the acknowledged center of avant-garde thinking within Catholicism." And then it goes on to quote Rev. Joos Arts, the priest-editor of the Catholic weekly over there, to this effect: "Orthodoxy is the tragedy of Christianity. What we need is a rethinking of all the basics of Christianity. We must break away from the formal dogma of the Catholic Church."

That such a startling statement was not without substance is evidenced by a letter received at the Vatican from those same Netherlands which ran in part:

> Holy Father, we the undersigned, kneel before the feet of your Holiness and, with great pain and sadness, write to you the following. In the last several years many Dutch Catholic authors and speakers, laypeople as well as religious and secular priests, have championed ideas that are irreconcilable with Catholic teaching — in fact they flatly contradict it. This has given rise to an ever growing scandal; it brings suffering and sorrow to many of the faithful.

> On 9 October 1966 a book entitled *The New Catechism* was published in the Netherlands; it had been commissioned by our bishops. The book presents many ideas that either blatantly contradict the faith or explain various truths of faith so ambiguously that every reader can decide for himself

whether they are orthodox or not. We single out the following examples . . . .

There then followed seven paragraphs of varying length on such topics as Original Sin, Virginity of Mary, the origin of man, the Holy Eucharist, the Resurrection, Angels, and birth control.

The authors of this letter concluded: "If this book is given a wider distribution — translations are already being talked of — it will certainly be a great danger to souls. We humbly entreat your Holiness to intervene, lest our faith be endangered and lest we be a source of danger to others."

Translations of this Catechism have been made. An English version is available. Professedly it is a Cathechism "for adults" — "for inquiring adults." But I, for one, say it is a book that will require vast theological knowledge by any teacher to explain many of its pages in the light of orthodox Catholicism.

Just what form of intervention the Pope made I do not know, but I do know a learned — and a labored — defense of the work was made by a capable Jesuit, Fr. Piet Schoonenberg. He showed how most of the unusual propositions could be held as "possible" opinions — I would dare say many of them at best are "highly improbable."

But that the petitioners were not alarmists can be seen from some of conclusions reached by so-called "lay theologians" over there. *Time* in its March 31, 1967 issue tells how "Dutch theologians" reject original sin as an "inherited spiritual stigma on the soul" . . . and . . . "for this reason question the need for infant baptism." And again: "Heaven and hell just do not preoccupy us any more." and later: "Mrs. Covaart, a mother of three, and a leading Catholic laywoman . . . challenges church teaching on the sinfulness of premarital sex."

Unquestionably, if the Press were right, we would have every reason to "lose our nerve," and conclude that not only we, like Peter that night on Lake Tiberias, are sinking, but that the bark of Peter is going under. If the Press gave us truth we would have little to live for. Look at *Time* for May 19, 1967. Under its column on Religion it has *New Views of Heaven and Hell*. It opens its long article by telling how, while millions of Christians affirm their faith in "God's promise of eternal paradise or perdition beyond the grave . . . many theologians are now attempting to redefine heaven and hell in this worldly terms — not as places where humans somehow survive after death. . ."

With that before you, you can see why Lucile Hasley, in her own witty way, has said: "It might be helpful, if not feasible, if our speculative theologians, with a lust for breaking into sensational print while the iron is hot, were transported to a South Sea island with coral reefs and palm trees . . . there they could work quietly and happily under those palm trees, disturbing no one until, mayhap, they came up with a 'richer and deeper' interpretation that had passed a majority vote. At which point, said interpretation could be forwarded, by carrier pigeon, to the mainland for weighing . . . instead of flashing out, in a half-baked verion, in *Time*."

Lucile had another "revolutionary suggestion" for our speculative theologians. She asked "why can't they use little words to *begin* with" instead of the current theological jargon which few, apart from professional theologians, understand — and perhaps only of a few of them can cope with it. Mrs. Hasley ends with a remark as sharp as a surgical scalpel: "Christ managed" to do it — in simple language. I am aiming to do the same — use little words to keep things clear. Christ did it. Why can't we Christians as least attempt to imitate Him — even in this?

Dan Herr, publisher of *The Critic* advised these speculative theologians to stop gadding about the world giving lectures and making headlines, and go home to truly "theologize." That kind of thing must be done "far from the maddening crowd." It calls for prayer, reading, rumination, deep thought, fierce and consistent logic, unswerving fidelity to tradition. That cannot be done gadding about. So Dan Herr is right. They should "go home" — and even stay at home tending to their real business.

But the point here is that if they stay at home — or even go to Lucile's South Sea Island — there will be less "shifting of cargo" in Peter's bark, with consequent better sailing on more even keel. And yet that is not the sharpest point we wish to make at the very outset of this assurance and reassurance that "all is well" with the helm, the helmsman and the ship he steers. No. The piercing point we wish to make here is that theologians, en masse or individually, are not the *officially* Teaching Church. Never forget that.

Pius XII, as gifted and as graced a man as ever put hand to the rudder of the Church, stated almost twenty years ago, in his Encyclical called *Humani Generis:* "The deposit of faith our Divine Redeemer has given for authentic interpretation not to each of the faithful, *not even to theologians*, but only to the Teaching Authority of the Church."

With paternal gentleness this same kind Pontiff did say: "Although we know that Catholic teachers generally avoid these errors (the very ones you read in the reports of the present day journalists) he immediately added: "it is apparent, however, that some today, as in apostolic times, desirous of novelty, and fearing to be considered ignorant of recent scientific discoveries, try to withdraw themselves from the Sacred Teaching Authority, and are in danger of gradually departing from revealed truth and of drawing others along with them."

Knowing human nature and the temper of the times, Pius XII told us then just what is going on now. He said: "Theories that today are put forth rather covertly by some, not without cautions and distinctions, tomorrow are openly and without moderation proclaimed by others more audacious, causing scandal to many, especially among the young clergy and to the detriment of Ecclesiastical Authority."

Paul VI has echoed and reechoed this truth again and again this current year — for human nature does not change and there is, in our day, a veritable passion, a lust for novelty — and, as is to be expected, especially among the young — laity as well as clergy.

We have good, and even great theologians in the Church today, sincere men who, as Pius XII said, put forth their theories covertly, cautioning all readers that they are only theories, and then adding careful distinctions along with exact definitions. But then along come those others Pius told us about. These all but call a Press Conference to tell the world — without definitions, distinctions, care or caution, and usually along with name-dropping of recognized thinkers — that some tentatively suggested theory of these real thinkers is fact for these "audacious" youngsters. You know the results. Pius XII called them "deadly fruit," and asserted that they can be found "in almost all branches of Theology."

So, as we go along examining the various changes that have been brought about by Vatican II, and showing that there is no need whatsoever for growing excited, we will distinguish clearly between what the Council said — and what some pseudo-theologians say it said. We will go even further and distinguish always between the authentic Teaching Body of the Church and those mere helpers of that Teaching Body — the capable theologians. Finally, we will never allow room for anyone being taken in by those who claim they are appealing to and interpreting the "spirit" of the Council. The letter of the Council's decrees is clear. The "spirit" is no less clear. And any interpretation of either letter or spirit can be given authentically only by those in authority ,in the Church — The Pope, the Bishops in union with him, and the Commissions he has set up for specific purposes. The Council called for "updating"; it never wanted an upheaval.

John XXIII requested that windows be opened, but all he desired was a bit of fresh air. He did not want the "winds of change" to blow off the roof and knock down the walls. Paul VI has put it pithily, pointedly, and with real penetration: "We are to have evolution, but never revolution." That is the "spirit" of the Council, and that is why I can assure youth, middle age, and all senior citizens who are members of the Mystical Body, that "all is well." Peter's bark is seaworthy. The hand on the helm is strong — and steady. That is why we can tell all to "Relax!" and assure the world that the visible Church, instituted by Christ, amidst all the changes, within and without, is as basically changeless as is the Changeless Christ, as timely and as timeless as the ever-living, eternal God — and just as indestructible.

But that is not to deny that the *National Review* had very valid grounds for blazoning on its cover, not long back, the pointed query: *"What in God's Name is Going On in the Catholic Church?"* For, according to reports (all unofficial, of course) Doctrine as well as Discipline was changing, and the insider as well as the outsider came to suspect that not only the Cult and the Code, but the Creed itself of the One, Holy, Roman Catholic Apostolic Church was being tampered with. Nothing could be farther from the truth. And the best answer to the above query is "What is going on in the Catholic Church *is* going on *'in God's Name'*."

It was Christ, you may recall, who commanded the disciples to get into the boat that night they were buffetted by the sea. Obviously we are in the same position and condition thanks to the same Commander. For John XXIII, in the address he made to the Conciliar Fathers on the opening day of the Council, October 11, 1962, confessed that "As regards the initiative for the great event which gathers us here, it will suffice to repeat as historical documentation our personal account of the first sudden bringing up in our heart and lips of the simple words, 'Ecumenical Council'. We uttered those words in the presence of the Sacred College of Cardinals on that memorable January 25, 1959, the feast of the Conversion of St. Paul, in the basilica dedicated to him. It was completely *unexpected*, like a flash of *heavenly* light . . ."

The sophisticated and superior may smile at the italicization of Pope John's words, and say to themselves: "Such naiveté!" How can anyone be so credulous, even gullible, in this Age of the Atom and Era of the Jet?" Let them. Should any such ask: "What do you make of the changes in the Catholic Church?"

answer: "I take them as sure sign that God is not 'dead'; an irrefutable proof that 'religionless Christianity' is a mental aberration, and 'The Secular City' is more phobia than fact." They need that kind of reply, for too many have read Bishop Robinson, Dietrich Bonhoeffer and Harvey Cox; not enough have read Paul VI, John XXIII, Pius XII and those other God-given Pontiffs of this twentieth century — men wise with the wisdom of two thousand years and not mere dilettantes mesmerized by the highly sophisticated developments of science in the last few decades.

God is Real — He is the one Great Reality. It is He who runs and rules the world. That is why John XXIII was always optimistic, never given to pollyannic pap, but at times even brutally realistic. He opened the Council with words that make excellent opening for this book: "In the daily exercise of our pastoral office," he said, "we sometimes have to listen, much to our regret, to voices of persons who, though burning with zeal, are not endowed with too much sense of discretion or measure. In these modern times they see nothing but prevarication and ruin. They say that our era, in comparison with past eras, is getting worse, and they behave as if they had learned nothing from history, which is, nonetheless, the teacher of life. They behave as though at the time of the former Councils everything was a full triumph for the Christian idea and life, and for proper religious liberty. We feel we must disagree with these prophets of gloom who are always forecasting disaster, as though the end of the world were at hand. In the present order of things, Divine Providence is leading us to a new order of human relations which, by men's own efforts and even beyond their very expectations, are directed toward the fulfillment of God's superior and inscrutable designs. And everything, even human differences, leads to the greater good of the Church."

See what Pope John saw: Christ walking on the troubled waters of our turbulent times. Hear what John heard: "Fear not! Take courage! It is I." Think as this wise Pontiff thought, and you will gladly realize that what we call "History," is in all truth, "His Story" — and ours; naught but the steady, straight narration of "Salvation History"; nothing other than the gradual, guided working out toward fulfillment of that mysterious plan conceived before Time was by Him who is Eternal. Over that plan and that mystery One alone is Master; for Divine Providence, to which John XXIII referred, is no empty phrase, but rather that heart-lifting, soul-thrilling reality of the governance of everything in being, from split-second to split-second, by Him who gave all things being, directing each and all to that final end He had in Mind when He, who is by nature Being, decreed to give being to others. We know that end. God Himself told it to us through St. Paul when He had this man from Tarsus write: "He (God) purposes in His sovereign will that all human history will be consummated in Christ, that everything that exists in Heaven or earth shall find its perfection and fulfillment in him." (Eph. 1:10 Phillips trans.)

There you have revealed by God the end of Creation — and implied in that revelation you have the specific end of the Council: changes that will mature you more rapidly and surely into the maturity of the Changeless Christ. Consequently you can see that your real concern, thanks to the Council, is not with the "new breed"; not with the "new theology"; not certainly with the "new morality" — all of which have been played up so sensationally in our ever-sensation-seeking press. Your concern is only with the "new man" spoken of by St. Paul — and that "new man" is to be you. You have been made a Christian by Baptism. You are to be made more Christ by the Council. Therefore you can see that it is to Changelessness that the changes lead, and that the call to renewal can only be answered by grasping more firmly what is "ever ancient and ever new" — the tried, the traditional, the true.

"The greatest concern of the Ecumenical Council is this: that the sacred deposit of Christian doctrine should be guarded and taught more efficaciously. That doctrine embraces the whole of man, composed as he is of body and soul. And, since he is a pilgrim on this earth, it commands him to tend always toward heaven." Thus did John XXIII speak on the very first day of the Council. As you will admit, it has all the familiar ring of the first pages of the old Baltimore Catechism: we men are "creatures, composed of body and soul, made by God, to know Him, love Him and serve Him in this world, and to be happy with Him forever in the next."

Listening to the "instant theologians" or reading the Press who would ever think that John XXIII went on that same day to tell the assembled Bishops that "it is necessary, first of all, that the Church should never depart from the sacred patrimony of truth received from the Fathers." Sitting in on any discussion among the younger clergy who would ever dream that the official call of the Church was — and is — to fidelity to Tradition made explicit by John XXIII, who, after telling of our "renewed, serene and tranquil adherence to all the teaching of the Church . . . as it still shines forth in the Acts of the Council of Trent and the First Vatican Council," asked for a "step forward toward a doctrinal penetration and a formation of consciousness in faithful and perfect conformity to the authentic doctrine, which, however" — and here comes the new element — "should be studied and expounded through the methods of research and through the literary forms of modern thought." To make clarity doubly clear on this issue, he added: "The *substance* of the *ancient* doctrine of the deposit of Faith is one thing. . ." and I hastily add: One thing that cannot be changed! . . . then the Pope concludes: "the way in which it is presented is another."

"*Aggiornamento*" then, that much used and abused word, does not mean uprooting, but only updating; not revolt, but revision; not rebellion, but renewal; not revolution, but simply renovation, rejuvenation, reanimation.

The above is from the official text of the Council. Look at one unofficial interpretation as it appeared in our Press: "The Vatican Council's documents spoke of renewal, but their substance is reform. The Pope, once an isolated prince of God surrounded by his ecclesiastical court, is now apt to govern with the consent as well as the advice of his varied, worldwide hierarchy. In turn the bishops are learning — often painfully — to consult their priests, nuns to speak up to their superiors, and alert laymen to criticize the entire church establishment. In short, a church that has long since sought to be one, holy, catholic, and apostolic, is trying to be more democratic, too." Thus, *Newsweek* for March 20, 1967.

Not a single sentence in that subtly worded paragraph is correct. Yet, so carefully have the words been chosen, and so slyly the sentences shaped, that the impression made on most readers would be that the Catholic Church is suffering something close to a cateclysm. Further on this same slanted article says: "A new force has entered the Church. And few reformers are willing to predict how much of the old Church will remain." Then, to frighten more fully the not so fully informed, these insidious men slip in this remark: "Observes the historian, Msgr. John Tracy Ellis: 'This is not a time of change, but a time of revolution.'" That is not only unfair to the Monsignor, but most unfair to the normal, hurried reader; for it condemns the first by association (placing his name in a paragraph telling of clerical extremists), and confuses the second by using a respected name in so sly and insinuating a manner that the unwary could be led to believe there is real substance to what is at best mere conjecture.

Knowing something of what you have had to face in recent years — and something of what has been thrown in your face by mass communication media — we used as the first word in this book: "*Relax!*" We will show you, as we analyse the changes that have been made, and some that will yet be made, that you have every reason to relax. The last word in this book is to be "*Rejoice!*" — And if you will come along with us, you will see that you have every reason to do just that. For we will prove to you that the Council was a gathering of Bishops from all over the world to discuss *you!* Every change has been made — or will be made — for *you!* The whole purpose of the Council was personal — and *you* are the person it was concerned about. You are the person the "mothering" Church, the "teaching" Church, the "changing, yet ever changeless" Church wants to bring to maturity; you the one she wants to help "grow up in every way into Christ"; you the one she wants to show how "to hold firmly to the truth in love." (Eph. 4:15) In short, you are the one she wants to bring to God through Christ, and bring Christ, our Lord and God, to you.

The position we take is the only position allowed the people of God — the position of the Council itself: not only respect, but true reverence for the past, eager enthusiasm for the present, and truly sanguine hope for the future. Open-mindedness, open-heartedness, genuine tolerance for all of good will, but no hestitation about asserting truth, nor any doubt whatsoever about her own identity. We will be as liberal as the Church, as conservative as the Church, as moderate as the Church. That means change, but never without vital continuity with the past. By showing you what the Council said and why it said it, we will be showing you that the changes made prove that the people of God form one Body — the Mystical Body of Christ, which must change, because it is living, and yet retain its identity as the same Body, because it is His. So relax and rejoice as we first prove that change is not only to be expected, but gladly accepted since it is evidence that God is not dead — and that you are living the life of all living.

ABBEY OF GETHSEMANI
Trappist, Kentucky
Holy ground since year 1848

Chapter 1

"To live is to change . . .
        . . . and to be perfect is
                to have changed often"

(Cardinal Newman)

There are many new changes in the Church, but changes in the Church are nothing new. A vivid, firm hold on and true realization of this historical fact can give reassurance to each of us in this time of implementation of Vatican II. One other historical fact can also help us greatly the fact that there has always been a "new breed" in the Church, always some "new theology," always some "new morality." It was thus in the very beginning, and, I suppose, it will be so until the very end — human nature being what is is.

Maybe that last fact should be the first fact stressed: the People of God are human beings. They have been "divinized," as the early Fathers used to insist. But that "divinization" and "deification," effected by Baptism, did not destroy their human nature. Therefore, expect foibles, failings, and even real failures among the People of God. Not because they are the People of God, but in spite of it! For wherever you find human beings, you find human nature and wherever you find human nature, you find a certain amount of pride.

Christ had not been in Heaven long when there was trouble among His chosen ones on earth. The Acts of the Apostles makes reassuring reading for our day and our times precisely because they show us that we are not experiencing anything distinctly new in the Church these days when so many are saying that almost everything is brand new — and that never before was the Church asked to face such crises. The first Christian Community had hardly been formed when we had scandal. . . Luke tells us in his fourth chapter what he had first enunciated in his second; namely, that "the whole group of believers was united, heart and soul; no one claimed for his own use anything that he had, as everything they owned was held in common. . . None of their members was ever in want, as all those who owned land or houses would sell them, and bring the money from them to present it to the apostles; it was then distributed to any members who might be in need." Acts 4:32-35)

Magnificent picture of harmony. True communism. Unquestionably this kind of life and living brought forth that well known saying: "Behold these Christians. See how they love one another." But Luke opens his very next chapter with the story of Ananias and Sapphira. Selfishness, a desire for security, a touch of greed, led to the sudden death of both a man and his wife who, as Peter stated, had "put the Spirit of the Lord to the test." Then came the squabble between the Hellenists and the Hebrews. Charges of partiality were made. The oil poured on these troubled waters was the "deaconate." It is interesting to note that the first seven deacons had Greek names. We can only conclude that the Hellenists had been upheld in their battle against the Hebrews.

Not long after this we hear of Peter practically being put on trial by his own brethren. Peter was Pope at the time — though, of course, the name was not used. Nevertheless, on his return from Caesarea where he had baptised the Centurion, Cornelius, "the Jews criticised him and said, 'So you have been visiting the uncircumcised and eating with them, have you!'"

Suppose for a moment that there were magazines such as *Time* and *Newsweek* in those days. Can you not see their "cover stories"? POPE CONDEMNED — might readily be one. Now go on with the same supposition and come to that First Ecumenical Council — that of Jerusalem. Saul of Tarsus had been converted. With Barnabas he had worked an entire year in Antioch where the "Good News" had been enthusiastically received by many a Greek. But before long "some men came down from Judaea and taught the brothers, 'Unless you have yourselves circumcised in the tradition of Moses you cannot be saved'. This led to disagreement, and after Paul and Barnabas had had a long argument with these men it was arranged that Paul and Barnabas and others of the church should go up to Jerusalem and discuss the problem with the apostles and elders.' " It was this determination that led to the opening of the First Council in the Church. What a scoop that would make for any reporter in those days— and what sensational headlines for the daily press (had they had one) were in the making as "certain members of the Pharisees' party who had become believers objected, insisting that the pagans should be circumcised and instructed to keep the Law of Moses."

There were "conservatives" in the Church even in that day — and there were "progressives" or "liberals." At least so "the Press" would have called them. When "after the discussion had gone on for a long time, Peter stood up and addressed them" your supposed reporter would have every right and reason to hurry off his hot headline: *"Pope Interposes"* . . . and you can be sure there would be those who would ask: "What in God's name is going on in the Catholic Church?" Others who would accuse Peter, the Pope, of watering down the substance of the Faith, of compromising Doctrine, of being too "irenic" in his "ecumenism" as he said: "Men and brothers, you know that from the earliest days God chose me as the one from whose lips the Gentiles should hear the Word and should believe it. Moreover, God who knows men's inmost thoughts had plainly shown that this is so, for when he had cleansed their hearts through their faith he gave the Holy Spirit to the Gentiles exactly as he did to us. Why then must you now strain the patience of God by trying to put on the shoulders of these disciples a burden which neither our fathers nor we were able to bear? Surely the fact is that it is by the grace of the Lord Jesus that we are saved by faith, just as they are." Acts 15:8-10 (Phillips trans.)

As for "changes" in those days, and for "liberty," with the

consequent uneasiness among many of the faithful, read St. Paul's testimony in his Epistle to the Galatians — and conjure up what the editors of *Look*, or even *Jubilee* and *Ramparts*, let alone your Sunday Supplements would make out of Paul's testimony that "I laid before the Christians there (Jerusalem) in a general assembly the gospel I habitually preach among the Gentiles, and in a private session I laid it before those in authority, to make sure that my course of action was not and had not been in vain. But although Titus, my companion, was a Greek, he was not compelled to submit to circumcision. The question had arisen on account of the false brothers, who had been brought in on the sly, and had sneaked in to spy on the liberty which we enjoy in Christ Jesus, with the intent of reducing us again to slavery. To these people we made no concession; not even for a moment did we yield, in order that what the true gospel teaches might remain in your possession. Furthermore, the men in authority . . . when they recognized the grace given to me, James and Cephas and John, who were considered the pillars, extended to me and to Barnabas their right hand in token of perfect accord . . ." (Gal. 2:2-9) (Kleist-Lilly Trans.)

The most sensational article, though, has not yet been brought before you as we labor to show you that what is going on now is nothing new in the Church of Christ — not even among the hierarchy. The above would have been matter for a claim that the "Liberals" had won a great victory in the Council of Jerusalem — and "religious liberty" had been rescued by the boldness and tenacity of Paul. But can you imagine what a "meaty" article the journalists would have reported about Paul's words to the Galatians: "when Cephas came to Antioch I resisted him to his face because he was wrong. In fact, he used to take his meals with the Gentiles before certain persons came from James. But when these came, he withdrew and held himself aloof for fear of the advocates of circumcision. And with him the rest of the Jews failed to act according to their convictions, with the result that by their inconsistency they led astray even Barnabas. But when I saw that they were not acting straightforwardly in

[4]

keeping with the truth taught by the gospel, I said to Cephas in the presence of them all, 'If you, though a Jew, adopt the Gentile way of life and not the Jewish, how is it that you compel the Gentiles to adopt the Jewish way of life?' " (Gal. 2:11-14)

Obviously, post-conciliar trouble was being had even way back there. Believing, as I do, that Pope John XXIII had such facts in mind as he opened Vatican II and said that "the prophets of gloom . . . behave as though they had learned nothing from history, which is, nonetheless, *the teacher of life*," and that they "behave as though at the time of former Councils everything was full of triumph for the Christian idea and life and for proper religious liberty," believing this, I say, I have had you look at the actualities and the possibilities in the First Council of Christ's Church. For I would have you know genuine tranquillity in these tempestuous times, and one sure way to that quietness of mind and heart is to realize that changes are part and parcel of the life of the Changeless Church of the Changeless Christ.

I go further and point out that "post-Conciliar" times have practically always been just like our own. Read the Epistles of St. Paul, St. Peter and St. Jude — and without reading "between the lines" you will learn that there were "intellectuals" in their day, men who would give the Church a "new theology" because of their particular "insights". They were the "avant-garde" of the first century — and actually in their methods and their posturing were very like the "avant-garde" of our own day. They were known as the Gnostics. They considered themselves very "superior" men. They taught that only the "Initiated" really had the "full faith" — and "true spiritual powers," because only these had superior intellects and superior education. Does that sound familiar? Do the members of the avant-garde today think themselves in any way inferior to the "average simple Christian" — the ones with the "ghetto intellects" — and who have been "brain-washed" by total Catholic Education from Parochial School's first grade to Catholic College degree? Some Gnostics took the terminology of the true Christians, but

[5]

then used it in their own apocryphal gospels, claimed their own "esoteric" revelation, and circulated a very distorted form of Christianity. As you must see, "Gnosticism" is not dead. But you must also see that the Church of Christ has not only survived, but grown! So relax — and rejoice!

You must begin to realize that the "new" is really very, very old. If so you are on your way toward more than calm; you are on your way to courage. For you have seen how Christ's truth triumphed in the troublous times in and after the First Ecumenical Council, and can conclude that He and His Church will triumph over all the trials and troubles after the twenty-first. Heed those in and of the Church who can and do speak officially and you will never be confused. Take for example the words of two Pauls . . . one after the first Council and the latter after the twenty-first:

St. Paul in his first letter to Timothy writes: "I am repeating in this letter the advice I gave you just before I went to Macedonia and urged you to stay at Ephesus. I wanted you to do this so that you could order certain persons to stop inventing new doctrines and to leave hoary old myths and interminable genealogies alone. Such things lead men to speculation rather than to ordered living which results from faith in God. The ultimate aim of the Christian ministry, after all, is to produce the love which springs from a pure heart, a good conscience and a genuine faith."

Look at that "ultimate aim" and compare it with that of the "*aggiornamento*" of our day. How changeless is the ever changing Church of Christ! And to realize how changeless is the ever-changing human nature of the members of that same Church read Paul's next lines: "Some seem to have forgotten this and have lost themselves in endless words. They want a reputation as teachers of the Law, yet they fail to realize the meaning of their own words, still less of the subject they are so dogmatic about." This first letter ends with the appeal: "O Timothy, guard most carefully your divine commission . . . Avoid the Godless mixture of contradictory notions which is falsely known as 'knowledge' — some have followed it and *lost their faith*."

Paul's final directive to his beloved Timothy is one every preacher of the Word needs to heed today. "I solemnly charge you, Timothy, in the presence of God and of Jesus Christ who will judge the living and the dead, by his appearance and his kingdom, to preach the Word of God. Never lose your sense of urgency, in season and out of season. Prove, correct, and encourage, using the utmost patience in your teaching. For the time is coming when men will not tolerate wholesome teaching. They will want something to tickle their own fancies, and they will collect teachers who will pander to their own desires. They will no longer listen to truth, but will wander off after man-made fictions."

The date line on that letter is 65 A.D., not 1965! Yet how timely is this directive for today — and how faultessly descriptive of the mental attitudes of many in this post-Counciliar time.

Because St. Paul had to write such a directive in his day, it should not come as surprise that Pope Paul has had to do the same thing in our day. In an apostolic exhortation to the Bishops of the universal Church, dated February 23, 1967, Pope Paul VI called for the observance of a "Year of Faith" and wrote words very reminiscent of those the first Paul wrote to that early Bishop. His Holiness said: "It is Our desire to point out the opportunity which Divine Providence offers in this celebration to the People of God to examine their faith accurately, to stir it up and renew it, to strengthen it and profess it. We cannot ignore the fact that at the present moment such action is vehemently called for."

That last statement is explained by His Holiness by pointing to the self-idolatry of the modern world, thanks to its development by subjugating nature through ever new and astonishing discoveries. "In its increasing self-esteem it easily tends to a forgetfulness and even a negation of God. As a result of this tendency there has arisen to torment the world the intellectual, moral, and social conflicts which inevitably follow upon the advent of religious decadence. . . Where God is not found, there is lacking also the supreme insight of all *thought*, there is lacking the prime motive of *morality*, without which rightly ordered human relations cannot survive, there is lacking the ultimate key to *reality* as a whole."

That is accurate analysis. That is also implicit prescription for the cure of all intellectual, moral, and social ills: GOD . . . which means for us of today: FAITH.

But now comes what I am sure most Christians and all sincere Catholics want to hear: "Moreover, while the sense of religious devotion now declines in the world, thus depriving faith of its natural fundament, there are springing up here and there in the field of Catholic *doctrine* new theories pertaining to exegesis or theology, frequently borrowed from rash, inept, and profane philosophies which not only call into doubt or weaken the genuine meaning of the truths which the Church has been authoritatively teaching, but also, under the false pretext of adapting religion to the modern mentality, ignore the guidance of the *magisterium* of the Church, fully subject theological research to the principles of 'historicism', do not hesitate to strip Sacred Scripture of its sacred and seriously historical character, and seek to cultivate in the People of God a so-called 'post-conciliar' outlook, that is to say an attitude which, in spite of the solid coherence of the impressive *doctrinal* and *legislative* contributions of the Ecumenical Council with the sacred inheritance of Church doctrine and practice, aims at subverting the traditional spirit of loyalty towards the Church in order to spread the unbecoming and fantastic idea that a new interpretation of the Christian religion has been developed.

"If movements of this kind, divorced from the control of the *Magisterium* of the Church, should ever gain the upper hand, what would survive of the truths of our Faith, or of the theological virtue by means of which we are enabled to maintain them?"

Paul VI is asking for "one great Act of Faith" to restore to the modern world a sense of God. "A single profession of Faith —

one that is individual and collective, free and deliberate, internal and external, humble and frank. We want this profession of Faith to arise from the depths of every faithful heart and to resound with the same loving tones throughout the Church . . ."

The practical suggestions made by the Pope for the proper implementation of this Apostolic Exhortation are simple — and can be followed easily by all. He suggested that we recite "solemnly and repeatedly" — the 'Apostles Creed' contained in every catechism or the 'Nicene Creed' recited during Mass. . ."

That suggestion by His Holiness prompts me to say that if Peter and Paul were to return to earth during this "Year of Faith," they would not have as much difficulty recognizing the Church Christ founded on the one and propagated through the other as some might be led to suspect. The "Nicene Creed" was formulated long after they had gone to their reward (which was nothing less than God Himself for all Eternity!); nevertheless they would recognize the truths enunciated in it as the truths they themselves taught. The "Apostles Creed," of course, would sound more familiar, but were they to be present at a Mass in some Cathedral with the Bishop presiding, surrounded, as the Pope suggests, by his "college of priests, the seminarians, and the lay Catholics active in the promotion of the Kingdom of God, men and women Religious, and as many members as possible of the assembly of the faithful," these two great men of the earliest days of the Church, would recognize, in all essentials, the Creed, the Code, the Cult they had been commissioned by God to make known to their world.

That sounds incredible at first hearing. But the Creed has not changed since their day. The Mass is the one Sacrifice of the New Law. The Code — in basics — was the same in their day as can be gathered from a reading of Acts and the Epistles. They had no church buildings such as we have today; no parishes or parochial schools, no College of Cardinals or Roman Curia. But they did have "Churches," as St. John's Apocalypse makes evident. They did have a hierarchy, as the Council of Jerusalem demonstrates. They did have a Discipline along with

[9]

their Doctrine as practically every Epistle from St. Paul shows.

Neither Peter nor Paul ever assisted at a Papal Mass, a Pontifical Mass, a Solemn High, or a High Mass — but they did offer Mass. Were they to assist today at a Papal or a Pontifical Mass they would find the substance the same — only the non-essentials different. At the outset it is necessary that we note that the noun or *substantive* — Mass — is like Jesus Christ Himself — "the same today as he was yesterday and as he will be forever." (Heb. 13:8) (Jerusalem Bible) The adjectives, those words which *modify* the noun but do *not* change its *nature*, — such as Papal, Pontifical, Solemn, High or Low — have been added to Mass as the centuries advanced.

What has been said about Cult can be said about Code, and, to a certain limited degree, even about Creed. There have been additions, which brought some modifications, but never any real change in nature. You can reduce practically all the variations to what has been offered regarding the Mass — adjectives, as it were, have been added to some substantives. Which means that the substance — or essence — remains the same, while some accidental differences have come to be added to it. And that is, in ultimate analysis, what Vatican II has done for us of the twentieth century. *"Aggiornamento"* can be called "adjectival" — in the sense explained above; and the Catholic Creed, Code, and Cult, despite what the Press may so arrogantly assert, are "substantives."

This Apostolic Exhortation by Paul VI to a "Year of Faith" prompts me to say one thing more to clarify your minds in this time of confusion, and to confirm you in your trust in Christ. It prompts me to link Paul's Exhortation to John XXIII's remark about "history being the teacher of life." Some, even among the clergy, ask every now and then if we are in those days Christ Himself referred to when He asked: "When the Son of Man comes, will he find any faith on earth?" (Lc. 18:8) Jer.) A black picture can readily be painted of our paganistic times. Yet I dare say what chaplains often said to service men during World War II — when the GI's would grow dispirited; namely, "You never had it so good!"

If we look with open eyes at those centuries which have been named "The Ages of Faith," we will come to the grateful realization and the comforting conviction that we, who are now asked to make a "Year of Faith," "never had it so good!" For, first of all, we know quite definitely just who is Pope. That was not so during the "Ages of Faith." Take but one period: that between 1159 and 1179. In those twenty years there were four different anti-Popes. History's hindsight enables us to see clearly who was the legitimate successor to St. Peter, but the "People of God" at that time had no such clear vision. Indeed "we never had it so good."

Secondly, we have just closed an Ecumenical Council without a single condemnation, excummunication, or an "anathema sit." In the "Ages of Faith" that was never so. In the thirteenth, which has been called "The Greatest of Centuries," there were three separate Ecumenical Councils, and after each there were not only excommunications, but actual depositions of Kings from Denmark to Sicily, and from England and Portugal to the furthest eastern reaches of Germany.

We have our difficulties about "Church and State" relations, it is true. But what are they compared to that long, bitter feud between the Hohenstaufens and the Papacy? We have our Communism to battle today; and have had it for fifty years. But what is it compared to what the "People of God" had to face in the "Ages of Faith" when Tartars and Turks were truly "the terror of Christendom" — and were such for nearly three hundred years! Genghis Khan was no gentler than Stalin.

In our twentieth century we have been shocked by the anti-Semitism of a Hitler, but the anti-Semitism in the thirteenth, that "Greatest of all Centuries," was such that the Popes had to renew a Bull extending protection to the Jews five distinct times in fifty short years.

We have our Secularism, Indifferentism, and even our Atheism, to combat today, but we have nothing as formally heretical

[11]

and schismatical to face as they had in the "Ages of Faith."
Hence, we can open our "Year of Faith" with warm gratitude to
God for allowing us to be in such a state that we can honestly
say "we never had it so good!"

Confining ourselves to the Papacy alone during the almost
century that has stretched between Vatican I and Vatican II, we
can be firmly convinced that "all is well" and we have good reason not only to *relax!* but to *rejoice* as well. For in that time we
have never seen a Pope driven from Rome as was Gregory IX
in the early Thirteenth Century; we have never seen the Papal
Chair without an occupant for a stretch of twenty months at one
time and almost three years at another, as was the case in 1241
to 1243, and again in 1268 to 1271; we have never seen a man
who was not even a cleric, elected to the Papacy as was Gregory
X in 1271, and Honorius IV in 1285; we have never seen a very
reluctant hermit practically forced to rule the Church as was
Celestine V in 1294; nor have we seen any Pope do what he did:
resign because of his realization of his utter inability to lead the
"People of God" — then be imprisoned by his successor and
kept in confinement until he died.

History shows us that, troublous as our times may be, they
are relatively tranquil when compared to "The Ages of Faith."
Compare the words of Innocent IV as he opened the Church's
Thirteenth Ecumenical Council with those with which John
XXIII opened the Church's twenty-first. Innocent delivered a
talk that struck fear into the stoutest of hearts as he told of
The Five Wounds of the Church. They were: the evil conduct
of prelates and people; the attacks of the Saracens; the Greek
schism; the Tartar invasion of Hungary; and the Emperor Frederick Barbarossa's persecution of the Pope. We, the Mystical
Body of Christ, suffer today; in some members we even bleed —
for Pascal was right when he said, "Jesus Christ will be in agony
until the end of time," but who would ever preach today as Innocent IV preached then?

But that the Lord of History — Jesus Christ — not only
walks on water, commands wind and wave, but also changes

[12]

hearts and clears the minds of men, is evident from the fact that back there in the Thirteenth Century He brought it about that the Pope was not only able to make— and obtain — a request of the Khan of Tartary, but had the joy of seeing two of the Ambassadors from Tartary baptised during a session of the Council at Lyons. That fact proves that John XXIII, when he made that "opening to the left," about which the Press made so much, was actually following precedent.

More recent History will convince you that you have every reason not only to relax but also to rejoice; for it shows that persistent as men can be in erring, the Papacy can be just as insistent in pointing out their errors and showing them the road to truth.

During the entirety of our twentieth century there has been a "virus" in the air that has been picked up by many. It was isolated and studied by the Papacy from the 1860's on. Powerful "antibiotics" have been prescribed by Pope after Pope from Pius IX to Paul VI. When taken, the "virus" is impotent. But when not taken, that "virus" can be devastating. It is still in the air — and is affecting too many. It has been named "Modernism."

It is an insidious thing which began to affect men about the middle of last century and has continued on into our own. Pius IX recognized the sickness and warned the world of the deleterious effects it could have by attaching a *Syllabus of Errors* to his Encyclical *Quanta cura* back in 1864. But it remained for Pius X to give us the etiology of the sickness. In his Encyclical *Pascendi* of 1907, he wrote:

"The immediate cause is a certain perversion of mind. The remote causes are of two kinds: moral and intellectual. The moral causes are curiosity and pride, the first engendering a love of novelty and of vain knowledge, the latter begetting self-confidence, vainglory, and disobedience. The chief intellectual cause is ignorance of true philosophy and a vain endeavor to ally faith and false philosophy. Ignorance, coupled

[13]

with fear, begets in them a hatred of Scholasticism and contempt for the authority of the Fathers and for the tradition and the *Magisterium* of the Church."

As you see, it is not a physical, but a mental illness; more, it is a spiritual disease. Further, it is one that is spread by "carriers" — and knows periods when it reaches "epidemic" proportions. Ours looks like one of those periods. It may help you recognize these "carriers" by recalling what Pius X had to say of them:

"The Modernists carry on a very active and cunning propagandism to spread their tenets: they ignore redoubtable adversaries and extol to the skies those who favor their views — and among the latter, unfortunately, are to be found Catholics, even Religious, who by unwise and unduly liberal, though professedly well-intentioned, writings, encourage the Modernists."

The Pope then tells what some of those writings treat of, the symptoms and the syndrome of this sickness.

"The Modernists have a mania for fastening reform on everything Catholic —

on *Philosophy* — by aboloshing Scholasticism and substituting modern philosophies;

on *Theology* — by basing rational theology on modern philosophy, and positive theology on the history of dogma;

on *History* — by writing and teaching it according to their modern methods only;

on *Dogmas* and their evolution — by harmonizing them with modern science and history;

on the *Catechism* — by eliminating all dogmas not duly reformed and within the capacity of the people;

[14]

on *Worship* — by reducing external devotions and preventing their further increase;

on *Ecclesiastical Government* — by putting it in harmony with the public conscience, by giving a share in it to the lower clergy and even to the laity, and by decentralizing it;

on *Morals* — by attaching more importance to the active than to passive virtues, by bringing the clergy back to their ancient lowliness and poverty and imbuing them with modern ideas, and, according to some, by abolishing ecclesiastical celibacy." (XI, p. 15 — American Catholic Quarterly Review)

That reads almost like an Index for many of our slick periodicals of the present day, yet it was written in 1907. Modernism, then, is far from dead; and can yet be very deadly. Still, it can be avoided rather easily by those who wish to stay healthy and within the Holy, Roman, Catholic Church. The cure was prescribed by Pius X: *Scholastic Philosophy*. The preventive has been offered by every Pontiff from Pius IX to Paul VI: *think with the Church*. That means: listen to her authoritative Teaching Body, the *Magisterium*.

There will be those who will tell you that neither the *Syllabus* of Pius IX nor the *Pascendi* of Pius X is "irreformable." That is true about some of the propositions Pius IX condemned, and may be true of some of the sentences uttered by Pius X, but the fact is that the Church has been so consistent in it authoritative teaching in this matter of Modernism that chances of there being any "reform" of the "reformable" are meager indeed. For just as there is a strong, straight line running from Leo XIII's *Rerum Novarum*, down through Pius XI's *Quadragesimo Anno*, Pius XII's *Pentecost Broadcast* of 1941, on to John XXIII's *Mater et Magistra* and Paul VI's *Populorum Progressio* on the matter of Social Justice, so is there an equally straight and strong line running from the *Syllabus* of Pius IX down to the weekly *Allocutions* of Paul VI during 1966 and 1967 against Modernism.

For consistency we need but read one passage in Pius XII's *Humani Generis*. "Unfortunately," says the Pope, "these advocates of novelty easily pass from despising Scholastic Theology to the neglect of, and even contempt for, the Teaching Authority of the Church itself, which gives authoritative approval of Scholastic Theology. This Teaching Authority is represented by them as a hindrance to progress and an obstacle in the way of science . . ." You can hear the voice of Pius X in that passage. The voice of Pius XI comes through clearly in this: "It is not surprising that novelties of this kind have already borne their deadly fruit in almost all branches of Theology. It is now doubted that human reason, without divine revelation and the help of divine grace, can, by arguments drawn from the created universe, prove the existence of a personal God; it is denied that the world had a beginning; it is argued that the creation of the world is necessary, since it proceeds from the necessary liberality of divine love; it is denied that God has eternal and infallible foreknowledge of the free actions of men — all this in contradiction to the decrees of the Vatican Council. Some also question whether angels are personal beings, and whether matter and spirit differ essentially. . . Nor is this all. Disregarding the Council of Trent, some pervert the very concept of original sin, along with the concept of sin in general as an offense against God, as well as the idea of satisfaction performed for us by Christ. Some even say that the doctrine of transubstantiation, based on an antiquated philosophic notion of substance, should be so modified that the real presence of Christ in the Holy Eucharist be reduced to a kind of symbolism, whereby the consecrated species would be merely efficacious signs of the spiritual presence of Christ and of His intimate union with the faithful members of His Mystical Body. . ."

That is not from *Time, Life, Look* or *Newsweek*. That is from Pius XII's *Humani Generis*. Hence you can see how old the supposedly new is; recognize old errors even though sporting new labels; and know what is Catholic doctrine and what is mere sensational journalism or sheer speculative — and occasionally very dangerous speculations — in Theology. You will also realize that when John XXIII asked us to be modern, he was not asking us to become Modernists; that when Vatican II urges us to be liberal, it is not encouraging Liberalism; that when the Church exhorts us to be rational, it is not advocating Rationalism; when greater latitude is recommended to all, it is not Latitudinarianism.

With the official teaching of the Church on Modernism clearly in mind, you need never be taken in by the young intellectuals — some even Catholics and Religious — with whom this "synthesis of all heresies" as Pius X called it, is both camp and cant. Nor will you ever be "condemned by cliché" — a thing becoming all too common, yet which should be recognized as Communistic. They condemn their own by such terms as "Revisionist" "Divisive" etc. Some today, on campus and off it, condemn in like manner with such terms as "antiquated," "post-Tridentine," "out-dated," and defend themselves with such clichés as "Post-Vatican II," "Adapatation," "Renewal." There is nothing wrong with Trent or Vatican I; nothing wrong with the *Syllabus*, *Pascendi*, or *Humani Generis;* nothing wrong with Tradition. But there is often very much wrong with those who depart from any of the sound teachings in any of those Councils or documents of the *Magisterium.*

You have seen the wisdom in distinguishing between noun and adjective, between essence and accidentals, between what the Council said and what some say it said. You are now asked to weigh the worth of distinguishing between the concrete and the abstract in order to do away with what so many call "crises." You have read about the "crisis of Faith" — the "crisis of Authority," the "crisis of Morals" the "crisis of Religion" and many other such. But to be accurate, there is no such thing as any one of the above crises. Just as you have never seen love — but only those who love; never seen patriotism but only those who are patriotic; never seen heroism but only those who have been heroic; so also you have never faced any crisis in Faith, Authority, Morals, Religion — but only seen those individuals who were having difficulties with Faith, with those in Authority, with Morality, with being Religious. None of these abstractions need to be changed — for there is nothing wrong with Faith, Authority, Morality or Religion. But there is imperative call for a change of those human individuals who are experiencing crises in these areas. No new morality, new religion, new faith or new authority, but only what the Council calls for — the new MAN.

That call of the Council is nothing new. Paul of Tarsus issued it back in the days of the infant Church. And yet it is a call that is always new. Paul VI issued it afresh when he flew to Fatima for the Golden Jubilee of Our Lady's appearances there. He told the Press that he had gone there to pray first of all for "the internal peace of the Church." The Pontiff said: "We want to ask of Mary a living Church, a true Church, a united Church, a Holy Church." What is that but an echo of what St. Peter, the first Pope, said when he wrote his First Epistle? "Be holy in all you do, since it is the Holy One who has called you . . . your new birth was not from any mortal seed, but from the everlasting Word of the living and eternal God. . . You are new born, and like babies, you should be hungry for nothing but milk — the spiritual honesty which will help you to grow up to salvation . . . you are a chosen race, a royal priesthood, a consecrated nation, a people set apart to sing the praises of God who called you out of the darkness into His wonderful light."

That is the call of Vatican II — that we become what we are: "children of light," flames in Him who is "The Light of the World," so that, as Pope Paul said, ours will be a "world of true men, a world which can never be without the light of God on its horizons."

The Year of Faith, which is to run from June 29, 1967 to June 29, 1968, is to kindle anew that fire Christ came to bring to earth, the fire that purifies and inflames the hearts of men, the fire He lit on Calvary's Cross as He offered Mass, that Sacrifice of His which is very truly *the* Light of the world — *the* sun of God's great universe — the *one* Light that gives true life and real love.

[18]

Paul said he had decided to proclaim this "Year of Faith" in order "to give the minds of the faithful tranquillity." He told those who had come to his general audience that he had keen sympathy with them because of the "immense difficulties your minds must be experiencing, almost inevitably, immersed as they are in the stormy sea of modern thinking about religion and, more precisely, about faith." It was at this audience Paul saw fit to declare that Vatican II was anything but a "liberation from ancient dogmas" and to tell the world, through those who were present, that "while the Council does not treat of faith expressly, it speaks of it on every page of its Documents, recognizes its vital and supernatural character, assumes it to be integral and strong, and builds its doctrine upon it." He went on to say it was the "true faith," he was referring to, "that faith which has Christ as its Source and the *Magisterium* of the Church as its channel."

That is the clear voice of the man who has his strong hand on the tiller and is guiding the bark of Peter through the troubled waters of the twentieth century. That is the voice which gives you all the reassurance you need to know that the actual changes called for by Vatican II are to be welcomed; for they are proof that the Mystical Christ is doing today what the Physical Christ did in the long ago: "increase in wisdom, stature, and in favor with God and men." (Lc. 2:52) For the first thing you are to realize is that change in a living organism is a sign of growth, and you are a member of that living organism which is the Mystical Body of Christ — the Holy, Roman, Catholic Church.

A homely, but I hope a very helpful, example can be given to show why you should rejoice over the changes — the official changes — you are asked to make by the authoritative voice of the Council. Snapshots of yourself as you grew up are all you need to convince you of the truth of this statement. Look at the pictures of yourself as a baby, as a child, as an adolescent, as youth, as adult. Not one of them is alike. Not one of them is essentially different. The face and physical form of the adolescent are greatly changed from what they were in the baby. And

[19]

those in the adult are even more greatly changed than they were from babyhood to adolescence. You have been steadily growing because you have been steadily changing. Yet it has been the same you all the while.

Look now at the history of the Church — and see how the infant Mystical Christ has changed, century after century, year after year, moment after moment. It had to be. It still has to be. For He is living, and change is the sign of life. Yet amid all this changing there is a substantial changelessness — the Person who owns this Mystical Body is the Second Person of the Blessed Trinity; and the Eternally Living God is Changeless.

If you did not change when you were a child, your parents would worry. If you are a parent, you thrill to note the changes in your children; for those changes are proof that the child is growing toward maturity. So, too, with the Mystical Christ — He must change; for He must grow — and grow toward maturity. To aid in that growth the Vatican Council has decreed some changes — It is the part of wisdom to welcome them, to relax and rejoice as we adopt them, so that we might contribute to the growth of Him upon whose maturity depends the life and living of mankind — in time as well as in Eternity.

The same truth of our oneness with Christ Jesus is put before us in the parable of the Vine and the Branches. And if you would know why some things are being cut away in these days of renewal, Jesus will tell you in His own way: "I am the true vine, and my Father is the vinedresser. Every branch in me that bears no fruit, he cuts away, and every branch that does bear fruit he prunes, to make it bear even more. . . As a branch cannot bear fruit all by itself, but must remain part of the vine, neither can you unless you remain in me. I am the vine, you are the branches. Whoever remains in me, with me in him, bears fruit in plenty. . ."

That is the voice you are to hear in these tumultuous times; for He alone can give you true peace, even as He alone can give you real life. He tells you the purpose of all the "pruning." Welcome your opportunity to "grow up in all things into Christ."

Trappists and Trappistines are constantly praying for the people of the world.

Chapter 2

KNOW YOUR WORTH . . . and YOUR WORK

If you were asked: "What are you worth?" would you immediately think of your bank account and your other material possessions? Most would — and thus prove the necessity for the changes that have been given to us by Vatican Council II.

If you were asked: "What is your real work?" would you pause long enough to pinpoint for your interrogator the precise nature of the job that is yours in the workaday world? Most would — and again prove the imperative necessity for Vatican II and the changes it has recommended — especially those in the Liturgy.

The first subject discussed in the Council, and the first Constitution to be promulgated by the Council was on the Liturgy. The first changes you noted in the Church's *"aggiornamento"* — and the changes that have caused most of the discussion — not to mention fiery argumentation — among the People of God — were those in the Liturgy.

Those facts — all of them "firsts" — call for more than psychological and sociological study and comment. They demand first, and last, and all in between that beginning and end, a *theological* probing and penetration.

The query most often put to you since this Constitution began to be put into practice has been undoubtedly: "What do you think of the changes?" But that was not, is not, and never will be the proper query to put to a thinking man. The one question for all of us to face is *"How* do you think of the changes?" And there is only one correct reply: "I think *theologically"*. In passing it can be said that theological thinking is the only proper thinking for the "thinking animal" we call man. Being a "rational animal" he should think logically, of course; but being a creature his very logic will compel him to think theologically.

[23]

When you think theologically about the changes, you do not ask "what" . . . but "why" . . . *Why* have they turned the altar around? *Why* have they introduced the vernacular? *Why* the Lectors and Commentators? *Why* have us singing hymns — especially going up to, and coming back from receiving Communion? *Why* stand when receiving?

The answer to that persistent "Why?" is theological — and thrilling! The changes have been introduced to make you what you are: a being who was born human, but who has been re-born a "divinized" human; you were brought forth from the womb of your mother with a human nature, but when brought forth from the "womb" of your Mother, the Church, you were vibrant with a share in the very nature of God; for when you were "Christened" you were, as that word literally means, made Christ. But Christ is Son of God-made-Man. You, therefore, are man-made-son of God. And just as Christ's life was directed to, dominated by, and culminated in the one work He came on earth to do, so must your life be directed to, dominated by, and culminate in — the Sacrifice of the Mass.

That is why the two questions which opened this chapter can be answered only by one word: *infinite*. You are of infinite worth; and you have an infinite work to do. That is why Vatican Council II, in its first Constitution to be promulgated, ordered that the "rites be simplified" even as "their substance be preserved" so that you — as member of Jesus Christ, the Only Priest of the New Law, and as one who shares in His Priesthood — might be able to "take part *knowingly, actively, fruitfully.*"

The Council was very conscious of you — as a person of infinite worth having an infiinite work to do. If you saw the majestic assemblage at the opening, closing, or during any of its sessions, you, unquestionably, were awed by the presence of the Pope, the Cardinals, Patriarchs, Archbishops, Bishops, and Generals of Religious Orders, and looked upon the assembly as concerned with anyone but you. That is not thinking theologically. Therefore, that is not thinking!

FATHER M. RAYMOND, O.C.S.O.

The opening words of this Constitution speak of you, as well as to you. They say: "It is the goal of this most sacred Council to intensify the daily growth of Catholics in Christian living. . ." Stop there. Study those words. You are a Catholic. Therefore you should grow daily in Christian living. The Council has made these changes to "intensify your daily growth." Do you know what "Christian living" is? It is to live as branch on the Vine, member of the Body, flame in the Light of the World. More. It is to live as syllable in the Word! The Word is Christ. Therefore, your life is the Christ-life. You live "in Christ Jesus," and even as Jesus Christ — or you really do not *live*. He lived for one ultimate purpose: to offer Mass. For He came to earth primarily and principally to be Priest. You know where He offered His Mass. You know how He celebrated that Liturgy. The Cenacle saw Him "offering" Himself for immolation. Calvary saw Him "immolated" as Victim. The Empty Tomb saw Him "accepted." Daily, on the altars of the Church, through the instrumentality of priests, that Sacrifice is represented: the same Victim is offered by the same Priest to the same God. But with this difference: the Sacrifice of Calvary was our Redemption, the Sacrifice of Mass is our sanctification and means of salvation; on Calvary Christ was alone, in the Mass He has His members who offer themselves "with Him, through Him, and in Him." That means you — for you are both priest and victim, since you live "in Christ Jesus" — and Jesus Christ is really your life.

That is why the altar has been turned around — not so that you can see what the priest is doing in your name, but so that you can see what you are doing with him. That is why the language is now the vernacular — so that you can speak more easily and with greater understanding and meaning to your God. That is why you sing — because you are of that "chosen race, royal priesthood — of the people set apart to sing the praises of God. . . ," as St. Peter so emphatically stated (I Pet. 2:9)

The changes have all been made so that you can function more "knowingly, actively, and fruitfully."

[25]

KNOWINGLY — First of all you must know — and that means be aware with all your being — that you are a priest. That is no figure of speech. That is literal truth. You are a priest of the Most High God. You are a priest "according to the order of Melchisdech." You are a priest forever. Yes, forever. For that "character" which was stamped upon your being at Baptism is a stamp eternally ineradicable. Neither the Light of Glory under which those in Heaven live, nor the "fires of Hell" in which the damned spend eternity can burn that priestly character away. Yes, the sacramental character stamped into your being when you were reborn — and this time "born of God" — is a priestly character. True, you may not have received the Sacrament of Holy Orders, but that does not mean that you have not been "ordained." My ordination, and that of every man in Holy Orders, gives me and them a power "essentially different" from yours, as Pope Pius XII emphatically taught. But that does not minimize the reality of the fact that, as Pope St. Leo I, in his fourth sermon, so eloquently stated: "Baptism is the ordination of the laity." Nor was this sainted Pontiff alone in using such words. The early Fathers of the Church used it again and again. Saint Ireneus spoke of you when he said: "All the just have a priestly order." Saint Jerome spoke of "the priesthood of the laity, that is Baptism." St. John Chrysostom was even more explicit: "Thou wert made a priest by Baptism." What were they doing but echoing St. Peter, the first Pope, who told you that you were to "set yourselves close to him so that you, too, the holy priesthood that offers the spiritual sacrifices which Jesus Christ has made acceptable to God, may be living stones, making a spiritual house." (I Pet. 2:5) St. Thomas Aquinas etched this tremendous truth about you, your worth, and your work in the third part of his *Summa* in these words: "Now the whole rite of the Christian religion is derived from the Priesthood of Christ. Consequently, it is clear that the sacramental character is specifically the character of Christ, to whose character the faithful are likened by reason of the sacramental characters, which are nothing else than certain par-

ticipations of Christ's Priesthood, flowing from Christ Himself."
(6.63 a.3)

You were doubly stamped with this indelible character: at
Baptism, then again at Confirmation. But the principle work
of any and every priest is dramatically and unforgettably set
forth in the ordination ceremony of those receiving Holy Orders.
It is stated as the ordaining prelate anoints the ordinand's hands
and tells him that he is empowering him *"offerre sacrificium —
to offer sacrifice."* Since there is only one Sacrifice in the New
Law, that of the Mass, it follows that the principal function of
priesthood is to *"offer Mass."*

The changes in the Liturgy have been made to keep you from
ever again thinking about "going to Mass," "attending Mass,"
"hearing Mass," or "being present at Mass." They go even
further. They are being made to keep you from being satisfied
with the true, though not quite fully expressive phrase of "assisting at Mass." The Council will have you conscious of your
real worth, and have you say: "I go to Church to OFFER Mass."
You can add: "For I am a priest of the Great High God."

Those are truths you will seldom find in the secular Press.
Yet they are truths Vatican II stressed again and again. Read
chapter II of the Constitution on the Church if you would
learn your worth and your work. "See the days are coming —
it is Yahweh who speaks — when I will make a new covenant
with the House of Israel (and the House of Judah) . . . Deep
within them I will plant my Law, writing it on their hearts.
Then I will be their God and they shall be my people . . . they
shall know me, the least no less than the greatest — it is Yahweh who speaks." (Jer. 31:31-34 Jer. Bible) That is how the
Council stressed your call as member of the People of God.
"This was to be the new People of God," it goes on to say, "For
those who believe in Christ, who are reborn not from a perish-
able but from an imperishable seed through the word of the
living God, not from the flesh but from water and the Holy Spirit,
are finally established as a 'chosen race, a royal priesthood . . .'"
The Constitution then goes on to say: "Christ the Lord, High

Priest taken from among men 'made a kingdom and priest to God his Father' out of his new people. The baptized, by regeneration and the anointing of the Holy Spirit are consecrated into a spiritual house and a holy priesthood. . ."

Then, to avoid all misunderstanding, the Constitution repeats what Pius XI and Pius XII taught so insistently, namely that while the layman has a share in the priesthood of Christ, has been ordained to offer Sacrifice, his share differs from that of the man in Holy Orders, not only in degree but in very essence. These two real priesthoods are "interrelated" the Council says. "Each of them in its own special way is a participation in the one priesthood of Christ. The ministerial priest . . . acting in the person of Christ, brings about the Eucharistic Sacrifice . . . the faithful, by virtue of their royal priesthood join in the offering. . ." The man in Holy Orders consecrates, but all the faithful offer. Pius XII put it this way: "In this act of Sacrifice through the hands of the priest, whose word alone has brought the Immaculate Lamb to be present on the altar, the faithful themselves with one desire and one prayer offer it to the Eternal Father."

Now you can see one reason why the altar has been turned around: so that you, a priest, can see more clearly, and, as it were, come more near unto that which is not only the symbol of Christ, but upon which Christ will again represent His Sacrifice through you. That is the point of it all: *through* you — His priest on earth. Perhaps the importance of the altar can be brought home to you by the query — and the response — made by Pius XII as he addressed the First International Congress of Pastoral Liturgy which met at Assisi in September, 1956.

"Is the Tabernacle, where dwells the Lord who has come down amongst His people, greater than the Altar?"

How would you answer that question? It can be most interesting to hear discussion on it. For the wonder of God's condescension, not only to come down upon our altars, but to remain with us, to be truly *Emmanuel*, prompts one to select the Tabernacle as the more important. Further, the fact that we can always adore Him really present there in the Tabernacle, pay our homage, give our thanks, make our petitions — all but face to face — is another fact which impels one to choose the Tabernacle. Yet, it would be a wrong choice. Pius XII answered his own question very directly: "The altar is more important than the tabernacle, because on it is offered the Lord's Sacrifice."

Now you have official reply to those who make issue out of the fact that the Tabernacle, in practically all places where the altar faces the people, has been removed from that altar. The Tabernacle is the "resting place of the Lord," it is true. It is also true that the Tabernacle holds what is called the "Permanent Sacrament." But the point to be made is that it is not Christ's Presence that redeemed the world, but only His Sacrifice. So, too, it will not be the Sacramental Presence of Jesus Christ that will save mankind, but, again, only His Sacrifice of the Mass, which the Council has called again, and again: "the font and apex of the whole Christian life" (Const. on the Church 11) "No other action of the Church can match its claim to efficiency, nor equal the degree of it." (Const. on Liturgy 7) "The liturgy is the summit toward which the activity of the Church is directed; at the same time it is the fountain from which all her power flows." (Const. on Liturgy 10)

Do you begin to realize how wise the Council was in having the altar turned around, brought close to you, and everything that could block your vision of that Wondrous Place of Sacrifice from your view removed? Just as the Mass Christ offered on Calvary marked the midmost moment of time, is the very center of History, so the "aggiornamento" of Vatican II would have the altar the focal point of your life and all your living; for there is where you do your greatest work and are employed at your highest worth. Like Christ you came into the world, principally, to offer Mass. This change introduced by the Constitution on the Liturgy is aimed at having you come to that knowledge about yourself and to go about your one great work with clarity of mind.

[29]

RELAX!

You may read much history and come to know something of the myriads of millions of humans who have existed before you. You may be up to the minute on current events and realize that there are billions of other beings like yourself living on this whirling planet. And you may feel very small, utterly unconsequential, having next to nothing to contribute to the well-being or development of mankind. But if you think such a thought, you will be doing a great wrong not only to yourself, but to the God who made you and placed you in Time, as well as to the God who redeemed you and left you the potency to contribute mightily to Salvation History, and thus, not only help God saving man, but help man worshipping God.

The opening lines of chapter one of this Constitution on the Liturgy are to be read as the opening lines to your life's work. They run: "God, who 'wishes all men to be saved and come to the knowledge of truth' (I Tim. 2:4) 'in many and various ways . . . spoke of old to our fathers by the prophets' (Heb. 1:1). When the fullness of time had come He sent His Son, the Word made flesh, anointed by the Holy Spirit, . . . to be . . . the Mediator between God and man. For His humanity, united with the Person of the Word, was the instrument of our salvation. Thus in Christ 'there came forth the perfect satisfaction needed for our reconciliation, and we received the means for giving worthy worship to God.' . . . The wonders wrought by God among the people of the Old Testament were but a prelude to the work of Christ the Lord in redeeming mankind and giving perfect glory to God. He achieved this task principally by the paschal mystery of His blessed passion, resurrection from the dead, and glorious ascension, whereby 'dying He destroyed our death, and rising He restored our life' . . . Just as Christ was sent by the Father, so also He sent the Apostles filled with the Holy Spirit. He did this . . . so that they might *exercise* the *work* of *salvation*. . ."

You are one of those "apostles." For it can be said that you have been sent by God into this world to "exercise the work of salvation." For it can never be stressed too heavily that we who

[30]

have been redeemed have not yet been saved. The Redemption was accomplished by Jesus Christ alone — all, all alone. But Salvation is a co-operative. As St. Augustine remarked in the long ago: "God, who made you without yourself, will not save you without yourself." You have to "work out your salvation" as St. Paul told you.

Pius XI in a remarkable Encyclical *Misrentissimus Redemptor* set forth this mystery — about God and about yourself — very lucidly in the lines: "Though the ample redemption of Christ more than abundantly satisfied for all our offenses, nevertheless, by reason of a marvelous disposition of Divine Wisdom by which we may 'fill up what is wanting to the sufferings of Christ in our flesh, for His Body, which is the Church' (Col. 1:24), we are able, in fact we should add to the acts of praise and satisfaction which 'Christ in the name of sinners has presented to God' our own acts of praise and satisfaction . . . For this reason we must bring together, in the august Sacrifice of the Blessed Eucharist, the act of immolation made by the priest with that of the faithful, so that they, too, may offer themselves as 'living sacrifice, holy, well-pleasing unto God' (Rom 12:1) . . . The Apostle admonished us that 'bearing about in our body the mortifications of Jesus' (2 Cor. 4:2) and 'buried together with Him by Baptism unto death' (Rom 6:4) not only should we crucify our flesh with the vices and concupiscences (Gal. 5:24) 'flying the corruption of that concupiscence which is in the world' (2 Pet. 1:4) but also that 'the life of Jesus be made manifest in our bodies' (2 Cor. 4:10) and, having become partakers in His holy and eternal priesthood, we should offer up 'gifts and sacrifices for sin'. (Heb. 5:1)

There is your vocation. There is your work as a priest. There is the real meaning of life. That is why there have been changes in the Liturgy: to enable you to realize who you are and what you are on earth to do — and most especially how you are to do it. You are to carry on the priestly work of Jesus Christ. You are to be "mediator between God and man." You are to represent the Passion, Death, Resurrection and Ascension of

Jesus Christ — and thus pour out over mankind the merits He won on Calvary. In other words, you are to offer Mass.

The Church, which is "The People of God" is still the Mystical Body, of which you are a member and Christ is the Head. It is still the Mystic Vine on which you are the branch — and Jesus Christ the root and stalk. Hence you can recognize your work: to bring forth fruit for the Vine; to make the Body more healthy by being more holy yourself. As Pius XII said in his *Mystici Corporis:* "The Church becomes, as it were, the filling out and the complement of the Redeemer, while Christ, in a sense, attains through the Church a fullness in all things. Here we touch the reason why to the mind of Augustine the Mystical Head, which is Christ, and the Church, which on this earth as another Christ bears His Person, constitute *one new man,* in whom heaven and earth are yoked together in perpetuating the Cross' work of salvation. . ." (#93)

Even more explicitly was your life's work stated and shown to be priestly in this same document. "As He hung on the Cross," says Pius XII, "Christ Jesus not only avenged the justice of the Eternal Father that had been flouted, but He also won for us, His brothers, an unending flow of graces. It was possible for Him personally, and immediately, to impart these graces to men; but He wished to do so only through a visible Church that would be formed by a union of men, and thus through that Church *every man would perform a work of collaboration with Him* in dispensing the graces of Redemption. The Word of God willed to make use of our nature when in excruciating agony He would redeem mankind; in much the same way throughout the centuries He makes use of the Church that the work begun might endure." (#16 *Mystici Corporis* — italics added)

In other words He chose a Physical Body to *redeem* mankind: He has chosen a Mystical Body to *save* mankind. In that Mystical Body, *you* are a member with a definite work to do — a work which will glorify God and help save men. That work

[32]

is accomplished just as Christ's work was accomplished; that is, "principally through the Mass."

It always startles people to hear that the Omnipotent God *needs* them. As Pius XII points out: this is true because He willed it to be this way. "One must not think," says the Pope, "that He (Christ) does not require the Body's help. What Paul said of the human organism is to be applied likewise to the Mystical Body: 'The head cannot say to the feet: I have no need of you.' It is manifestly clear that the faithful need the help of the Divine Redeemer, for He has said: 'Without me you can do nothing.' . . . Yet this, too, must be held, marvelous though it appear: *Christ* requires His members.

"Deep mystery this, subject of inexhaustible meditation: that the *salvation* of many depends on the prayers and voluntary penances which the members of the Mystical Body of Jesus Christ offer for this intention, and on the assistance of pastors of souls and of the faithful, especially of fathers and mothers of families, which they must offer to Our divine Savior as though they were His associates" (54 *Mystici Corp.*)

The Council would have you realize that the one place best suited for the offering of your "prayers and voluntary penances," for offering all your "crosses," for offering all your joys, and your very selves, is on that altar that has been turned around, in that action which is the action of your life — Mass. "In this act of sacrifice," said Pius XII, "through the hands of the priest, whose word alone has brought the Immaculate Lamb to be present on the altar, the Faithful themselves with one desire and one prayer offer It to the Eternal Father . . . And just as on the Cross the Divine Redeemer offered Himself as Head of the whole human race, so in 'this pure Oblation' He offers not only Himself as Head of the Church, but in Himself His mystical members as well."

Take a clear-eyed view of that turned-around altar and realize it should be the center of your world. It is there you make your one great act of love — for God, for self, for all you love — and for all mankind. There you make your life of infinite worth; for it is there you do something that has value this world cannot compute. From the fact that you are a priest, share in the eternal priesthood of Jesus Christ, there comes to you a right, an obligation, a privilege, a pressing but very pleasurable duty to share fully in His Sacrifice. That means you are not only a priest who offers, but, like Christ, you are the victim who is offered. "In Christ Jesus" you become a sacrifice to be offered "with Him, through Him, and in Him" in the New Law's one only Sacrifice — the Mass.

That is what the Council would have you take to your heart. That is what it is saying in this Constitution. "The Church, therefore, earnestly desires that Christ's faithful, when present at this mystery of faith, should not be there as strangers or silent spectators. On the contrary, through a proper appreciation of the rites and prayers, they should participate knowingly, devoutly, and actively. . . They should give thanks to God by offering the Immaculate Victim, not only through the hands of the priest, but also with him; they should learn to offer themselves too." And why all this concern? "Through Christ the Mediator they should be drawn day by day into ever closer union with God, and with each other, so that, finally, God may be all in all." What an objective!

Talk about being at "the heart of the matter!" We are within the heart's most central core. Abbé Anger, an authority on the Mystical Body of Christ, once said, "The heart of Catholic Worship is the Mass — that full, efficacious representation and application of the one Sacrifice of Calvary. The active participation of the faithful out of the mandate, and of those rights which they received in baptism."

The Council was thinking theologically about you and your life. It would have you think the same way. But there is nothing new in this theological teaching of Vatican II. Back before the Fall of Rome St. Augustine, Bishop of Hippo, was saying with a stern directness: "God wants *you* — rather than your gifts." He was speaking about the offering of the faithful in Mass. St. Gregory the Great was saying the same thing in that "Thirteenth, the Greatest of Centuries": "We must offer ourselves; for the Mass will be sacrifice *for* us when we have made, in it, an offering *of* us." And Pius XI: "In the very august Eucharistic Sacrifice the priest and the rest of the faithful must join their immolation in such a way that they offer themselves as living hosts, holy and agreeable to God." *(Miserentissimus Redemptor).* Pius XII states the same truth in a more direct manner in his *Mediator Dei* — and gives clear indication of the purpose of the change from Latin to English: that you might know more surely just what *you are doing* in the Holy Sacrifice of the Mass. Pius was proving that the Sacrifice is offered by people as well as by priest. His last bit of evidence he took from the Mass prayers themselves, saying they "signify and show no less clearly that the oblation of the Victim is made by the priest in company with the people. For not only does the sacred minister, after the oblation of the bread and wine, when he turns to the people, saying the significant prayer: 'Pray, brethren, that my sacrifice *and yours* may be acceptable to God the Father Almighty;' but also the prayers by which the Divine Victim is offered to God are generally expressed in the plural, and in those it is indicated more than once that the people also participate in this august Sacrifice inasmuch as they offer the same. The following words, for example, are used: 'For whom we offer, or who offer up to Thee . . . We, therefore, beseech Thee, O Lord, to be appeased and to receive this offering of our bounden duty, as also of Thy whole household. . . We, Thy servants, as also Thy whole people. . .'" Pius added at the end of this convincing proof: "Nor should Christians forget to offer themselves, their sorrows, their distresses, and their necessities in union with their Divine Savior. . ."

Now you have one reason why the altar was turned around — That reason was *you*. The same reason prompted Vatican II to change the language for offering Mass from Latin to the vernacular, introduce Lectors, and bring on Commentators. All for you — that you might come to keener realization of who you are, and what you have to do as "Time marches on" . . . The

Lector clearly teaches you that *you* are *in* Salvation History. . .

Louis Veuillot, editor of the influential journal *L'Univers*, always kept a History of the Church on his over-crowded desk, "Because," he explained, "that is the Biography of my Mother." Vatican II would have us realize the truth in Pius XI's statement that we are all "spiritual Semites." Yes, we are the "children of Abraham," spiritually, just as we are the children of Adam physically. That is why you hear so much of the Old Testament read out to you and for you by the Lectors during Mass. It really is your "Family History" — for you are of the Family of God, made so by Baptism — and History, as we said before is truly "His Story" — the Story of His love for mankind as shown in sending His Son to be Saviour. As we listen we learn that it is the God of Abraham, Isaac, and Jacob, whom we are adoring; that the Patriarchs and Prophets are ours; that we are the "People of God" whom He is leading toward the real "Promised Land." Again you have reason to rejoice over another change Vatican II has made.

ACTIVELY . . . You have heard the Council saying that "in Christ we have received the means of giving worthy worship to God." It is a statement to be pondered; for you well know that the first commandment given to Moses was about worship; you also know the prime, as well as the ultimate purpose of your entire existence, both here and hereafter, is to glorify God. The Council helps you further by stating that "this is achieved principally by the Paschal Mystery;" that "the Liturgy is an exercise of the priestly office" and the "outstanding means for the faithful to express in their lives, and manifest to others, the real nature of the Church." All that should add up to a conviction that the changes recommended have as ultimate goal your *metanoia* — *your change* of mind, heart, and whole being, so that you can become who you are: God's son with a work to do for your Father — and all your fellow humans.

I have just received a letter from Uganda in East Africa, written by an American young woman who has learned first hand just how these changes — especially that of Latin to the vernacular — can help us all to *be* what we are. She writes: "I was able to assist at Mass in Kisoro last Sunday in a Church that seemed at least a half mile long. Because I am (still) white. . ." (She has been out in the Congo's sun for six months studying gorillas) . . . "I had to sit up front with the sparkling white nuns in my filthy dirty jeans. But I forgot my embarrassment when the first song — the Introit — broke loose to the accompaniment of six drums which, try as they did, could not drown out the voices of the 1500 (this according to the priest) which swelled from my seat by the altar to the distant back (which is the front door). Every one of those black shiny heads participated both in the responses and hymns as though they themselves, individually, were accountable to God for the worship of the world. It was awesome to feel their strength — and this experience was only exceeded by the one which came to me as I watched them go to Communion — which took all of forty-five minutes — most of them in rags and barefooted. There were some in 'City clothes'. There were also four mulattoes in the congregation, and on their faces I could really *see* Faith!"

That is the purpose of the vernacular: that you might praise God more knowingly and actively; that you might enable others to see *Faith* on your very face. Not many of us expected the Council to allow us the use of our mother tongue. When the Bishops of the United States went further and asked, then obtained permission to have the very Canon in English, all, even the most sanguine of Liturgicologists, were surprised — and grateful.

No one will now say that it is not more meaningful to pray "Lord have mercy; Christ have mercy" than it is to say *"Kyrie eleison; Christe eleison"*. Nor will any question the advantage it is to sing "Glory to God in the highest, and on earth peace to men of good will," over singing *"Gloria in excelsis Deo, et in terra pax hominibus bonae voluntatis."* Even those of us who know Latin can use our mother tongue with more ease — and even with more meaning. To sing the angels' song in English and have our whole hearts in our "Holy, Holy, Holy Lord God of Hosts. . ." enables us to give deeper resonance to our worship. When we all sing the *Our Father* as we learned it at our mother's knee, we realize with a more vital and vibrant realization that we are His children and are all one family. Think what a supersonic boom must break into Heaven as, after that high point of the Canon when the priest holds up the transubstantiated wheat and wine and we look upon the species under which He is present and the priest says, "Through Him, and with Him, and in Him be unto You, O God, the Father almighty, in the unity of the Holy Spirit, all honor and glory, world without end" we sing out "*Amen*" — ratifying Christ's action. Then dare anyone ask: "Why the change into the vernacular?" Hardly. For everyone knows that this is intelligent and heart-deep *participation*.

Admitted that there have been those who have roundly condemned the hymns that are sung, saying they are sentimental, poor translations, or borrowed from Protestants.

Admitted again that many have objected — and objected strenuously, to singing hymns going up to and returning from Communion. Admitted that there are real grounds for criticizing the musical ability of many in the congregation. It is still asked: Do you realize that "song belongs to the lover" as Augustine said centuries ago — and said wisely? It is also asked: Do you realize that Mass is our Act of Love — just as Calvary was the climax of His Loving Act? It is finally asked: Do you realize that only "practice makes perfect"?

There is nothing wrong with sentiment. Man is the only creature capable of manifesting it. There is nothing wrong with borrowing from Protestants. For just as we borrowed from the Jews our psalms and most of our liturgical acts, so they actually borrowed hymns and hymn-singing from us in the long ago. Finally, there is nothing wrong with allowing our hearts to find voice as we go up to and return from receiving the greatest Gift God can bestow: Himself!

Let us have done with carping at the "changes" and get with them so that we may change into what we are: Lovers in our

[38]

greatest Act of Love! Then we can realize the ultimate purpose
of the Council's changes: We will offer Mass more . . .

FRUITFULLY . . . You may read how some of the "new
breed" want nothing to do with such terms as "*ex opere operato*"
and "*ex opere operantis*," technical terms telling tremendous
truth in an unforgettable formula. But, say what they will, the
truth still remains. "*Ex opere operato*" means that the Mass, no
matter what the state of soul in the priest or the congregation,
gives "infinite glory *to God.*" The "*ex opere operantis*" however,
tells us a different story. That means that the fruit *we* receive
from Mass depends on our *dispositions.* Consequently you can
immediately see the wisdom of the Council in suggesting all
these changes. It would have us participate more knowingly and
actively so that our dispositions would be such that we can
garner the greater fruit from our offering. With head and heart
totally given to the discharge of our priestly function, we ourselves, the entire Mystical Body, and all mankind are bettered.
And that, in all truth, is the real purpose of "*aggiornamento*" —
not just to bring the Mystical Body "up to date" — but to bring
mankind up to God.

There have been mistakes, of course. Human beings will always
make mistakes. Some pastors had their people plunge into the
changes too precipitously. Further, some few took it upon themselves to initiate innovations. This was wrong. The Council empowered only those who have ecclesiastical authority — "that is,
the Apostolic See and, as laws may determine, the bishop". It
reiterated this fact in that passage which runs: "Therefore, ab-
solutely no other person, not even a priest, may add, remove,
or change anything in the liturgy on his own authority." That
is why this book has insisted from the outset that we distinguish
clearly, and consistently, between what the Council says, and
what some people say it says.

The secular press has made much of "Jazz Masses" — of
"Hootenanny Masses" — of the use of the guitar. The Council
said: "The Church acknowledges Gregorian chant as proper to
the Roman liturgy: therefore, other things being equal, it should

be given pride of place in liturgical service. But, other kinds of sacred music, especially polyphony, are by no means excluded . . . so long as they accord with the spirit of the liturgical action. . ." The Council missed nothing in its suggestions. Hence, it is not surprising that it said: "In the Latin Church the pipe organ is to be held in high esteem. . . But other instruments also may be admitted for use in divine worship, with the knowledge and consent of the competent territorial authority. . . This may be done, however, only on condition that the instruments are suitable for sacred use, or can be made so. . ." Did you ever know that the guitar is a descendant from the "cithara" we hear so much about in the psalms?

The Council wants nothing that is not "in accord with the dignity of the temple" or anything that does not "truly contribute to the edification of the faithful."

Be not impatient. Mistakes will be made before there is finality to our mode of worship. But, believe me, the ultimate will be dignified, enable you to act as priest, and enjoy your functioning as who you are. Just remember always that the changes are being made so that you can change into your changeless self — priest — thanks to share in the Priesthood of the Changeless Christ.

It can be done because it has been done. Here is a letter from a Catholic who was on vacation to the seashore:

Last summer we saw in action the splendid results of Vatican II as regards the "new" Mass.

This was at Sunday Mass in a popular oceanside resort where the Catholic Church we attended was huge, cathedral-proportioned. The church auditorium, its ample balcony, wide stairway, and aisles, were filled to capacity at the 9 o'clock Mass (one of five). Five priests distributed Communion.

But what so impressed us was that these people from many States were praying the Mass aloud in complete unison. It made one stop to realize the excellent job our priests have done in so short a time in inculcating the "new way" into a practicality for their parishioners.

It was one of those times when one becomes acutely aware of, and grateful for, the farsightedness of our Catholic Hierarchy in bringing functions up to date; for the communing of the people, gathered in the midst of vacation to worship God and to give Him thanks; for the complete freedom to worship for this huge congregation, and for the deep and hard sacrifices being made to help a far-distant small country in its effort to achieve the same freedom.

It was a moving and most impressive experience. After this, we couldn't help wondering why anyone would want to go back to the old way. . .

No one will want to go back when they realize the theological depth in these changes. We have already referred to *"ex opere oprato"* and *"ex opere operantis."* Let us return to it once again to pinpoint the deepest, personal, theological reason we can have for adopting these changes whole-heartedly. Every Mass offered will be acceptable to and accepted by God — because of the Victim offered by *the* Priest — Jesus Christ. Every Mass will be acceptable to, and accepted by God — because of the holiness of the Mystical Body of Christ, His Church, one of whose distinctive and distinguishing marks is holiness. But we must be keen enough to realize that the holiness of the Mystical Body will vary because of the holiness or lack of holiness in its members. Therefore, — and you should take this inevitable conclusion to your heart — the efficacy of the Mass, any day, and every day, depends upon *you.*

From early days you, no doubt, have known that while every Mass is efficacious and acceptable to God, the holier the priest offering it, the more efficacious and acceptable it will be. Now that you have been made to realize that you are a priest, it behooves you to become as holy as possible just that God may have that much more accidental glory, and every Mass may be that much more efficacious for mankind.

RELAX!

The Blood of Christ cries to Heaven from all our altars, but we must never forget that it cries through our lips and through our hearts. Therefore, the purer our lips, the holier and warmer our hearts, the more eloquently will that Blood plead.

Life becomes more serious, and living becomes more challenging when you realize who you are and what you can do. That is the purpose of all the changes. Change with them and through them.

Concelebrated Mass at Gethsemani

Chapter 3

COME, LET US ADORE HIM

We have not completed our examination of the changes suggested by the Council concerning the Eucharist. Far from it. But, by this time, you must have seen that the final purpose of them is to make you much more keenly Christ-conscious. This consciousness is what pinpoints for you your dignity, with the consequent effect of showing you your highest duty. For to be Christ-conscious is to be keenly Mass-conscious; which, in its turn, makes you intensely aware of your priesthood and your victimhood.

But before we go further let it be said that your hesitancy in immediately accepting all the changes that have been made proves that, maybe unknown to yourself, you are almost passionately attached to Mass. We do not resist changes in things we do not greatly value. We would be utterly unconcerned about any changes the Moslems might want to introduce in their manner of doing things. We would not be greatly concerned about any changes the College of Cardinals might want to make in their way of meeting and discussing matters. But when changes are made in what is personal, dear to our hearts, and highly valued, we are hesitant to accept the change until we understand its purpose. Once we realize that every change that has been introduced by those who have competence to make changes is for our good, for the better discharge of our duty, for our more intimate, and fruitful manner of functioning as priests of the Most Migh God, then, far from resisting them we give them hearty welcome.

Never think that you were alone in your uneasiness with the changes. Have you ever thought what it must have cost priests to adopt them? Some of us have been offering Mass for twenty, thirty, forty, and even fifty years in one way. Latin was very much our "natural" milieu, our second "mother-tongue". The rubrics had become second nature to us. Suddenly, and I mean suddenly for most of us, we were facing the people — and had to check ourselves at every *"Dominus vobiscum"* lest we turn our backs to them as we said the words. That was bad enough. But when, almost as suddenly, we had to say certain parts in English — and others in Latin — believe me we often got confused. So much so that there is justice in the jest that we priests "looked better" with our backs to the people, and that some in the congregation thought it a "real mistake" — an injustice to us (and to them!) to have us "look so bad" by "turning the altar around."

When later changes were introduced and we had to struggle with two Missals, folders with the vernacular (to help us out), allow a Lector read the Epistle, have our minds distracted from what we were doing by some Commentator telling the people what they should be doing, and often be startled to say the least by some hymn by the entire Congregation, many of us appreciated the remarks by Father Bernard Basset, S.J. "Sanity and serenity can come from realizing there is a difference between private and liturgical prayer." To be honest, many of us experienced real difficulty in doing what Pius X had exhorted all to do, back before World war I; namely, to "pray the Mass."

But practice does make all things easier — if not perfect. . . Even to the singing of hymns. As one parishioner put it: "Before this congregational singing began I could not sing at all. Now, after only a few weeks, I find that I have advanced to the stage where I can sing terrible." He may have meant "tolerably" — but he said "terrible."

Yet, joking aside, I believe all will admit that the changes have made Mass much more meaningful. At least the National Conference of Catholic Bishops here in the United States felt reasonably confident that they could say; "The Mass has a new experience for the people of God, bishops, priests, Religious and

[46]

laity together." They then listed the reasons for this "new experience": "We listen to more of the Scriptures and to homilies that proclaim the wonderful works of God. The priest speaks in the language of the people, and they respond and sing according to their proper role. The liturgy of the Word of God, with the priest presiding, stands out more clearly; the celebration of the Eucharist, with the priest facing the people, has genuine pastoral value."

The Conference did not hesitate to admit: "We experience difficulties, but many of these are the inevitable problems of transition and growth. Old liturgical defects, of which few were aware, are coming to light as we use the vernacular. Gradual and uneven liturgical changes have to be appreciated for what they are — first steps."

That is an important final phrase. Little has been made final in this matter of offering Mass as a Community. We are in the transitional stage — and should be open to every change that can enable us to fulfill our marvelous duty and express our surpassing dignity with greater meaning for self, for others, and especially for God.

In the opening pages of this book it was said that we can see Christ "walking on the waters of our world" — and hear Him giving us His usual greeting and heartening: "Peace — Courage — It is I". Now I believe we can go further and say that once we enter into the changes with our whole heart and being we can see Christ in every Mass, not as the disciples saw Him that night of storm, but more truly as Thomas saw Him that night in the Cenacle — one week after the Resurrection: His hands and feet and side aglow with the glory of Resurrection — and yet memorials of His Passion and Death. With Thomas, at the Elevation, we can say: "My Lord and my God."

That is one of the most thrilling effects of this renewal: our Faith in His Real Presence under the species of the consecrated wheat and wine. But there is more. We have been alerted to His presence in the people, in the priest, and in ourselves. We have been impressed by the truth that Mass is a *communal* action, not a private devotion. We know that He said: "Wherever two or three are gathered in My name, there am I in the midst of them." We know now that more than two or three are gathered for the common offering and the offering of a community and as a community. That makes us realize the sacredness of every human being, and deepens our reverence for every human person. We hear now the Canon of the Mass as never before and listen to the plural nouns and pronouns throughout. More, we are made vividly aware that Christ Himself is acting, in Person, in and through the person of the priest who consecrates. Thus does our Christ-consciousness grow, and Religion becomes what in fact it is: life with God, life for God, life in God. With the important correlary that we will live more for our neighbor.

If we are honest, we will admit that heretofore Mass was not always the communal celebration it should have been. We were not too conscious of the congregation forming a unit, a whole, one body with one mind, will, heart, and soul bent on adoring God, making reparation for sin, thanking Him for His mercies, and begging Him for more of the same. But with all now acting in unison, all saying and singing the same words, all lifting minds and hearts to God in the one great Act of Love, we realize Mass is the source of our strength and ability to live for others. Having heard the word of God more clearly; having offered ourselves "through Him, with Him, and in Him"; having received Him into our beings, we go forth with ever increased love not only for God and self, but for all men. Hence, we can never close our eyes or our ears, let alone our hearts, to the needs of others.

As the Conference of Bishops said "the involvement of the whole worshipping congregation is being accomplished," but then quickly pointed out that this was but the "first liturgical aim of the Council." It went on to indicate the second by asking such questions as: "How much more committed are we to the needs of all mankind?" and "How much better do we manifest to others the true meaning of the Church?" It does add: "Unquestionably we are more conscious of the universal claims of Christian faith and love. If the liturgy has been speaking more clearly of these claims, and if it has moved us to step toward the great goals of the Council, then the renewal may be said to be under way."

If there is one teaching of Christ that can frighten as well as stimulate and console it is that about "Whatsoever you do to one of these, the least of my brethren, you do to Me." That is but an application of the truth about the Vine and the Branches, the Body with Him as Head and us as members, the Light of the world made up of many flames. This was the truth that changed Saul the persecutor into Paul the Apostle. That is the truth that can change us from uncommitted individuals who are always taking good care of themselves into open-handed, open-hearted, spirited workers for the rest of the world. It is the Mass that should move us out to the masses — each in his or her own way. It is the Mass which has already done so for thousands and even tens of thousands. It is the Mass, consciously lived, that will yet move more millions. For there is nothing like the Mass to make each of us realize that we *are* our brother's keeper — since Christ has already been ours — especially through His Mass.

The Bishops have told us that "the liturgical program is a positive effort of the Church" and that "it must express faith and piety and bring us all to a greater awareness of full Christian responsibility." That last phrase really says that every Catholic, by virtue of his calling to the true Faith, is really an Atlas with the world on his shoulders — and those shoulders cannot be shrugged. Nothing will keep them steadier than an ever deeper, personal, active, intelligent participation in the Eucharist.

That last word brings us to something that must have bothered many: some speculations on the Eucharist that have been played up by the popular press; and some unwarranted stress on the Eucharist as a Banquet.

These have not only upset you, they have saddened Pope Paul VI — even as they stirred Pope Pius XII long before him.

[49]

That is point number one: these speculations are not new — despite what the press may tell you.

You may hear much today about Mass being a "Banquet." It is not simply a "Banquet." It never was and never will be that. It is a *Sacrificial* banquet — and that adjective really has more force here than the noun — "Banquet." For without the Sacrifice you would never have the "Banquet." Some of the "new breed" have gone so far as to say that if you do not participate in the "Banquet" — that is, if you do not receive Holy Communion — you do not offer Mass. That is false — unqualifiedly false. Do not be taken in by such talk no matter from whom it comes — even from a Doctor of Divinity. They may put forth their arguments suasively, telling you how Christ said: "Take and *eat* . . . Take and *drink* . . ." He did. But He added "Take and eat. This is my body *which shall be given for you* . . . This cup is the new covenant in my blood *which will be poured out for you*" (Lc. 22:14) clearly showing that the *offering* He made in the Cenacle looked toward the *immolation* on Calvary. In other words, what the Apostles received in the Upper Room was the Body that was yet to be immolated and the Blood that was yet to be poured out. What you and I receive is the Body that has been immolated and the Blood that has been poured out. Both are oriented to the *Sacrifice* of Calvary. Which means there never would have been, and there can not now be, any Sacrament without the *Sacrifice*. The Mass is, and ever will be the *Sacrifice* of Calvary. Holy Communion was and ever will be the Body and Blood of the Victim offered by Calvary's immolation. The Banquet is had because the Sacrifice was made.

This subject is so important that it is necessary to orient you rightly by giving you the authentic teaching of the infallible Church, so that you will never be misled, never be confused, never be in error about this truth of truths, this love of all loves, this life-giving source of real life.

Two decades ago the errors which the "new breed" are now putting forth as "new theology" were shown to be centuries old, and were roundly condemned by Pius XII who was but echoing the condemnations of the holy — because God-guided and God-guarded — Council of Trent. Because he put it so pointedly and pithily; because he presented it so theologically; because he covered the matter so thoroughly, it is the part of wisdom and practicality to give you the Pontiff's own words. In his Encyclical *Mediator Die of* November, 1947, Pius XII said:

> "The Mystery of the Most Holy Eucharist which Christ, the High Priest, instituted, and which He commanded to be continually renewed in the Church by His Ministers, is the culmination and center, as it were, of the Christian religion. . .
> "Christ the Lord, 'Eternal Priest according to the order of Melchisedech' 'loving His own who were in the world' 'at the Last Supper, on the night He was betrayed, wishing to leave His Spouse, the Church, a *visible sacrifice* such as the nature of man requires, that would represent the bloody *Sacrifice* offered once on the Cross, and perpetuate its memory to the end of time, and whose salutary virtue might be applied in remitting those sins we daily commit . . . offered His Body and Blood under the species of bread and wine to God the Father, and under the same species allowed the Apostles, whom He at that time constituted the priests of the New Testament, to partake thereof; commanding them and their successors in the priesthood to make the same offering'."

There is a paragraph that is what the modern man likes to call "dense" with theological truth. Do not read it too rapidly. You should re-read it slowly and make an effort to catch all that is said therein. The word "Sacrifice" is italicized because that is the one word the "new breed" omit all too frequently when speaking of Mass and the Eucharist. The word "Banquet" is not used at all by His Holiness, though the "meal," of which the "new breed" make so much, is indicated in the clause "allowed the Apostles to partake thereof." The Pope did not even employ the word "Sacrament" — as if, by design, he would bas-relief for us the main truth about the Eucharist; namely, that it is a Sacrifice first and foremost. So be wise enough to hold on to the truth you have always held; that is, that the Mass "is the representation of the *Sacrifice* of the Cross."

Although His Holiness has presented almost the entirety of the theological truth and reality of the Eucharist in that one paragraph, he saw a pressing need to go on patiently and almost ploddingly to unravel all the magnicent reality by saying:

"The august *Sacrifice* of the altar, then, is no mere empty commemoration of the passion and death of Jesus Christ, but a true and proper act of *sacrifice*, whereby the High Priest by an unbloody immolation offers Himself a most acceptable Victim to the Eternal Father, as He did upon the Cross. 'It is one and the same Victim; the same Person now offers it by the ministry of His priests, Who then offered Himself on the Cross, the manner of offering alone being different.'

"The Priest is the same, Jesus Christ, whose sacred Person His minister represents. Now the minister by reason of the sacerdotal consecration which he has received, is made like to the High Priest and possesses the power of performing actions in virtue of Christ's very Person. Wherefore in his priestly activity he, in a certain manner, 'lends his tongue, and gives his hand' to Christ."

There again is "density." The first quote in that last paragraph is from St. Thomas Aquinas who lived in that "Greatest of Centuries." The second quote goes back to St. John Chrysostom, who died in 405 A.D. The combination tells you clearly why you can see Christ so vividly in the priest who bends over wheat and wine to utter the very words Christ Himself uttered "the night before He died" in that Upper Room which saw the first "transubstantiation." Christ is using that priest's lips, tongue and very life-breath as His own. That priest, when he utters those words of consecration, is speaking, not in his own name, but in that of Jesus Christ. Realize then, that it is Christ who speaks today even as He spoke the first Holy Thursday evening — He says the same words, with the same effect — and

He speaks them for you. Indeed Mass "is no mere empty com-memoration," as the Pope says. He goes on:

"Likewise the Victim is the same, namely our Divine Re-deemer in His human nature with His true Body and Blood. The manner, however, in which Christ is offered is different."

Now comes another most important passage; one that gives you the true doctrine on the Mass as a *Sacrifice*. Read it slowly. Read it assimilatively. Read it gratefully. . .

"On the Cross He completely offered Himself and all His sufferings to God, and the immolation of the Victim was brought about by the bloody death, which He underwent of His free will. But on the altar, by reason of the glorified state of His human nature, 'death shall have no more dominion over Him', and so the shedding of His Blood is impossible; still according to the plan of Divine Wisdom, the *Sacrifice* of our Redeemer is shown forth in an admirable manner by external signs which are symbols of His death. For by the 'transubstantiation' of bread into the Body of Christ and of wine into His Blood, His Body and Blood are both really pres-ent: now the Eucharistic species under which He is present, symbolize the actual separation of His Body and Blood. Thus the commemorative representation of His death, which ac-tually took place on Calvary, is repeated in every *Sacrifice* of the altar, seeing that Jesus Christ is symbolically shown by separate symbols to be in a state of victimhood."

The importance of the fact that it is Jesus Christ, as Priest and Victim, who offers and is offered in every Mass, must not escape you. For each of us must realize that as creatures we owe adoration to our Creator. But how could we, finite beings, ever offer Him due praise and glory? The answer is obvious: we simply could not. Secondly, as recipients of life from the One Source of all being and life, our debt of gratitude is evident. But, once again we ask ourselves: how can we express adequately our thanks for the gift of being, and of life? The answer is the same:

we could not. But more; we are not only creatures who have received all that we have from the Creator, we are sinful creatures, from the very moment of our conception. We have been conceived with sin upon our souls; consequently, we came forth from the womb enemies of God, with the inevitable need for reparation and reconciliation. Yet, we were helpless to make the due apology, effect the necessary reconciliation, win again favor and friendship with Him who is our Maker. Finally, who is there among us who could cast the first stone at that poor, weak woman whom the Scribes and Pharisees had taken in adultery? We not only were stained with sin at our conception, we have sinned since our birth, and need to cry to Heaven for forgiveness. But what value our voice in the halls of Heaven? Without Christ, "through Whom, with Whom and in Whom" we can adore, give thanks, make reparation, and implore, we would be in a sorry state. But since He is our Priest and Victim in Mass, since He is the Vine and we the branches, He the Head and we the members of His Body, we can know a soul-deep confidence that God will hear us, see us, accept us, and answer us.

Pius XII stated all this magnificently, as he summed up his teaching on the four ends of the Mass, showing them to be identical with the four ends of the Sacrifice of the Cross, saying: "Christ, on the Cross, 'offering prayers and supplications with a loud cry and tears, has been heard for His reverence,'. *Likewise* upon the altar He is our Mediator with God in the same efficacious manner, so that we may be filled with every blessing and grace." (#74)

Small wonder St. Augustine cried out to his people back at the time of the fall of Rome: "See how we were bought: Christ hangs upon the Cross. See at what a price He makes His purchase: He sheds His Blood, He buys with His Blood, He buys with the Blood of the Spotless Lamb, He buys with the Blood of God's only Son. He who buys is Christ; the price is His Blood; the possession bought is the world." (Enarr. in Ps. CXLVII, n. 16)

Pius XII in anticipating the objection that would arise since the purchase has been made, and the purchase price already given, there is nothing for us to do, wrote: "This purchase, however, does not immediately have its full effect; since Christ, after redeeming the world at the lavish cost of His own Blood, must still come into possession of the souls of men. Wherefore, that the redemption and salvation of each person, and of future generations unto the end of time, may be effectively accomplished, and be acceptable to God, it is necessary that men should individually come into vital contact with the Sacrifice of the Cross, so that the merits which flow from it, should be imparted to them. In a certain sense it can be said that on Calvary Christ built a font of purification and salvation which He filled with the Blood He shed; but if men do not bathe in it and there wash away the stains of their iniquities, they can never be purified and saved."

That clarifies, perhaps, as it substantiates, what was said earlier in this book; namely, that while each and every one of us has been *redeemed,* — and that without our cooperation! — no one of us who yet breathes the air of earth has been *saved.* Salvation demands our cooperation — the Mass is *the* Act in which we best cooperate and through which we are most surely saved.

That truth ought to show you why the Church, which, as Pope John XXIII made manifest by the very title of his magnificent Encyclical *Mater et Magistra,* is both Mother and Teacher, has changed the Liturgy. She would have you more "intelligently, actively, and fruitfully" *participate.*

Long before Vatican II was called, Pius XII told you the identical, life-giving, and life-saving truth. In so doing he really was but echoing Pius X. Liturgical change is no novelty. It has been going on for over a hundred years. Yet, we must admit that it has been the latest changes that have enabled us to realize the exactness of Pius XII's statement: "Through this active and individual participation, the members of the Mystical Body not only become daily more like to their Divine

[55]

Head, but the life flowing from the Head is imparted to the members, so that we can each repeat the words of St. Paul: 'With Christ I am nailed to the Cross: I live, now not I, but Christ liveth in me.' "

Then, as if mindful of old errors, and as if by some special sense he realized there would be a "new breed" who might attempt to put new labels on those errors, Pius XII went on to say: "The august Sacrifice of the altar is, as it were, the supreme instrument whereby the merits won by the Divine Redeemer upon the Cross are distributed to the faithful. . . This, however, far from lessening the dignity of the actual Sacrifice on Calvary, rather proclaims and renders more manifest its greatness and its necessity. . . Its daily immolation reminds us that there is no salvation except in the Cross of Our Lord Jesus Christ, and that God Himself wishes that there should be a continuation of this Sacrifice 'from the rising of the sun till the going down thereof', so that there be no cessation of the hymn of praise and thanksgiving which man owes to God, seeing that he requires His help continually, and has need of the Blood of the Redeemer to remit sin which challenges the justice of God." (#79)

Have you noticed how insistent the Holy Father has been on the idea that the Mass is a *Sacrifice?* Not a word has yet been said about it being a "Banquet," yet we are far along in His Holiness' exposition of the true nature of Mass. Before he nears that fact the Pontiff roundly scored some other erroneous opinions the "new breed" continues to air. One such was the age-old error of confusing the priesthood of the laity, which is a real participation in the Priesthood of Christ, with the priesthood the ordained minister enjoys. They are not the same. Far from it. Pius XII insisted in season and out of season that they differ "not only in *degree*, but in *essence*." All, lay and cleric, *offer* the one Victim; but only the ordained priest *consecrates*. "The unbloody immolation at the words of consecration, when Christ is made present upon the altar in the state of a Victim, is performed by the priest and *by him alone*, as the representative of Christ and not as representative of the people." Only the man who has received the Sacrament of Holy Orders can make Christ present on the altar; for he alone can consecrate. But once that Victim is present, then all can *offer* Him.

"It is clear," says Pius XII, "that the faithful offer the Sacrifice by the hands of the priest from the fact that the minister at the altar, in offering a Sacrifice in the name of all His members, represents Christ, the Head of the Mystical Body. Hence the *whole Church* can rightly be said to offer up the Victim through Christ. But the conclusion that the people offer the Sacrifice with the priest is not based on the fact that, being members of the Church no less than the priest himself, they perform the visible liturgical rite . . . rather it is based on the fact that the people unite their hearts in praise, impetration, expiation, and thanksgiving with the prayers or intention of the priest, even of the High Priest Himself, so that in the one same offering of the Victim, and according to a visible sacerdotal rite, they may be presented to God the Father."

Therein you see why there have been changes. You must participate. You must be united with the priest who consecrates and with the High Priest, Christ, who is the principal agent, inasmuch as He is, strictly speaking, the One Priest of the New Law, who now acts in and through the person of His ordained ministers.

Pius XII, perhaps one of the profundest theologians we have had on the Chair of Peter in centuries and centuries, did something the "new breed" of theologians seldom, if ever, do. He went on say: "In order that the oblation by which the faithful offer the Divine Victim in this Sacrifice to the Heavenly Father may have its full effect, it is *necessary* that the people add something else, namely the *offering of themselves as a victim.*" Then, practical man that he was, he immediately added: "This offering in fact is not confined merely to the liturgical Sacrifice. For the Prince of the Apostles wishes us 'as living stones, built upon Christ the cornerstone, to be able, as a holy priesthood, to offer up spiritual sacrifices, acceptable to God by Jesus Christ.' St. Paul the Apostle addresses the following words of

[57]

exhortation to Christians without distinction of time: 'I beseech you therefore . . . that you present your bodies, a living sacrifice, holy, pleasing unto God, your reasonable service.' "

Everything that you do, everything that you are, day after day, should be "wheat and wine" for your Sacrifice. To us who have been ordained, words were addressed that spell life for us in time and promise life eternal. Since you were "ordained" by Baptism and Confirmation, the identical words apply to you: "Understand what you do, imitate what you handle, and since you celebrate the mystery of the Lord's death, take good care to mortify your members with their vices and concupiscenses."

Before saying a single word about the "Banquet" Pius XII wisely summed up the true teaching on the Mass by saying: "Let the faithful, therefore, consider to what a high dignity they have been raised by the Sacrament of Baptism. They should not think it enough to participate in the Eucharistic Sacrifice with that general intention which befits members of Christ and children of the Church, but let them further, in keeping with the spirit of the sacred Liturgy, be most closely united with the High Priest and His earthly minister, at the time the consecration of the Divine Victim is effected, and at that time especially when those solemn words are pronounced: 'By Him, and with Him, and in Him, is to Thee, God the Father Almighty, in the unity of the Holy Spirit, all honor and glory for ever and ever.' To those words, in fact, the people answer: 'Amen'. Nor should Christians forget to offer themselves, their cares, their sorrows, their distress and their necessities in union with their Divine Saviour upon the Cross." (#104)

It was only after all that, that His Holiness turned to the Banquet. But to pinpoint error first of all . . . an error to which you have already been alerted, I believe. There are those who even today dare to say that "unless you receive Holy Communion at Mass, you do not offer Mass." Know how "new" that kind of "theology" is? — Almost half a millenium "new." Back in the early part of the sixteenth century there were those who endeavored to make the same point. The Council of Trent felt forced to say: ". . . none of the faithful can hold that private Masses, in which the priest alone receives Holy Communion, are thereby unlawful, and do not fulfill the idea of the true, perfect, and complete unbloody Sacrifice instituted by Christ our Lord." Pius XII was even more explicit. He said: "They therefore err who do not want to have Masses celebrated unless the faithful communicate; and those are still more in error who, in holding that it is altogether necessary for the faithful to receive Holy Communion as well as the priest. . ." He gave the exact doctrine with clarity and brevity when, in a single sentence he stated: "Holy Communion pertains to the integrity of the Mass and to the partaking of the august Sacrament; but while it is obligatory for the priest who says the Mass, it is only something earnestly recommended to the faithful."

Before addressing ourselves to other "new labels on old, old errors," let us recall what Pius XII taught about something that seems to be going out of use: Thanksgiving after Communion.

"When the Mass, which is subject to special rules of the Liturgy, is over, the person who has received Holy Communion is not thereby freed from his *duty* of thanksgiving; rather, it is most becoming that, when the Mass is finished, the person who has received the Eucharist should recollect himself, and in intimate union with the Divine Master hold loving and fruitful converse with Him. Hence, they have departed from the straight way of truth who, adhering to the letter rather than to the sense, assert and teach that when Mass has ended, no such thanksgiving should be added, not only because the Mass is itself a thanksgiving, but also because this pertains to a private and personal act of piety and not to the good of the community."

That may shock you, if you have not heard of it before. But it is fact. The so-called "new breed," carried away by the communal aspect, forgetting that a community can only be made up of individuals, seem to want to do away with everything that is personal, individual, and truly intimate. They have used the wildest arguments for doing away with "thanksgiving after

[59]

Communion." Some try to prove that Christ remains sacramentally present only for the briefest amount of time; saying that the species are assimilated in less than three minutes. Therefore — and what a "conclusion" that is! — therefore, thanksgiving would not only be out of place, it would be "out of context" — since the Person you would be conversing with would not be present! That is utterly illogical; for, even it were true that the species have been assimilated, Christ is present, *really* present, in a non-sacramental manner.

Pius XII, with his usual honesty and true logic and theologicallity, went on to say: "Admittedly the congregation has been officially dismissed, but each individual, since he is united with Christ, should not interrupt the hymn of praise in his own soul 'always returning thanks for all in the name of Our Lord, Jesus Christ, to God and the Father.' The Sacred Liturgy of the Mass also exhorts us to do this when it bids us pray in these words: 'Grant, we beseech Thee, that we may always continue to offer thanks . . . and may never cease from praising Thee!'"

"Wherefore," concludes His Holiness, "if there is no time when we must not offer God thanks, and if we must never cease from praising Him, who would dare to reprehend or find fault with the Church, because she advises her priests and faithful to converse with the Divine Redeemer for at least a short while after Holy Communion . . . ?"

Pius XII was being gentle in that passage, as becomes a Pope and Pastor. He well knew, as many of us know, that there are those who "dare reprehend and find fault with the Church" for so advising. But now that you have the authentic and authoritative statement of the Church, you need never be misled by the "intellectuals" who say that "thanksgiving after Holy Communion" is wrong "because" — and do grasp their "reason" — "because the congregation has been officially dismissed." Dismissed from Mass, yes; but from the Liturgical act of *Sacrifice;* not from the duty, the privilege, the instinctive response to having received the *Sacrament.* Of course these "intellectuals" disdain distinctions such as that between the Sacrifice and the Sacrament; failing to realize that in the first we give ourselves to God, and in the second He gives Himself to us; that there is a real distinction between the two, albeit the one is "confected" in the other — and there is an "inseparable" connection between the two. They "pertain," as Paul VI has said, "to the same Mystery," nevertheless they are clearly distinguishable. When you receive the Sacrament you do one thing. When you offer the Sacrifice you do something definitely and clearly distinct from that. And that is the one basic error that is made by those who teach that the Mass is a "meal." It is not. It never was and never will be. You can offer the Sacrifice without receiving the Sacrament. And, under certain circumstances, you can receive the Sacrament without offering the Sacrifice.

It is distressing to find intelligent men — some who have even studied Theology formally — falling for such rhetoric and falsity as that put forth by a certain psychologist named Ernest Ell. First of all, what has a psychologist to do with Theology? But let that pass and read his "drastic formula." The Catholic Church, he says, went from "the meal to the mass; worse still, from the meal to high mass; and worst of all, from the meal to Pontifical High Mass. In this way, from age to age, the meal was increasingly obscured by the spectacle, until, in the end, only the spectacle remained . . . without the meal for the community." He does not stop at that distortion of truth. He goes on to say that this development of Mass from the meal was "a tactical plan for the clericalization of the Church." He regretted, he says "this development from meal to mass and, correspondingly, from house to cathedral; from table to altar; from the toga, ordinary dress for the Roman, to the chasuble; from the presbyteros to the clergy; from the laying on of hands to ordination; from the 'People of God' to the hierarchy; from the Church to religion; from Christ's command to 'eat' His meal to the 'vocation' to the clerical office."

Take those steps in reverse, and you may see what I mean by "no idea being without influence." Go from Mass to meal (as so many of the "new breed" have done); then from cathedral to house (as some more have attempted); from altar to table (as too many have taught); from chasuble to everyday dress; from the clergy to the presbyteros; from ordination to the laying on of hands; from the hierarchy to the "People of God"; from "vocation" to the clerical office to Christ's command to "eat" His meal — which, they claim, is the actuality as Christ instituted it! and you can see what is left of Truth, let alone of the Catholic Church as founded by the Son of God.

Whether this Psychologist is aware of it or not, he has but repeated that which was commonly heard in the mid-sixteenth century. It is Lutheranism in purest form. Luther would do away with the sacramental priesthood, with all Masses that were said in privacy with only a server assisting, would do away with the hierarchy — and did to his own satisfaction. But the Catholic Church did not disappear — nor did the clerical priesthood, the Mass, or the hierarchy.

But that such errors come not only from those outside the Church is evidenced by all that has been quoted from Pius XII as put forth in that 1947 Encyclical *Mediator Dei*. Just three years later the same Pontiff had to write his monumental *Humani Generis* and draw up a whole long list of errors contained in "opinions" — and that is the operative word! — of scholars and even men who rated the name of "theologians." His Holiness began with "philosophers and theologians" and admitted that "although we know that Catholic teachers generally avoid these errors, it is apparent, however that some today, as in apostolic times, desirous of novelty, and fearing to be considered ignorant of recent scientific findings try to withdraw themselves from the sacred Teaching Authority and are accordingly in danger of gradually departing from revealed truth and of drawing others along with them into error." After treating of many errors attributable to students of Sacred Scripture His Holiness tells how "novelties of this kind have already borne their deadly fruit in almost all branches of Theology" . . . Then after giving quite a number of examples, he came to the matter we have been examining and said: "Disregarding the Council of Trent,

[62]

some pervert the very concept of original sin, along with the concept of sin in general as an offense against God, as well as the idea of satisfaction performed for us by Christ. Some even say that the doctrine of Transubstantiation, based on an antiquated philosophic notion of substance, should be so modified that the real presence of Christ in the Eucharist be reduced to a kind of symbolism . . ."

Fifteen years later we hear the same tone of sorrow from the reigning Pope because of some of the intellectual waywardness of certain individuals who must consider themselves superior to the *Magisterium* of the Church. For Paul VI had to say: "Indeed we are aware of the fact that, among those who deal with this Most Holy Mystery (of the Eucharist) . . . there are some who, with reference either to Masses which are celebrated in private, or to the dogma of transubstantiation, or to devotion to the Eucharist, spread abroad such opinions (and again your attention is called to this very important word) as disturb the faithful and fill their minds with no little confusion about matters of faith, as if every one were permitted to consign to oblivion doctrine already defined by the Church, or to interpret it in such a way as to weaken the genuine meaning of the words or the approved import of the concepts involved."

Then the Pontiff went on in his marvelously clear Encyclical *Mysterium Fidei*, to enunciate again the Dogma you have held since childhood about the "Real Presence" and the adoration you should give the Lord there under the sacramental species. In his paternal gentleness he commended these men for their efforts to "investigate this lofty mystery . . . and to explain its meaning to the men of today . . ." But he immediately added: "However, we cannot approve the opinions (that word again!) which they express, and we have the duty to warn you about the grave danger which these opinions involve for correct faith."

You must realize of course that between opinion and truth there is a difference as wide as the sky. We all have opinions on this, that, and the other thing. But so long as it is only an "opinion," there is a lack of certainty about this, that, or the other thing concerning which we have the "opinion." Further, there is always present a degree of *doubt*. Once we are certain about anything, all doubt vanishes; for we have truth. For instance, you have truth about your own existence. You are certain of it. You have not the vaguest doubt about it. But even in the soundest and most solid of opinions there is always a remaining doubt that the opposite opinion to yours may be true. Opinion is a state of mind in which you adhere to, or accept, some proposition as *probably* true; but you are not *certain* it *is* true. There is always some doubt about it. Certainty, on the other hand, leaves no room for doubt; no room for mere probability. You are certain the earth is round, that the sun gives heat, that rain is wet. You have only probability that democracy is the best form of government, only an opinion that we will put men on the moon within the next few years. You have no certainty. There is room for real doubt. Next, you must realize that while there can be sound opinions, high probability that they are corect, there are also opinions that are highly improbable, and others that are simply erroneous.

So, too, in the study of Theology. There are certainties — Christ presence in the Blessed Sacrament is one such. There are sound opinions — such as that the Upper Room saw the "ritual offering" of the one Sacrifice of Calvary, as Father de la Taille holds. Then there are erroneous "opinions" such as the one Pope Paul spoke of in his Encyclical; namely, that "Christ, the Lord, is no longer present in the consecrated hosts which are left after the celebration of Mass is ended." The point is that you are to distinguish between mere "opinion" and actual "truth."

The Eucharist is exactly what Paul named it in naming his Encyclical, and what every priest names it at the very moment of consecration — it is *"the* Mystery of Faith." It will always be beyond our comprehension — else it would not be a mystery. But, as St. John Chrysostom said: "Let us submit to God in all things and not contradict Him, even if what He says seem contrary to our reason and intellect; rather let His words prevail over our reason and intellect. Let us also act in this way with regard to the (Eucharistic) mysteries, looking not only at what falls under our senses but holding to His words. For His words cannot lead us astray." St. Cyril advised the same: "Doubt not whether this be true; but take rather the Saviour's words with faith, for since He is Truth, he lieth not."

It is as true today as it was when Christ first promised the Eucharist: "This is a hard saying." Indeed it is; and many say today what was said then: "who can listen to it?" (Jno. 6: 61) There are those who do today what was done then: "many of his disciples left him and stopped going with him." But we, just as Peter did then, when Christ asks us: "What about you, do you want to go away too?" answer: "Lord, to whom shall we go? You have the message of eternal life, and we believe; we know that you are the Holy One of God" (Jno. 6:69 — Jerus. Bible)

The point is that, as Pope Paul said: "It is a logical conclusion, then, that we should follow as a guiding star in our investigations of this mystery the *Magisterium* of the Church, to which the Divine Redeemer entrusted for protection and for explanation the word of God written or handed down, having this firm conviction that 'what since the days of antiquity was preached and believed throughout the whole Church with true catholic faith is true, even if it is not comprehended by reason, even if it is not explained by means of words."

But the integrity of the faith is not the only thing that is to be safeguarded against the "opinions" of philosophers and theologians of the present generation, we must also safeguard the very words used to express this mystery. Paul VI showed us why "transubstantiation" is to be kept — and not "transignification" or "transfinalization." It is the one word, consecrated by Trent and by usage, that explains clearly what it is that takes place, and what makes this Sacrament different from all others. Paul cited Theodore of Mopsuestia, "a faithful witness to the faith of the Church" as having said: "The Lord did not say: 'This is a symbol of My Body, and this is a symbol of My Blood,' but: 'This is My Body, and this is My Blood'. He teaches us not to look to the nature of the thing which lies before us and is perceived by the senses; for, by the prayer of thanksgiving and the words spoken over it, it has been changed into Flesh and Blood." The Pope then went on to say: "To avoid misunderstanding . . . we must listen with docility to the voice of the teaching and praying Church. This voice, *which constantly echoes the voice of Christ*, assures us that the way Christ is made present in this Sacrament is none other than the change of the whole *substance* of the bread into His Body, and of the whole *substance* of the wine into His Blood, and this unique and truly wonderful change the Catholic Church fittingly and *accurately* calls transubstantiation." *(Mysterium Fidei —* #44-46)

You have seen the Tabernacle removed from the altar that has been turned around, and you may have wondered if this meant a change in your adoration of God really and substantially present in the Blessed Sacrament. You have seen, or heard, of special chapels — usually to the side of the church — being the place where the Blessed Sacrament has been placed, and you may have wondered if this was not a lessening of the truth of the Real Presence. Not at all! As we have already noted, the changes have been made to increase your realization that Mass is the pulsing heart of our Religion; that the altar is the place of Sacrifice — and Sacrifice is the very essential core of all Religion; that you have been led on to participate as priests — according to your "ordination" in this Act of Love. Now you must be convinced that all these changes, and the one we are now considering, have been made for you — your greater sanctification, thanks to greater identification to Christ the High Priest and the Victim of the New Law's one Sacrifice. Your dignity concerns the Church. She would have you realize with ever fresh and deeper, keener realization just who you are, Whom you have been made by Baptism — namely, *Christ*. As Pope Paul put it: "to extol the dignity of all the faithful, and to spur their spirit toward the attainment of the highest sanctity, which is nothing less than the total offering of oneself to the service of the Divine Majesty." (M.F. — #31) But the Church does not stop there. She goes on to point out other ways for you to grow in Christness. Here are her words from the pen of Pope Paul: "It is to be desired that the faithful, every day and in great numbers, actively participate in the Sacrifice of the Mass, receive Holy Communion with a pure heart, and make fitting thanksgiving to Christ Our Lord for so great a gift. . . Moreover, in the course of the day the faithful should not omit to visit the Blessed Sacrament, which according to the liturgical laws must be kept in the Churches with great reverence in a most honorable location. Such visits are a proof of gratitude, an expression of love to Christ the Lord present in the Sacrament, and a duty of the adoration we owe." (ib #66)

Perhaps some have been upset by certain statements and actions regarding the Blessed Sacrament — especially about Its reservation and the many devotions we have always cultivated toward Him really, substantially, present therein. You may have seen the Tabernacle removed, the altar rail disappear, been made to receive Holy Communion standing, missed the annual Forty Hours Devotion, the processions on Holy Thursday to the Repository, and the well-established custom of having a Corpus Christi Procession. Such "innovations" could be very disturbing; for one could reasonably wonder about the Doctrine on the Real Presence. But once again you can be told to "Relax!" and even to "Rejoice!" For after some of the more impetuous pastors and priests had done the above things, and some avant garde "Theologians" had gained notoriety for their speculations on the manner of Christ's presence etc. the authoritative voice of the true Teaching Body of the Church has spoken out.

Paul VI had heard all you have heard — and more. He may not have seen all that you have seen, but he was cognizant of what was going on. Hence, his Encyclical *Mysterium Fidei*, which told us to keep the word "transubstantiation," that "the Church has always offered — *and still offers* — the cult of *latria* to the Sacrament of the Eucharist, not only during Mass, but *also outside* of it, reserving Consecrated Hosts with the utmost care, exposing them to solemn veneration of the faithful, and carrying them in processions. . ." His Holiness saw fit to mention the "feast of Corpus Christi, which was first celebrated in the diocese of Liege . . . and which our predecessor Urban IV extended to the universal Church. From it have originated many practices of Eucharistic piety which, under the inspiration of divine grace, have increased from day to day, and with which the Catholic Church is striving ever more to do homage to Christ, to thank Him for so great a gift, and to implore His mercy." (#65)

Then he exhorted all the Bishops (and through them those pastors and priests who have been somewhat impetuous) "to preserve this faith in its purity and integrity — a faith which seeks only to remain perfectly loyal to the words of Christ and of the Apostles and *unambiguously rejects all erroneous and mischievous opinions.* Tirelessly promote the cult of the Eucharist, the focus where all other forms of piety must ultimately meet and converge." (#64)

The Pope exhorted you, personally, and all other members of the People of God to visit the Blessed Sacrament; for such visits, he said "are a proof of gratitude, and expression of love . . . and a *duty of the adoration we owe.*" If we are to be human, we simply *must* adore. If we are to be Catholic, we must realize "the incomparable dignity" as the Pope put it, "the divine Eucharist bestows upon the Christian people. For, "as long as the Eucharist is kept in our churches and oratories, Christ is truly the Emmanuel, that is 'God with us'." Small wonder His Holiness ended this section with the statement that "there is *nothing* more consoling on earth, nothing more efficacious for advancing along the way of holiness, than this devotion to the Blessed Sacrament." So you can indeed "Rejoice!"

The bark of Peter is, indeed, sea-worthy. On the Feast of Corpus Christi, May 25, 1967, there came from the *Consilium* — for the Implementation of the Constitution on the Liturgy, a document that should help you to relax and rejoice, for it states in clearest terms that the Mass is a *Sacrifice* — in which the Sacrifice of the Cross is perpetuated; that it is at the same time and inseparably a *memorial* of the death and resurrection of the Lord, who said: "do this in memory of me" (Lc. 22:19) — and a sacred *banquet*. Once again this official document taught what we have always held, but which some seemed to have loosened their grasp upon; namely, that "the Eucharistic *Sacrifice*" (not the banquet) "is the source and the summit of the whole of the Church's worship and of the Christian life."

Of course the *Consilium,* far from denigrating Holy Communion, insisted upon it — but in its proper place and with its proper reference to the Sacrifice, saying: "The faithful participate more fully . . . not only when they offer the Sacred Victim, and in it themselves, . . . but also when they receive this same Victim Sacramentally." Then obliquely referring to some sophistical arguments this official body went on to say "that all the faithful ought to show to this most holy sacrament the worship which is due to the true God . . . Nor is it to be adored any the less because it was instituted by Christ to be eaten. For even in the reserved Sacrament He is to be *adored.*"

The immediate aim of all this is set forth in the paragraph which says that "what the faithful have received by faith and Sacrament in the celebration of the Eucharist should have its effect on their way of life." That is why it is said once again that Vatican II had *you* in mind; that the real purpose of all changes is to change you; that all these "new" things are ultimately for the "new man." That truth was put forth officially by this same *Concilium* in this same document when it said: "everyone who has participated in the Mass should be 'eager to do good works, to please God, and to live honestly, devoted to the Church, putting into practice what he has learnt, and growing in piety.' He will seek to fill the world with the Spirit of Christ and 'in all things, in the very midst of human affairs to become a witness to Christ."

Read that last sentence again and realize that you are being challenged to manifest to your world the dignity that God has bestowed upon you by calling you to be a member of His People.

Some of you have been puzzled by the "newness" in standing to receive Holy Communion. But once again "His — Story" teaches us that it is kneeling that is really "new." Standing has been the practice in the Eastern Church for twenty centuries — and it was the practice in the Latin rite for thirteen centuries. So you see, it is not new. Further, standing is a mark of respect and reverence. Not that kneeling is not the same. But, do not let a change of custom upset you. God made us humans the only living creatures who can really stand erect. It is our normal posture. However, let it be said that standing to receive is not universally mandatory. The *Consilium* has just said that "In accordance with the custom of the Church, Communion may be received by the faithful either kneeling or standing. One or the other way is to be chosen according to the decision of the Episcopal Conference . . ." Then it kindly and prudently adds: "The faithful should willingly adopt the method indicated by their pastors, so that Communion may truly be a *sign of the brotherly union* of all those who share in the same table of the Lord."

After all, does it really matter whether you stand or kneel — or even receive lying down? Hardly. The real thing is to receive HIM.

The *Consilium* then added what you have already been advised by Paul VI — and by your own innate and instinctive sense of the proper: Thanksgiving after Holy Communion is encouraged. But the Consilium went one step further and said: "But union with Christ, to which the Sacrament itself is directed, is not to be limited to the duration of the celebration of the Eucharist; it is to be prolonged into the *entire Christian life*, in such a way that the Christian faithful . . . may make their life a continual thanksgiving."

Now it can be said that your life should be Eucharistic in the fullest sense of that word — not only as priest and victim "in, with and through" Jesus Christ, but in the completest meaning of Mass: life should be adoration, thanksgiving, reparation, and impetration. And in that order! We should give before we ever ask; be donors before being recipients; love before being loved! If you make Mass your life — and that is very precisely what Vatican II desires — then you will make your life "Mass."

The *Consilium* closed its long, authentic instruction on "Worship of the Eucharistic Mystery" with prescriptions for Reservation, Exposition, Processions of the Blessed Sacrament. All that has been part of your life as a Catholic has been preserved. How could it be otherwise when, with repeated insistence, Vatican II taught again, again, and again that "the Eucharistic Sacrifice is the source and summit" . . . the "Center of the entire life of the Church" — "the true center of the whole Christian life both for the universal Church and for the local congregations of that Church" — "the summit of both the action by which God sanctifies the world in Christ, and the worship which men offer to Christ, and through Him to the Father in the Spirit." Finally it has been pointed out that the celebration of the Eucharist is "the supreme means by which the faithful come to express in their lives, and to manifest to others, the mystery of Christ and the true nature of the Church."

We have spent a long time on this study of the changes in the Mass; for "it is the Mass that matters." — Matters to you — else you would never have been so stimulated by the changes. Matters to you — yes, to the extent that it is a "matter of life or death" — You can live by the very life of Christ thanks to the Sacrifice of Mass and the Sacrament confected therein. You can cling ever more closely to the Vine — and have His "sap" run through you as a branch, with ever greater fecundity the result.

If you have thought, now and then, that I have been a bit hard on some of the speculative theologians, let me cite Bishop John Wright in his Statement on the "Year of Faith" given to his Diocese of Pittsburgh on June 22, 1967, touching the same subject: the difference between Theologians and the Authentic Teaching Body of the Church. After first questioning whether we are, as yet, in a real "crisis of Faith," and not rather in a "crisis of hope" Bishop Wright said: "Much of the present crisis in religion is due perhaps to confusion arising from failure to keep clear these distinctions between the 'theologies' and the Faith. . . The exciting years of the Council experience . . . have stimulated minds, and dizzied some imaginations with the theoretical speculations, reasonings, wit, wisdom, subtlety, and, occasionally, aberrations of scores of theologians who suddenly became popular lecturers, authors of best-sellers, and TV personalities. . . Theologians are men; and the thoughts of men are many and divided. Theological *theories* set forth aspects, elements, corollaries of the Faith. They provide reasonings about the Faith. But theologians are not sources of Faith, nor are their speculations the object of Faith. . . *Only* what the Church teaches *authoritatively* as the mind and the will of Jesus Christ is the object of Faith; all the theologies . . . are secondary and peripheral; related to the Faith, perhaps, but not to be confused with it."

That is the point we have been laboring to make as we called attention to the Press. Bishop Wright goes on to say that "such a confusion *has* taken place." We have been endeavoring to unscramble that "confusion." Therefore, we close this long chapter, and this long examination of the Liturgical changes with this quotation. The words are Bishop Wright's; the thought comes from the bottom of my being:

"Suddenly caught up in the intricacies and fascinations of theologies, people have supposed the Faith to be at issue in the speculations they have found so heady. And so it is well to recall, as should be obvious, that Father Baum or Monsignor Bandas, Father Häring or Father Connell, Hans Küng or Cardinal Brown, Fathers Congar or de Lubac, either or both of the Rahners, Charles Davis, the Council Press Panels (including Bishop Bekkers or even me), Teilhard, Scotus, Bonaventure, Aquinas (not to mention Bonhoffer, Cox, Altizer and Who Not?) may be scholars, but they are also fallible men; some are professional theologians of measurable competence and degrees of insight, perhaps (as we have discreetly suggested) degrees of Faith. In any case, they are the objects of such attention, gratitude, and agreement as the critical, intelligent listener or reader may deem them to deserve. It is *entirely different*, as any one of these would, please God, be the first to confess, with Jesus Christ and the *authentic* teaching voice of His Church. Christ and what God teaches through the channels of revelation committed to the care and judgment of the *Magisterium* in the Church, are the objects of our Faith.

"The various theologies may be freely examined, freely espoused, some freely rejected; not so with the Faith itself. Here, as Pope Paul has recently pointed out, freedom takes on other formalities so far as the Christian is concerned. Although we are free (psychologically, though not equally so morally) to accept the Faith of Jesus Christ or not, we are not free in the formulation of the content of the Faith; we are not free to pick and choose among the articles of the Faith, as we would be to choose critically among the contentions of the theologians. . . The Faith . . . is a total commitment that the Christian can give to no man, to no theological opinion, and, therefore, to no theologian."

Bishop Wright then went on to make the point I have already made, please God; namely, that "any crisis in the Church arising from confusions among theologians and rival commitments to theological parties or personalities is no *new* thing." He then cites as example what you have already read about St. Paul and his times. Then he concludes: "Clearly, this is an old story — and a new one. Theological debate, lively and fruitful, is indispensable to religious progress and to the renewal of Christian life, thought, and values; but the loving service of the Faith, and unqualified adherence to the univocal teaching of the Church concerning the undivided Christ, who alone was crucified for us, and to Whom alone we are committed by Faith at Baptism — these are the basic, the essential, the enduring needs, demands, joys of the Christian Creed and Code.

"That is why we who dearly love freedom, cherish Faith even more passionately. That is why we who rejoice in the renewal of theological studies in and around the Council, welcome even more the 'Year of Faith' by which Pope Paul hopes to make secure the good coming out of the Council, and fortify that authentic teaching of the Church, without which theological discussions and speculations become unsubstantial and fanciful, like to the fragile writings of so many romanticists and aesthetes who speak nostalgically, but unprofitably, of the beauty of a Faith which they no longer believe as true, or live as good and essential to salvation."

With that in mind you can relax and rejoice as you read to-day's presentation of religious news. Theologians are only theologians and not the authentic teaching body of the Church — and the opinion of each is only an opinion — and as Aquinas taught so long ago: "worth as much as the *reasons* behind it." These men, some of them at least, may speak with "authority" (for they are learned in their science) but they can never speak "authoritatively." That can be done only by the *Magisterium.* So, despite what you may read in the popular press about the Church, you can relax and rejoice — for "all is well" with the bark of Peter — no matter how strident the winds whipping up the waters of the world in which she moves.

A Concelebrated Mass

Chapter 4

ALL THE NEWS THAT IS PRINT TO FIT

This chapter, after all that has been said about the priesthood — both yours and that of the men in Holy Orders — was
to have been on celibacy, a subject over which the Press has
had a noisy time of late. But His Holiness, Paul VI has made
a chapter on that "brilliant jewel" unnecessary. Yet a few words
on the way the subject has been handled in the popular periodicals may be in place.

Undoubtedly there have been those in the Church who may
have felt as did one of the characters in the play *Green Pastures*
and concluded, after reading all that was printed about defections from the priesthood for the sake of a woman, and the observations of priests, young and not so young, about the need
for change in this matter, that "De levees is gonter bust, an'
everything dat's fastened down is comin' loose." But now that
the Pope has spoken on this matter with such clarity and firmness, after such an exhaustive study, we can relax — and even
rejoice that this is one of those things that is "fastened down,"
and which no pressure will make "come loose."

But what pressure you have been subjected to! To read the
secular press you would think there was a wholesale abandonment of celibacy by the clergy — just because a name "theologian" went off with an American woman, and some English priest
flew to California to "marry" some Oriental, or some Chancellor
of a Diocese took to himself a divorcee.

There have been defections. No one denies that. Rome even
admitted that some four thousand cases had been looked into
since 1964 — some of which have been hanging fire for three
decades. The number may shock some of the less well-informed,
and the more idealistic. But taking statistics for what they are

worth, what is the percentage derived from that number four thousand when the total number of priests in the world runs well over hundreds of thousands?

Yet, it hasn't been the secular press alone that has added to the uneasiness among Catholics; pronouncements in their own press have been disturbing. Undoubtedly the effort of the Jesuit Father Fichter to question some three thousand priests, and the conclusion the press gave out that "two out of three voted for the freedom (of the clergy) to choose marriage" was unsettling. When this was followed by the poll by the National Association for Pastoral Renewal in twenty-two dioceses in the United States on the question of "optional celibacy," and the press told you that the "response was overwhelmingly favorable," you must have begun to think that maybe "the levees is gonter bust." When you read that "an official" (how wonderful a word, and how cowardly a reporting!) "of the National Council of Catholic Men stated that about six hundred priests in the United States are already married"; then read how "more than ten thousand petitions for release from priestly vows have been received at the Vatican during the past decade" and that "a Vatican official (again that wonderful word — and that some cowardly reporting!) "admits that such requests are piling up," you must have thought that "the levee had already busted."

What has been most illogical in the whole matter has been the way these advocates of change in celibacy have claimed to be following "the questioning spirit of Vatican II." That is not only illogical, it is illegitimate. One would have to suppose that both Father Fichter S.J., who is usually identified in the news as "Professor of Sociology at Harvard," and Monsignor John A. O'Brien, who wins from the press the by-line of "author and research Professor of Theology at University of Notre Dame," had never read the Decree on Priestly Formation, promulgated by Pope Paul October 28, 1965, nor the Decree on the Ministry and Life of Priests, promulgated December 7, 1965 by the same Pontiff acting as the one official voice of the Second Vatican Council, and, finally, that they had missed the explicit reference to celibacy in the Dogmatic Constitution on the Church. For in all three documents celibacy was presented as beyond all questioning. That is the "spirit of the Council" in this matter; just as it is its "letter."

The Council said: "Students who, according to the holy and fixed laws of their own rite, follow the revered tradition of priestly celibacy should be carefully trained for this state. By it they renounce the companionship of marriage for the sake of the kingdom of Heaven (cf. Mt. 19:12); they devote themselves to the Lord with an undivided love which is profoundly proper to the new covenant; they bear witness to the state which the resurrection will bring about in the world to come (Cf. Lc. 20:36); and they gain extremely appropriate help for exercising that perfect and unremitting love by which they can become all things to all men through their priestly ministrations." (#10 Priestly Formation)

Anyone thinking theologically can see from the Scriptural references, that priestly celibacy is freely chosen for the kingdom of God. It has been amusing to note how infrequently — one might say, "almost never" — has any allusion been made to the passage in Matthew to which the Council would have us look. It is a very interesting passage — and should command the attention of anyone who would talk intelligently on this matter of celibacy. Christ had been challenged by some Pharisees on the matter of divorce. His reply was one that needs to be repeated day in and day out: "what God has united, man must not divide." (Mt. 19:6) Christ went on to tell them very directly that "the man who divorces his wife — and marries another, is guilty of adultery." This uncompromising assertion of the indissolubility of marriage set even the disciples saying: "If that is how things are — it is not advisable to marry." Then comes the key text for all who would talk theologically about clerical celibacy: "It is not everyone who can accept what I have said, but only those to whom it is granted. There are eunuchs born that way from their mother's womb, there are eunuchs made so by men, and there are eunuchs who have made themselves that way for the sake of the kingdom of heaven. Let anyone accept this who can." (Mt. 16:10-12)

In that last sentence Christ invites to perpetual continence those who would consecrate themselves entirely to the Kingdom of God. No candidate for the priesthood in the Latin rite has been ignorant of this fact. If he accepted the invitation, he did so freely and with full knowledge of just what was entailed. That is why Paul VI could say in his Encyclical *Sacerotalis Caelibatus:* "the law requiring a *freely chosen* and perpetual celibacy of those admitted to Holy Orders remains unchanged."

The Council spoke very directly to aspirants to the priesthood, saying: "Seminarians should be duly aware of the duties and dignity of Christian marriage, which bodies forth the love between Christ and the Church (Cf. Eph. 5:32 sqq). Let them perceive as well the superiority of virginity consecrated to Christ, so that by a *choice* which is maturely thought out and magnanimous they may attach themselves to God by a total gift of body and soul." (#10) But that high idealism was accompanied by almost brutal realism as the Council went on to say: "Let them be warned of the very severe dangers with which their chastity will be confronted in present-day society. Aided by appropriate helps, both divine and human, may they learn so to integrate the renunciation of marriage into their life and activity that these will not suffer any detriment from celibacy; rather, that they themselves may achieve a greater mastery of soul and body, and added growth in maturity; and may comprehend more profoundly the blessedness promised by the gospel."

The Council all but repeated itself on this subject when it came to make a Decree on the Life of Priests. It exhorted all priests "who, trusting in God's grace, have freely undertaken sacred celibacy in imitation of Christ" to "hold fast to it magnanimously and wholeheartedly." (#16) It ended the paragraph by asking "not only priests, but all the faithful to have at heart this precious gift of priestly celibacy. Let all beg God that He may always lavish this gift upon His Church abundantly."

FATHER M. RAYMOND, O.C.S.O.

With that before you, how do you feel when you read the following: "A decision on the question of whether priests should be permitted to marry is long overdue, a prominent Catholic theologian told *Chicago's American today*. 'For far too long, the subject of celibacy has been swept under the rug,' said the Rev. John A. O'Brien." But that is not all of it. The *American* goes on to say that the Monsignor added: "Sincere and honest treatment has been frowned upon. The refusal to permit rational inquiry on any man-made legislation, such as this, only begets suspicion that the law in question cannot stand close scrutiny and honest examination. Thank God the Vatican Council has opened that door for such discussion, and that door can never again be closed upon free men."

Let us hope that the good Monsignor was talking "off the top of his head"; that some reporter for the Chicago *American* caught him somewhat off guard; and that further study of the Council Documents would have convinced him that the mind of the Church was very clear and the heart of the Church truly devoted to clerical celibacy.

But that kind of a statement by the *American* was mild compared to many others in, perhaps, more distinguished media. The *Saturday Evening Post* carried an anonymous article: "I Am a Priest, I Want To Get Married." Then about a year later *Look* magazine had a truly sensational article by this same writer who did not stay anonymous this time. Father James Kavanaugh allowed his emotions and imagination so to run away with him that he wrote a whole book which he rather arrogantly and presumptuously titled A MODERN PRIEST LOOKS AT HIS OUTDATED CHURCH. Monsignor Kennedy aptly summed it up by saying the two adjectives in that title tell you the book's whole story. The priest in question may be quite "modern" but he is most obviously none too "priestly." As for the Church he found "outdated," perhaps she could not but find him rather emotionally — and intellectually, immature. But what intrigues the thinking man is the fact that while *Look* was evidently anxious to get that article from Father's book

[81]

before the public, it was not even interested in running a critique of the book in any other of its issues. Gerald Renner, an associate director of the U.S. Catholic Conference Bureau of Information, asked William Arthur, *Look's* editor, if he would publish a critique of Kavanaugh's book in his magazine. The answer was distinctly negative. Yet this same magazine, presumably with the same editor's approval, introduced Fr. Kavanaugh's article with such fulsome praise as "With courage and candor a Roman Catholic priest pleads for reforms in his Church." One wonders where *Look's* "courage and *candor*" is when it refuses to publish a critique of this "great" book.

Of course journalism has always adhered to the old saw about "man bites dog" being *the* news. But one may ask: *Is it American* to be slanted, unfair, or to refuse to report that some "dogs" bite the man back? We Americans believe in freedom of the press — but we often wonder if the press knows what freedom it is that we so wholeheartedly believe in. Certainly not many Americans would approve of the "freedom" shown by the editor in the case above: freedom to do what he *likes* — and not the freedom to do what he *ought*. We Americans like fair play — and it is that fair play which our freedom demands.

How many articles by Psychiatrists have you read making out a case *for* celibacy? I need not ask the number you have read by the same type of men *against* celibacy; for it is all but axiomatic with such practitioners that "sexual abstinence means sexual denial; but sexual denial means sexual repression; and, of course, sexual repression means *neurosis*." Celibates, therefore — the conclusion is inescapable — are *sick*. And yet there is before me an article by Jean B. Rosenbaum, M.D., Instructor in the Department of Psychiatry, Wayne University College of Medicine, and a frequent contributor to psychoanalytical journals — which makes out a strong case for celibacy.

Dr. Rosenbaum confesses that he practices no religion himself, yet has been chosen by some Religious Superiors as the man their subjects should consult. Further, he has had many clergymen in his classes as Wayne University. This twofold experience with patients and pupils led this scientist to note two things: first, that just as there are many sexually active people who develop mental illness, so, secondly, there are sexually abstinent people who obviously do not. This set him saying: "when any theory contradicts obvious reality, either the theory must be modified, or it will crumble." He changed his theory; for the facts were against it. His conclusion, arrived at after many cases and long study was: "Sexual abstinence which serves well and which is based on a unique makeup is not only healthy, but it is *vitally necessary* for the fullest living by a religious, for it is the precondition of his ability to most fully love, work, and create within the structure of the Church."

Dr. Rosenbaum said: "The priest loves, but he has transformed the basic male need to have intercourse with one woman and produce a son, into a desexualized love for all women, and a sense of benevolence toward all men. The nun loves, but she sublimates her need to be pregnant by a man and raise his family, into feminine work for all men, and a maternal affection and attention to all children."

That kind of thing is seldom found in the modern day press, while its opposite, as stated explicitly by Pope Paul VI, is too often found. The Pope said: "There are also some who strongly maintain that priests, by reason of their celibacy, find themselves in a situation that is physically and psychologically detrimental to the development to a mature and well-balanced human personality." You cannot say that His Holiness is not up on the modern jargon. He has not missed a word that is "in" today. Nor can you say that the Pontiff simply "repeated and reaffirmed an ancient rule." Obviously Paul VI did what he says he did: "Examine clerical celibacy more penetratingly than ever before, from the doctrinal, historical, psychological, sociological, and pastoral points of view." That is why he could state: "After what science has now ascertained, it is not just to continue repeating that celibacy runs counter to lawful physical, psychological and affective needs, or to claim that a completely mature human personality demands fulfillment of these needs." But

[83]

that statement was not enough for His Holiness — nor for you Catholics who have always revered your priests. Paul continued: "Man, created to God's image and likeness, is not just flesh and blood; the sexual instinct is not all that he has; man is also, and pre-eminently, understanding, choice, freedom; and, thanks to these powers, he is, and must remain, superior to the rest of creation; they give him mastery over his physical, psychological, and affective appetites."

As the Council, so the Pope, was realistic — very realistic. He said: "The choice of celibacy does not connote ignorance, or the despisal of the sexual instinct and affectivity. That would certainly do damage to the physical and psychological balance. On the contrary, it demands clear understanding, careful self-control, and a wise sublimation of the psychological life on a higher level and makes an effective contribution to his own perfection."

The Pope sounds like a psychoanalyst in that passage — and rightly so; for he had left no avenue of investigation in this matter of celibacy unexplored. But did you notice how the professional Psycholanalyst quoted above, all but echoed both the Council and St. Paul when he said his observation in long clinical practice enabled him to say that priestly celibacy and the virginity of nuns enabled these real persons to be "all things to all men" — and women!

Even before the Pope's Encyclical, Jean Guitton had written: "I would like to say one last word on the much discussed problem of priestly celibacy, and this from the point of view of a married man. If in this aphrodisiac world of ours, people can practice pre-marital chastity, conjugal fidelity and chastity, without heroic effort, it is because they see people living outside of cloisters who are young, strong, manly, open, and warm, cheerfully and almost spontaneously chaste: priests. The abnegation of a few raises and purifies the atmosphere for all. Without these men, who, while very human, have yet inscribed in their flesh the token of the Absolute, and whose conduct would be absurd if there were no Absolute, the spiritual level would

[84]

fall immediately. Flesh would little by little overcome the spirit, for we would be quickly convinced that the spirit cannot overcome the flesh, at least without the exceptional conditions of the monastery or the religious life. There would be a decline of freedom in souls — of this I am convinced."

So should any thinking man be. Celibacy in a few strengthens freedom in the souls of the many. As one woman in Pennsylvania, when questioned by one of the Louis Harris and Associates interviewers for the poll taken by *Newsweek*, replied: "They freely chose the life of a priest with all its blessings and restrictions. We look up to them as such and expect them to be different from every other man." She has not been disappointed too often. A book such as Father Kavanaugh has written will not help such people — nor anyone else, for that matter. As one has observed the book is "the work of an exploited man, a man blinded by emotion, who has stopped thinking creatively, who is faltering in faith and hope. In such a state he can only mislead, not lead, God's people." But this criticism by Fr. Thomas E. Clarke S. J. was immediately followed by "For their sake, as well as for his, I pray he will receive the support he needs: guidance from God, and the sympathetic presence and advice of friends."

The Pope sounded the identical note toward the close of his Encyclical on Celibacy saying: "Now with fatherly love and affection our heart turns anxiously and with deep sorrow to those unfortunate priests who always remain our dearly beloved brothers and whose misfortune we keenly regret: those who, retaining the sacred character conferred by their priestly ordination, have been or are unfortunately unfaithful to the obligations they accepted when they were ordained. . . The Church is very conscious of the sad state of these sons of hers and judges it necessary to make every effort to avert or to remedy the wounds she suffers by their defection."

That is honesty. That is also being Christlike: loving the sinner with warm, paternal — almost maternal — love, but never condoning the sin; never saying it was inevitable, psychologically

[85]

necessary, the only way to fulfill your person! The Church has always been a depth psychologist of the first water — deeper far than anything the science of the day has yet brought to light, but never one to indulge in jargon to hide reality. Sin she has always called sin — and never a mere physiological-psychological compulsion!

It was refreshing to read in a small Catholic publication at the time so much was being made in the secular press of the defection by Father Charles Davis in England and of the article by the priest who proclaimed that he wanted to marry, the following witty, in the truest sense of that word, testimony by Father Norbert Sharon, M.S.SS.T. —

"I am a Catholic priest — never wrote for the *Saturday Evening Post* — never organized a union for discontented priests — never even had an 'identity crisis' . . . Just a happy priest, thankful for the privilege of working full time for my God.

"My life has meaning. . . Each morning I offer the Holy Sacrifice of the Mass. The Bread of Life is present upon the altar through me.

"I am not 'half a man' anymore than Christ was 'half a man' (for not being married). His thirty years of preparation were matched by my own long Seminary training. These were happy years. I knew what I was doing.

"Neither my parents nor any 'well meaning advisors' kept me from entering the Seminary. (Otherwise there would be one less priest.)

"The Church that baptised me is the same that ordained me. It is the very same Church that I see today — perhaps the 'building' has been repainted a little with a pleasant coating of English here and there, plus a nice new floodlight shining on (that same old) Bible. People seem to be singing a little more (still off key), but the essentials remain the same.

"I guess I will just never make the news, because I am like so many thousands of other priests who are happy in God's service.

"Well, if the Lord Himself had an 8% rate of defects (among

His very own Apostles), I guess I shouldn't be too concerned
that the same problem continues (but happily on a smaller
scale.) It wouldn't keep me from following Him. I sure hope
it won't stop others. The odds still seem to be better than 11 out
of 12 for success!

"Thank You, God; I'm glad I am Your priest."

That is something quite different in tone — and in truth —
from what Charles Davis released to the press in his statement
"Why I left the Roman Catholic Church"; different in tone —
and, again, in truth — from anything Father Kavanough has yet
written. And never forget that for one Father Kavanough, there
are thousands, and even tens of thousands of Father Sharons.
But, as the witty Father Sharon said: he would "never make the
news." Would it be wrong to suggest that the reason is journalistic: he is a "*man* — who does not bite dogs?"

It was also gratifying to read — again at the same time —
and again in a larger though still relatively small Catholic publication — a less jolly but nonetheless jolting piece about the
press, albeit obliquely. A woman from Lowell, Massachusetts
had written in to the Question Box of the magazine *THE SIGN*:
"Would you please say something about the Father Charles
Davis affair. I am confused. I get the impression that too many
Catholics, especially supposedly learned ones, have minimized
what he has done, and have been too busy excusing him. One
well-known theologian even praised Father Davis' fidelity to his
'singular' vocation. What is wrong with our theologians? Don't
they have any sense of responsibility for the Church any more?"

This individual had reason to be confused — and very sound
reason for questioning in this manner. Too many failed to make
the necessary distinction between the sin and the sinner. We
can never love the first. We must always love the latter. But
other leading Catholic periodicals, *Commonweal*, of course
Jubilee, and to some extent, even *America* contributed to this individual's confusion. The priest who answers questions in *THE
SIGN* was forthright. His reply ran in part: "*Touché!* While I
have read no outright approval of Father Davis' action . . . I

[87]

must agree that there has been an extraordinary outpouring of sympathy for him. It seems more attention has been given to why he left the Church than to the fact of his apostasy. Why? . . . a psychologist might be able to throw light on this phenomenon. It seems to be that Father Davis . . . has become a symbol for some people . . . but he cannot serve as such . . . Father Davis is no prophet, at least not according to any traditional canons of Catholic theology. What is the supposed 'singular vocation' that he is being faithful to? What theologian can really support such a notion? Father Davis has abandoned his vocation as a priest. He has reneged on his promise of celibate dedication. Without any possibility of a plea of ignorance, he has rejected the divine origins and instrumentality of the Church. Fidelity to his conscience? — I fervently hope that he is being true to his conscience. That is his hope for salvation. But can we encourage Father Davis to consider his conscience as a reflection of Catholic Faith? No, Father Davis as a symbol of the suffering servant of God is not theologically acceptable. . .

"Sympathize with Father Davis? One must cry for him. Such a shipwreck is soberingly tragic. But we must not make him what he is not. He will not do as a Christian hero. There are others much more worthy of the honor — men who have suffered more, believed more tenaciously, and loved more generously."

That is the kind of writing you seldom find in the secular press. That is the kind of straightforwardness you find too seldom in the Catholic press. And since every effect must have a proportionate cause, I am going to suggest to you that it is not the cause usually given by journalists; namely, the case of "man biting dog." At least not ultimately.

Of course there are more immediate causes for this kind of reporting in both presses. John Leo, in the December-January (1966-67) issue of *The Critic*, gives you one such "cause." He rather triumphantly tells that there is in America today a self-appointed coterie of "liberal" Catholics consisting of several dozen scholars, journalists, activists, and publishers who, in his own words, are "the Establishment." He claims that they are the ones who publicize and shape the issues that "dominate American Catholic life today." It is too large a claim, of course; but there is some substance in it. They are the articulate minority whose words have an outrageously disproportionate weight to their worth. Mr. Leo used to be quite a frequent contributor to *National Catholic Reporter* wherein he could really "ventilate." But even there he went too far with his sneers. This same writer elsewhere has sneered at the "paper thunderbolts" that fly out of the "world of Romanita" and even claimed the utter "irrelevance" of "the Italian Church." Bishop Helmsing, with whose blessing and practical support the paper was founded, disassociated himself from it because of the "wild speculations and reporting" on such matters as birth control, priestly celibacy, and Church Authority — done by this same "Establishment." Mr. Leo then became connected with the New York *Times* in — of all capacities — the role of Religious Editor! In this capacity he had a whole page on Priestly Celibacy in the *Times* just a fortnight before the Pope's Encyclical — and Paul proved John Leo not only not a prophet, but not even a good prognosticator; aye, even lacking in ordinary perception. Yet it is from such reporters and editors more often than from Pope Paul that you hear in the press — and read about the changes. So let us speculate a bit on the possibility of an unsuspected source of the slant in much reporting.

Why, for instance, did *Newsweek* publish a dark — though not actually scowling — picture of Pope Paul VI — and opposite it a bright, smiling snap of one Father Gregory Baum — and then caption them: *"Pope Paul: The law continues . . . But, asks Baum, is it valid?"* Why begin this article with the title *In Defense of Celibacy?* — a strong caption. But then end it with almost a sneer, quoting Father Baum as saying: "The Pope has simply reaffirmed a rule, but we will have to study the arguments of the Pope to see if they are valid." If that last remark sounds arrogant to you, your hearing is excellent.

Why did *Look* pay good — and much — money to Fr. Kavanaugh for excerpts from his book, then refuse to accept — even for free — Father Bernard Cooke's S. J. critique? Why should the New York *Times* run an ad with almost the largest print available for Kavanaugh's book, shouting "THIS BOOK WILL MOVE THE WORLD" — then have laudations for Kavanaugh from a host of well-known liberal Catholics and avant gardists such as Father Baum, Michael Novak, Thomas Merton, Bishop James A. Pike. Why did the same *Times* give a whole page to its religion editor's soon-to-be-exploded prognostications of priestly Celibacy — and only a few columns, low down on a page to the forthcoming Encyclical itself? "Man bites dog" explains to some extent; but not to be full extent. Hence you are asked: Could it be '*Pax*'?"

There is an organization whose origins are, to say the least, dramatic. One Boleslaw Piasecki, a Pole who had been active in the resistance, was caught by the Soviets and condemned to death. But the cunning Communists saw possibility for use in this man. They promised life if he would infiltrate the Catholic Church and implement Lenin's recipe for destroying the Church *from within* — by creating and promoting artificial divisions between Bishops and Bishops; between Bishops and their own clergy; between clergy and laity.

Lenin's recipe is well known the world over. But the *Pax* Movement is hardly known outside of Europe. Yet evidence is not wanting that it is highly active in Latin America, the United States and, to a lesser degree, Canada. Cardinal Wyszynski, with his usual prudence, boldness and bravery drew up a long, detailed and accurate account of the organization of *Pax*. This he sent to Rome. In it he named "the Communist Party, the Secret Police of the same, and the Bureau of Religious Affairs, as the real leaders of this "Movement." Orders are issued from Communist Headquarters. Piasecki answers directly to the Security Office (U.B. — the Secret Police). He poses as a Catholic, ingratiates himself with Catholic "intellectuals" — especially if they are writers — and pays them well for every "progressive" article they write. Since his organization has absorbed all the Catholic publications in Poland, and since he has the financial backing of the Party, he is really "Lord of the Press" — He pays well. What strength of character it would take for a hungry writer to refuse such a lure. But the people of Poland have not been taken in. They know that without money Piasecki would be without writers. So they pay little attention to what is published — especially since the 1956 "thaw."

Prior to the thaw there was a real freeze. Stalin went on one of his rages. Cardinal Wyszynski was imprisoned. Piasecki tipped his hand! He wrote a book titled THE ESSENTIAL PROBLEMS. Of course they were the Church and Religious Education. The Poles knew now what the Pax Movement was. Piasecki's usefulness was almost at an end. There came the period of de-Stalinization — and Piasecki had a new mission. His tactics:

1) Form cells of disunity among the Faithful.

2) Promote discord between Seculars and Regulars.

3) Divide the Bishops into "Integrists (Conservatives) and "Progressives."

4) Set Priests against Bishops.

5) Drive wedge into masses by contrived distinctions between "Progressives" and "Obstructionists."

6) Never attack Church save "for her own good"; to help her "clear away antiquated structures"; and do away with all "abuses which disfigure her."

7) Promote confusion by creating ambiguities.

Thus "condition Church by interior fragmentation for service of the Communist Revolution."

To any one acquainted with Communistic tactics, each step is normal; the ultimate end in view, well in line with all the

Party has ever and always aimed at. To anyone unacquainted with Communism and its tactics, it must read like a "pipe dream" — and the pipe not loaded with tobacco. But Rome, never known to be exactly gullible, saw fit to send a letter, signed by the Vatican Secretary of State, to the Papal Nuncio in Paris with instructions that he acquaint the French Episcopacy and the Major Superiors of all Religious Orders residing in France with the contents of this letter. That letter contained all of Cardinal Wyszinski's report. So you are not dreaming. Neither am I. We are dealing with *Pax* — and it does not spell peace for us.

At times Piasecki and his minions have been diabolically clever. After Pope John XXIII's dramatic act of receiving Kruschev's son-in-law, and making what has been called the "opening toward the left," *Pax* flattered all Popes, and Poland, itself, by insisting it and they had been granted by Divine Providence the role of saviour. Poland was to be the "Model of Coexistence between the Church and the Communistic State." But the Poles have longer memories than Mr. Piasecki credits them with. They were not taken in by any of his flattery and by any of his rhetoric.

Thereupon Piasecki showed himself true to Communistic tactics. He turned around and instead of flattering the Poles, he charged them with being in "opposition to the Pope.'" John XXIII was "The Pope of Co-existence." To fail to cooperate with the Polish Communistic Government was to oppose the Pope. "Just look at the intelligent, open, progressive French Episcopacy, and you'll see how far afield you are. See how they collaborate. See how they are ready for new moves."

The Poles hardly heard him. But then came John XXIII's Encyclical *Pacem in Terris*. Piasecki wrote: "The Head of the Church has decided in favor of those who promote the ideology of co-existence and collaboration with persons who profess other ideologies."

No one should have any difficulty deciphering that sentence. Mr. Piasecki is more Catholic than Cardinal Wyszinski. Mr.

Piasecki and his *Pax* movement is much more progressive and loyal to Rome than the Polish Episcopacy. As for the Polish laity . . .

Mr. Piasecki openly asserted again and again that "the good Pope John XXIII" had ended the Tridentine era in the history of the Catholic Church, and opened a new epoch in which the Church would be "much more open and tolerant — ready for compromise."

How familiar those words sound! What follows? you may ask. Maybe nothing. Maybe mere coincidence. But then, again, maybe *not!*

The *Pax* Movement, which made so much of *Pacem in Terris*, refused to so much as allow *Mater et Magistra*, by the same "good Pope XXIII," to be published. In the field of journalism, the Communists "print *only* the news that *fits*."

When Cardinal Wyszynski and the Polish Episcopacy protested quite vigorously against the way the Government was legislating for religious instruction, *Pax* and Piasecki, again tipped their hands. Once they openly supported the Government in this matter all further attempt to mask themselves as other than Communistic was futile. It was curtains for *Pax* in Poland — but rising curtain for *Pax* in France.

In the country of "Le Grand Charles" *Pax* members set up and maintained permanent contact with certain groups of "progressives" and won real sympathy from the same "because of the awful persecution these *Pax* members had suffered from the backward, conservative, and even recalcitrant Polish Episcopacy — and especially that Cardinal Wyszynski."

It was not difficult for *Pax* to organize tours into Poland — and to make them very carefully "Guided Tours." On such jaunts "progressive priests" were numerous. The result was that in 1962 *La Croix* ran a series of very carefully documented articles giving the real position of the Catholic Church in Poland. Father Wenger, Editor-in-Chief of *La Croix*, was immediately buried under mail — most of it from priests who had "been there, and had seen with their own eyes" — charging *La Croix* with gross misrepresentations. *La Croix*, far from retracting, had Cardinal Wyszynski read the articles and comment. His comment ended all protest. But not before it was proved that all the protesters were individuals who had been sympathetic to, or duped by — *Pax*.

The fascinating — and enlightening — follow-up on this story is that when the author of the articles gathered these articles and submitted them to the Diocesan Censor for his approbation, so that he could publish them in book form, he received the slightly unusual, to say the least, reply that "while there was nothing doctrinally erroneous in the articles, hence, the 'nihil obstat' could not be refused, still the Censor hoped that Pierre Lenert would have the courage to suppress the chapter dealing with *Pax*."

Pierre did not have that kind of courage; but for the more courageous kind he manifested in publishing the truth he and his book were the objects of a fierce campaign led by *Pax* and *Pax's* followers. Vilify Lenert and *La Croix*, they did; but deny a single fact these two had published, they did not.

Pax and Piasecki dread being exposed in France as they were in Poland. For that will certainly mean final curtain. Let the Catholics of the West recognize the Movement for what it actually is, and Mr. Piasecki would not only lose his income and his job; he might well lose his life. Let Western Catholics awake to the reality that the Press is being used as an instrument of Moscow and an implement in the policy of Lenin to infiltrate and split the Church — and *Pax* will really have to go to war to save its life.

Why all this about *Pax*, Poland, and France in a book addressed to Americans and all English-speaking readers? Because the parallels give any thinking man pause: *Pacem in Terris* has been used here in America in a manner very like to the way *Pax* has used it in Poland. John XXIII has been held up as "the good" while Pius XII has been condemned for his centralization. Vatican II, according to many of the "Establishment," has done precisely what Piasecki claims it has done — ended the

Tridentine era — as if that era could ever really end! — and opened an epoch when the Church must "compromise." Magazines like *Continuum, The Critic,* and *Jubilee,* not to mention *Ramparts,* periodicals and papers such as *Commonweal, National Catholic Reporter,* and occasionally *Ave Maria* and even *America* read as if *Pax* members were on their staffs. As for *Look, Time, Newsweek, Saturday Evening Post,* with contributors such as Frs. Kavanaugh and Baum — whose theological acumen has yet to strike many as equal to Aquinas or Scotus or several other "ancients" — there is hardly need for Piasecki. Yet the tactics of these news media appear no whit dissimilar to those of the *Pax* Movement: publish what confuses and divides, refuse to publish what will clarify and possibly unify.

Now of course it may be only a case of parallels — and we all know that parallels never meet. Yet what if these "parallel" lines actually crossed? There is an American *Pax* Association in the United States. There is a group called SLANT in England. There is John Leo's "Establishment." There are "liberal" papers and magazines that, quite obviously, labor to blur the basic incompatibility between Catholicity and Communism. Terence Eagleton, head of the SLANT group in England, boasted publicly of being on the best of terms with Piasecki's *Pax.* Then look how that Center for the Study of Democratic Institutions has used John XXIII's *Pacem in Terris . . .*

Robert Hutchins, the man behind this organization, has been known to the *Chicago Tribune* for over 30 years — very well known, as is evidenced by the *Tribune's* prognostication before the first Convocation on *Pacem in Terris;* which was held in New York City, I believe. Said the *Tribune:* "Any seminar promoted by the Center will certainly preach the wickedness of the United States and the nobility of the Viet Cong. The Center has already said that American anti-communism is just plain fascism, and no more respectable than Communism itself." If you read any of the reports on the first Convocation you know what accurate prognosticators the *Tribune* proved to be. But in case you have missed such reports let me give you the very latest from the second Convocation or Conference on the same Encyclical, spearheaded and sponsored by the same Hutchins and his Center for the Study of Democratic Institutions. . . It happened at Geneva. . .

Both sides were invited to the conference, but the free-world's representation was limited almost exclusively to ultra-liberals. Prominent among the free-world "defenders" were such noted American "doves" as Senator William Fullbright, Senator George McGovern, Justice William O. Douglas, the Rev. Eugene Carson Blake, Dr. Martin Luther King, Bishop James Pike, John Kenneth Galbraith, Linus Pauling. . . Need one go on? The Government at Washington did not send a representative; for it well knew what the atmosphere would be like. . .

Harry Ashmore, chairman of the Executive Committee for the Center said that Ho Chi Minh is revered in his own right . . . that he has "brought liberation to the Vietnamese three times; that he will rank historically with Gandhi; no one else around the world today in any country seems to provide a similar blend of spiritual and political power."

Ho Chi Minh has been an atheist for over half a century. Yet Harry Ashmore says he is a spiritual leader. Gandhi is known for his non-violence. Yet Harry Ashmore says Ho Chi — who is still somewhat violent in South Vietnam — and has been hardly less violent for almost half a century — will rate historically with Gandhi. Ho Chi has been such a splendid religious leader that he has closed every religious school, most churches, and even some pagodas in North Vietnam — yet Harry Ashmore says . . . But why go on?

The remarks of Supreme Court Justice William O. Douglas, Chairman of the Board of the same Center, were even more amusing — and *Pax*-like. As one would expect from a Justice, his Honor called for a rule of law in international affairs, and not the rule of force. But one would also expect that a Supreme Court Justice of the United States would be somewhat cognizant of the United Nations and its efforts to keep peace by law — and even by law-enforcement — One would expect it especially in these times when a former colleague of Mr. Douglas' on the Supreme Court bench plays no minor role in the U.N. But the most amusing part of Justice Douglas' remarks came after his praise of Ho Chi Minh and Nikita Khrushchev and his denouncement of Chiang Kai-shek (That is some combination of figures, is it not?) It was here that William O. Douglas told the assembly that eighty-five percent of the human race lives in intolerable conditions — which can be remedied only by revolt. Yes, those are his words — just after asking for the rule of law! and not of force!

Robert Hutchins, President of the Center, spoke — and made it quite clear that the real aim of this Conference on John XXIII's *Pacem in Terris* was the neutralization of Southeast Asia — Proving once again how accurate the same John XXIII was when, on opening Vatican II, he spoke of those who "had learned nothing from History." Mr. Hutchins need only look at the not too distant past to learn that neutralization means Communistic take-over. It has always meant that to date. It seems obvious that it will mean that for some time into the future. But the Center for the Study of *Democratic* Institutions asks for neutralization. Who said *Pax?*

But the best is yet to come — and again the "parallelism" makes one think of parallax. Pope Paul VI saw fit to send an official representative of the Vatican to this Conference. After all, why not? Was it not his Predecessor's Encyclical that was to be discussed? And had he himself not shattered all precedent by flying the Atlantic to stand before the U.N. and plead for peace on earth? At any rate, His Holiness sent Cardinal Journet to Geneva — not to honor Hutchins and the Center for Study of Democratic Institutions, but to say something about *Pacem in Terris*, which might be something a bit different from the line usually followed by *Pax*. Cardinal Journet never spoke!

Another man who might have spoken with some authority was Monsignor Francis Lally, Editor of the Boston *Pilot*. Monsignor Lally was asked *not* to speak. But Bishop James Pike was. Of course this illustrous retired Bishop was much more able than

Cardinal Journet or Monsignor Lally to discuss *Pacem in Terris.*
Of course he could give better, more accurate, more profound,
and deeply theological commentary on Pope John's Encyclical
than either of the Roman Catholic prelates.

Maybe the lines are only parallel to *Pax.* If so, of course they
never will meet. But after watching the tactics and hearing some
of the views expressed at Geneva; after noting the manner of
proceeding among the "Establishment," SLANT, some Publishing Houses, and the secular Press, we cannot but say our minds
are not blind to the parallelism — in fact they are almost par-
alyzed by the similarities.

Of course that attack on the Press — and that is what it is
meant to be — may be shrugged off by some as "Just a monk's
talk. What can he know locked up in that monastery of his?"
So let us have more expert testimony . . .

Howard K. Smith is no monk. Howard K. Smith has never
spent years behind a cloistering wall. Howard K. Smith may
not be as interested as I in American Catholics who can be confused by the Press, nor about the Roman Catholic Church and
her mighty effort, God-inspired, I am sure, at her *aggiornamento.*
But Howard K. Smith is as ruthless, if not more ruthless than
I, in his attack on "all the news that's print to fit" . . .

Howard K. Smith has been a columnist for years and a well-
known ABC-TV Commentator. His profession has been journalism. Yet before 1968 was two months old this liberal journalist
openly professed that he was disillusioned with his profession,
and had been disillusioned precisely by professionals in his
chosen field. For years, he confessed, he had had "the exhilarat-
ing feeling of being a tiny part in a great age of journalism."
But, he went on to say, "I miss that feeling now." Why? Because
he came to realize all that I have been endeavoring to make you
realize throughout this chapter — and this book; namely, that
the American Press — as well as that of the Press in many other
parts of the world — has contributed to what Smith called "the
confusion and frustration now damaging the nation's spirit."

He gave as one example the "elevation of Stokely Carmichael

into a real force in our nation." He rightly called that elevation the result of "an irresponsible journalistic building-up." Again very rightly he contended that Carmichael is "basically a nobody who, before the Press took notice of him, had achieved nothing." And a "nobody" this same Carmichael would have remained "except for us" says journalist Smith, "with our cameras and note pads." He went on to give another example of this "irresponsible" and "exaggerated" journalism by pointing to the way the so-called "credibility gap" has been handled by the Press. Smith calls it "one of the most distorting oversimplifactions of the time." Then goes on to say that the President of our country has to make decisions on matters about which those not high up in Government know little or nothing. "Yet," says Smith as he turns to his fellow journalists, "we tend to call it calculated deception if he (the President) does not provide conclusive facts and admit failure. If he does not keep a frozen consistency, he is held to be lying." That would be unjust enough to the President, and horribly unjust to the citizenry of the country who reads the Press distortions, but Smith went on to point to a truth many of his fellow journalists ignore or are actually ignorant of: namely that "no Government ever has been run that way and none ever will." His third indictment is devastatingly true and truly devastating. He says that the coverage of Vietnam has been full of "one-sided journalism." Need I add that the other side, which is very definitely *our* side, has suffered because of this?

Take another professional's word before my own on this whole matter. Kent Cooper, one of the last of the truly big men in the Associated Press wrote a book which he titled THE RIGHT TO KNOW. That sounds like but another plea — or demand — for "Freedom of the Press," but that sound is deceptive. Cooper warned his colleagues about the possibilities of news produced by themselves for what "the public ought to want." Not too many of his colleagues heeded, or now heed, that warning. Too often, bare-facedly and with an arrogance hard to believe, they do produce just that kind of "news". Kent Cooper gave them an example of what he meant, and of what they should avoid, when he

[99]

went back to 1917 and showed how "news propaganda to incite the country to demand a declaration of war" had been used.

Only last week, March 24, 1968, Frank Cullen Brophy, wrote to an Editor of one of our Catholic papers to say: "I am surprised that you are just discovering that the Associated Press, CBS, NBC, the *New York Times*, and other mass media, distort news, and, in some instances, actually falsify it for the purposes of furthering leftist or liberal causes. . ." Then, after citing a few cases, he concludes: "Without the planned and consistent efforts of the Associated Press, the radio and TV networks, and the liberal Press, these synthetic and divisive efforts would get nowhere."

But perhaps the most telling testimony, and one that will soften the charge in Mr. Brophy's words: of all this being "planned and consistent," is that of Senator Thomas Dodd, given in New London, Connecticut, at the Communion Breakfast of the Holy Family Retreat League, March, 1968. After referring to Howard K. Smith's disillusion with, and withdrawal from, American Journalism, the Senator went on to say: "Mr. Smith is not the only outstanding member of his profession to complain about slanted or inadequate reporting in certain crisis situations. I recall, for example, that the prize-winning Scripps Howard correspondent, Jim Lucas, who is widely recognized as one of the greatest war correspondents of all times, recently complained that the Vietnam war was one of the worst reported wars in history."

The Senator then went on to make what he called "a casual examination of recent history" to show how the public has been badly misinformed by the Press in real crises. He took the Greek Communist insurrection in 1944 as one example and showed how editors and public opinion moulders attacked Prime Minister Winston Churchill for his courageous decision to employ British troops to put down the insurrection. The press coverage was so bad that many had been led to believe that Churchill was intervening against the heroic Greek resistance fighters — and not against a Communist insurrection in which there had already been mass executions of thousands of anti-Communist Greek citizens. Today, of course, everyone knows how right Mr. Churchill was.

But then Senator Dodd comes closer home as he takes up the case of China and shows how American newspapers held Chiang Kai-shek as a "crook" and the Chinese Communists as nothing more than "agrarian reformers." Who does not know today what kind of "reformers" they were, and what a staunch patriot Chiang Kai-shek was and is? The Senator went on to say: "Had we made a tenth of the effort in China that we are today making in Vietnam, China could have been saved from Communism, and the world would have been spared the horrors of the Korean and now the Vietnam War." Slanted reporting can have worse effects than confusion, can't it?

Think of how we were duped by our Journalists about Cuba. According to our leading journals Castro was anything but a Communist; he was more nearly a Robin Hood or a Thomas Jefferson. It would be asking too much to request a return to the information the Press gave us on the Spanish Revolution back before World War II, but it is not too much to ask anyone to think back on the misinformation that was constantly given us on the so-called Buddhist crisis in Vietnam — and which led, directly or indirectly, to the murder of President Diem. When the U.N. got around to sending an international fact finding committee it was learned that the alleged persecution of the Buddhist was non-existent . . . and that all the agitation was purely political. But that discovery came only after the assassination of the best man Vietnam has ever had as head of state. What horrible consequences can follow from irresponsible journalism.

Senator Dodd made the point I have been making, even though he did not mention PAX, when he said: "Communist propaganda, when it is clearly identified as Communist propaganda, the free world can counter. But the trouble is that 99% of the articles, and publications, and radio and TV programs, that serve the Communist cause cannot be clearly identified as Communist propaganda . . . and those who are used to transmit the Communist propaganda line are not Communists, nor pro-Communists, but simply 'innocents'."

That is the piercing point of all I have been trying to say. Many of these good men *are* innocent — because ignorant of PAX.

The Senator closed his address with a simple suggestion: "Try to read two newspapers a day, preferably one which reflects the so-called liberal viewpoint and one which reflects a more conservative viewpoint." He went on to say the same about magazines. I dare be more specific and tell you, if you want to avoid PAX reports and reportings, read such orthodox Catholic papers as *Twin Circle* and *The Wanderer*, such magazines as *Triumph* for religion, and *National Review* for politics.

But the purpose of this chapter was to prepare you in such a way that you will, from now on, be enabled to read the Press with a new acuity and you will quickly perceive any and every slant — and may even be moved to chuckle as you say to yourself: "Baseball has its Leo Durocher. Boxing has its Cassius Clay. I suppose we have to have our Father Gregory Baum — and his like."

Again the purpose has been to give you grounds to relax and rejoice as you have once more been alerted to the fact that opinions are only opinions — and never truth, that theologians — even the greatest of them — are only theologians, helpers of the *Magisterium*, but not the *Magisterium;* finally, that what we are most interested in is not what some say the Council said, but what the Council actually promulgated.

As Father Baum, the great Gregory — and not Gregory the Great — examines Pope Paul's arguments, to "see if they are valid," we can go on peacefully and examine Authority in the Church — and see if there really is such a thing as a "crisis in Authority."

Canonization of Twenty-Two African Martyrs
Integration?

Chapter 5

"HE WHO HEARS YOU, HEARS ME"

The papers seem full of stories about the defections of some priest for the sake of some woman, or that of some young cleric who considers himself the recipient of some charism which obligates him to publicly disobey his Bishop, or, more common still, that of the pseudo-intellectual who deems himself so endowed with superior understanding that he hesitates not to disagree with the Doctors, the Councils, and, most especially, the latest pronouncements of the reigning Pontiff. This last, as you can see, is an atack upon *authority*. Were it ever to be a successful attack — which is utterly impossible seeing that Christ promised to be with us all days — then, truly, the Church would — as one worried missionary wrote me — be "ready to fall apart."

What would my Missionary have said had he heard the keynote speaker at the meeting in St. Paul, Minnesota which was to formulate the *National Association of Laymen?* That speaker told that convention that "The Church is much too valuable to be entrusted to the clergy." Obviously, then, it must be entrusted to the laity — and, obviously again, to such laymen as those who make up the National Association of Laymen. The speaker, with his accustomed modesty, said "The Church is sick ... and it is to this Church that *we* come *to teach.*" A new *Magisterium* for the fortunate People of God in the late Twentieth Century!

True it is that the president of the Association of Christians for Church Renewal, the organization which hosted this convention the last week of June, 1967, did insist that the newly formed National Association of Laymen intended to cooperate with the priests and Bishops, nevertheless the keynoter, expressed open dissatisfaction with the fact that the direction of the Church has been, and still is, "in the hands of a professional caste separately trained, speaking a separate language, holding a separate view of reality, and employing a separate method of operation." Would one be wrong to hazard the hesitating opinion that such kind of talk smacks slightly of anticlericalism? If that surmise be off target then we can take comfort in the fact that that man has his plan to care for things — with or without benefit of Clergy. He says: "We do not intend to bring Christ to the world. He is there already." Rather, went on this prodigy, "it is the Church that we (the laity) come to teach."

Bravo, for him. He is not going to Christianize the world, but, rather, his work is to Christianize Christ's own Church. How? By breathing into this all-but-defunct organism (he would say "organization") a "new form of life, a new training, a new language and theology, a new world view, and new methods of operation." That is no little amount of newness, is it not? Can this brilliant man be contemplating the creation of a NEW Church? That "breathing a new form of life" makes one think of Genesis and God the Creator. And that constant reiteration of "new" stirs up echoes of that second last chapter in the Apocalypse when "The One sitting on the throne spoke: 'Now I am making the whole of creation new'." Our keynoter does not go that far. He only wants to make the Church new — or a new Church. How? Simply. All he has to do is to bring into being what he terms "a new kind of *community* structure" (Most likely that means a structure composed mostly, if not exclusively, of laymen.) This "structure" (the "in" word of the moment) will "assist in dismantling the old structure" and "do away with the caste system until the Church again becomes a community."

Now it is true that Vatican II in its Dogmatic Constitution on on the Church opened with a somewhat different approach. Instead of beginning with a discussion of the hierarchial structure, it began with the idea of the Church as the people to whom God communicates Himself in love. Thus a foundation was laid for a clarion call to the laity to assume their responsibility, recognize and live up to their dignity, and aid in their own way the accomplishment of the total mission of Christ. But this same Constitution, after asserting that "an individual layman, by reason of the knowledge, competence, or outstanding ability which he may enjoy, is permitted, and sometimes even obliged to express his opinion on things which concern the good of the Church," immediately added: "When occasion arises, let this be done through the agencies set up by the Church for this purpose. Let it always be done in truth, in courage, and in prudence, with reverence and charity toward those who by reason of their sacred office represent the person of Christ." (#37)

This same Council issued a marvelous Decree on the Apostolate of the Laity, but one will look in vain for any line in that Decree which empowers or encourages any layman to restructure the Church, let alone to arrogate to himself the role of teacher of the Church. One may find a pseudo-courage in our speaker's remarks, but one will hardly find the truth, the prudence, the reverence and the charity the Council requires of those who feel obligated to express thir opinions.

No on should realize more vividly and vitally the responsibility which is theirs for the true *"aggiornamento"* of the Church than the laity. For the specific Decree on their Apostolate is far from the only document of the Council in which the laity is directly referred to. Martin Work put forth a true and touching statement when he said: "The renewal of the Church, called for by the documents of the Council, *depends in great part* on a laity that fully understands not only these documents, but also their own *co-responsibility* for the mission of Christ in the Church and in the world." And yet that really is but echo of what the Council itself said in the very opening sentence of this Decree: "Wishing to intensify the apostolic activity of the People of God, this most holy Synod earnestly addresses itself to the laity, whose *proper and indispensable role* in the mission of the Church it has already called to mind in other documents." — Those Documents are The Constitution on the Church, that on the Sacred Liturgy, the Decree on Social Communications, the one on Ecumenism, even the Decree on the Bishops' Pastoral Office in the Church, the Declaration on Christian Education, the Decree on the Missions, that on Priestly Life, and especially in that Pastoral Constitution on the Church in the Modern World. As you see, the role of the laity is all pervasive. Small wonder the Council said: "The layman's apostolate derives from his Christian vocation, and the Church *can never be without* it." Today, more than ever before, perhaps, that apostolate is an imperative need. The Council said as much: ". . . modern conditions demand that that apostolate be thoroughly broadened and intensified. The constant expansion of population, scientific and technical progress, the tightening of bonds between men have not only immensely widened the field of the lay apostolate, a field which is for the most part accessible only to them, but these developments have themselves raised new problems which cry out for the skillful concern and attention of the laity. . . Besides, in many places where priests are very few or, in some instances, are deprived of due freedom in their ministry, the Church could scarcely be present and functioning without the activity of the laity." (#1)

No lay person can read this Decree without feeling his heart expand with wonder and gratitude to God for the call He has issued to each to help His Son in the Salvation of mankind. In this Council document each will learn that he or she is somewhat of an Atlas — shouldering the very world; for the assembled Bishops declared: "On all Christians, therefore, is laid the splendid burden of working to make the divine message of salvation known and accepted by all men throughout the world." (#3) The Council then went on to speak of "charisms" — those special gifts the Holy Spirit gives to individuals — and to say: "From the reception of these charisms or gifts, there arise for each believer the right and duty to use them in the Church and in the world for the good of mankind and for the upbuilding of the Church. In so doing, believers need to enjoy the freedom of the Holy Spirit who 'breathes where He wills'. At the same time, they must act in communion with their brothers in Christ, especially with their pastors. The latter must make a judgment about the true nature and proper use of these gifts, not in order to extinguish the Spirit, but to test all things and hold fast to what is good." (ib.)

That brief passage is enough to show the essential notes required for proper lay activity. The vocation is there. God wants each layman to help in the work of Salvation. But the necessary relationship is also there. It is the "pastor" who judges the genuinity of the gift — and the place for its use. Further on this same document will say: "No project, however, may claim the name 'Catholic' unless it has obtained the consent of the lawful Church authority." (#23)

That last word is one of those "nasty" words to the modern generation. One could go much further and say that human nature, ever since that first revolt against Authority, has been truly allergic to all authority. Yes, it is in our tainted nature's blood. And perhaps most noticeably in this "land of liberty," "the home of the free. . ." But that capitalization of the word a few lines above really settles the whole matter. Authority is a word derived from *Author* — and, if we are to think theologically, which once again we say is the only way to think truly, we know that God alone is Author.

Authority is a reality, a personal reality, more substantially related to us than our bones. It goes as deep as our *being*. We are finite beings. We are beings who received our all from the Creator, the Author of our beings. Therefore, authority involves the very mystery of Creation, and the very Love of the Creator. Since God alone is absolute Author, St. Paul was making something of an obvious inference when he said to the Romans: "all legitimate authority is derived from God's authority" (13:1 Phillips), and Jesus Himself was voicing an inescapable truth when, at that solemn moment in His Passion, He said to Pilate: "You have no power at all against me, except what was given you from above." (Jno. 19:10 Phillips). That this Authority is still on earth is clear from Scripture which tells how Christ commissioned His Apostles as Teachers: "Absolute authority in heaven

[109]

and on earth has been conferred on Me. Go, therefore, and make all nations your disciples: . . .teach them to observe all the commandments I have given you. And mark: I am with you at all times as long as the world will last. (Mt. 28:19, 20 — Kleist-Lilly)

That being the truth, Bishop John Wright was most perceptive when he remarked that since "authority is bound up with the origins, divine and human, of our being, contempt of the authority of parents grows fatally in proportion as our recognition of the mystery of creation, and the fact of God grow more and more agnostic, however sentimental, and finally atheistic."

That is not exactly a digression; for just as our origins were Divine, so were those of the Church; and just as all authority comes from God, that in the Church is more expressly derived from Him who said "Go . . . teach." And there is the "center's central core"; for, since God is Love, and Authority is from Him, it follows ineluctably that all authority, ultimately speaking, is to enable us to *grow* (the root from which the word 'authority' comes — *augeo)* in love and come ever closer to Him who is Love.

It is not often that we myopic and ever selfish individuals look upon Authority in this light. But it is the only light in which to see it correctly and clearly. It is an accepted and well-established Catholic truth that one who has authority stands "in the place of God" for those who are under that authority. The one who is vested with legitimate authority truly "represents God." That means he or she represents Divine Love — Divine Mercy as well as Divine Justice — and ultimately and in all truth and reality, the *life-giving power of God*. That is why we say that Authority is for our good, our growth — and most especially our growth in love.

One homely example that has helped teen-agers to realize that Authority is given to help us and not to hinder is that of traffic signals — or the traffic cop. Red lights do stop us — but only that we may go on more safely. Traffic cops, at times, hold us up, but only to wave us on in a flow of traffic that ultimately

[110]

enables us to move on not only more safely, but even more speedily. So with all Authority — there will be occasions when it has to forbid something, but that will be only that we may grow more readily into what we are supposed to be. The way Vatican II expressed this truth is well worth remembering: ". . . obedience will not diminish the dignity of the human person, but rather will lead to maturity in consequence of that enlarged freedom which belongs to the sons of God" (Decree on Religious Life #14)

Again we have to clear our myopic vision to see that freedom is a correlative of acceptance of authority; obedience leads to greatest freedom — and actually is an exercise of that distinguishing prerogative of man. Again the homely example of traffic lights and traffic laws will aid us in grasping this truth. Why do we in America have to drive on the right side of the road? Is it a hindrance or a help? Does it crib, cabin and confine us, or does it set us free? The answer to those questions is obvious. Imagine the chaos and the utter impossibility of any free travel if there were no laws and no lights! How exact is the inscription seen over the Court House in Worcester, Massachusetts: "Obedience to law is the greatest liberty." That copula "is" can be taken in more than one sense; for obedience is not only an exercise of liberty, but it assures us of liberty. Therefore we are to recognize Authority not as a "necessary evil," not as a "lesser good," or the consequence of some deficiency. No. Authority in itself is an unqualified *good*. How could it be otherwise when it comes from God who is Good, and is to lead us to God who is Love?

We are back again to the notion that he who holds authority is vicar for Him who is Author of life, liberty, and love; therefore in the exercise of authority he should give life, enable one to be free, and lead on to love.

Love — that word abused as much as *liberty;* that word in whose name as many crimes have been committed as in the name of Liberty; that word which, for our twentieth century has been made a synonym for lust. For how many that word connotes only one thing — sex; selfish sex at that. In other

[111]

words, too many of our contemporaries have so distorted the notion the word is meant to give, that they have made it come to mean its opposite. Love *gives* — that is obvious for anyone who thinks theologically; for God is Love and God is forever giving. Creation was an Act of Love. What was Redemption but another Act of Love? And what is the sending of the Holy Spirit upon us but Love again giving — and giving Himself! Yes, love *gives* — but for most moderns love means only to *get*.

Love serves — that is the truth taught us by Him whom St. John the Beloved called Love. It was amidst very human happenings that Christ taught this quintessential truth about *Authority and Love*. (That is the point of this whole passage: that Authority, in all truth, is "the Servant of Love.") Zebedee's wife had come to Jesus with the request that her two boys, John and James, be given preferential treatment: seats on the right hand and on the left of Jesus in the Kingdom of God. It is understandable in the mother. Christ quietly and kindly told her she really did not know what she was asking for. However when the "other ten heard this they were indignant with the two brothers." That is human nature, too — and quite understandable though not exactly pardonable in grown men. But Jesus seized the occasion to teach us a truth about authority which should set all mature minds and hearts not only reverencing those in authority, but welcoming every exercise of that authority with love. Jesus called the twelve to Him and said: "You know that among the pagans the rulers lord it over them, and their great men make their authority felt. *This is not to happen among you.* No; anyone who wants to be great among you must be your servant, and anyone who wants to be first among you must be your slave, just as the Son of Man came not to be served but to *serve*, and to *give* his life as a ransom for many." (Matt. 20:24-28 Jerus. its. added)

Love *serves*. Love *gives*. The lesson is not mine; it is that of Jesus Christ, Incarnate Truth, Incarnate Love. But note well the purpose of this giving and serving: Christ "emptied Himself" as St. Paul tells us in his Letter to the Philippians, and

[112]

"assumed the condition of a slave, and became as men are. . ."
but not that men might remain as they were, not that men might
remain slaves in any sense of the word, but that by loving them
to Death — even to Death on a Cross — by serving them, by
giving His very life for them, He might lift them to a level "a
little less than angels" — as David, His ancestor sang. This
Servant of men, this "Suffering Servant" as foretold by Isaias,
is the same Christ to whom "all authority in Heaven and on
earth was given" — and in whose place, and as whose representative, certain individuals exercise authority today. That exercise has the identical ultimate purpose — to raise men to a level
"a little less than angels." And now we have a new element in
love — Love *suffers*. True, that is only another aspect of love
serving and love *giving;* but there is an added nuance to the nature of love and one that will lead us ultimately to a very exact
definition of love. Love *suffers* — and to save time let us focus on
the greatest Act of Love ever offered by undergoing the greatest
suffering ever experienced by a human being — Jesus Christ's
love for mankind led Him to that suffering which we know as the
Sacrifice of the Cross. Now we can say that Love serves, Love
suffers, Love sacrifices, and thus Love saves. But, as yet, we
have not said just what Love is . . . Still, it is from this saving,
sacrificing, suffering and serving Act of Love, called the Passion
and Death of Jesus Christ, that we can come to the most exact
definition of Love one can desire: Love is the *union of wills*.

When Christ was in the Garden of Olives — that "place called
Gethsemane" — He prayed as no other human had prayed and
as no other human will pray. It was not only an anguished
prayer, but an agonized and agonizing prayer — and from it we
learn what Love really is: "Father," he said, "if you are willing,
take this cup away from me. Nevertheless, let your will be done,
not mine." (Lc. 22:42) That prayer came from His tortured
being shortly after He had said in the Upper Room: ". . . the
world must be brought to know that I love the Father and that
I am doing exactly what the Father told me." (Jno 14:31)

In many other ways Christ taught the same truth about love

[113]

being a union of wills. What else is that unforgettable line "If you love me, keep my commandments," but a definition of love as a "union of wills?" The Commandments are the express Will of God. Our keeping of those Commandments is an expression of our wills and a manifestation of love that will win Eternity.

Vatican II taught all this in a passage directed toward Religious, but a passage that can be directed to every human being on earth. For while it is true that not all have a vocation to the Religious Life there is no one who has not a vocation to a life that is religious. Since some derive the very word religion from *re-ligare*, and say it means "being bound to God," it should be obvious to all that the very call to being, the very call to human existence, is a love-call on the part of God that should evoke a returning call of love from every human. Hence this quote has personal pertinence for any and every human being: "Through the profession of obedience, religious offer to God a total dedication of their wills as a sacrifice of themselves; they thereby unite themselves with greater steadiness and security to the saving will of God." Pause there and recall our definition of love as a "union of wills," and you will see why we insist that Religious Life — and every human life should be religious — is naught but an Act of Love; and since Love's fruit is Joy, no human should ever live one single moment without genuine Joy bubbling in his heart.

This is especially true of those who are Christians; for Vatican II goes on, in this same passage, to say: "In this way they follow the pattern of Jesus Christ, who came to do the Father's will. . . Under the influence of the Holy Spirit, religious submit themselves to their superiors, whom *Faith* presents as God's representatives, and through whom they are guided into the *service* of all their brothers in Christ. Thus did Christ Himself, out of submission to the Father, minister to the brethren. . . Therefore, in a spirit of *Faith* and love for God's will, let religious show humble obedience to their superiors. . . For his part . . . each superior should himself be docile to God's will in the exercise of his office. Let him use his authority in a spirit of *service* for the brethren, and manifest thereby the charity with which God loves them." (#14)

Authority, then, is the "servant of Love." Obedience, then, is an act of Love. But before either will be recognized for what it is, or exercised in the way it should be, *Faith* is required. Paul VI knows that his authority is being questioned, challenged, and even ignored by some. He realizes what this can mean for God, the Church, and all mankind. That is one of the reasons he asked for a "Year of Faith" in 1967-1968. For Faith means *life* — "The just man *lives* by faith" (Rom. 1:17) Consequently, since life is for love, man cannot love save by having lively Faith. But Faith is light — it enables us to see what otherwise we could never see. That is the kind of light our dark, and ever darkening modern mind, modern man, modern world needs. With that light he can come to see that Authority is the "servant of love," and obedience to legitimate authority the greatest liberty, the truest life, and the most magnificent love.

Since this rather long and somewhat labored passage is to lead you to a realization of what the *Magisterium* of the Church is, and very especially just what the Supreme Authority of the Pope is, it may be well to have you recall under what circumstances Jesus Christ conferred supreme authority on the first Pope, Peter the Fisherman. It was after a night at sea — a miserable night; for the fisherman had caught nothing. In the early dawn as they were nearing shore they saw someone who hailed them and asked them about their luck. When they admitted to utter failure He, for it was Jesus, told them to throw their net out to starboard. They did and they found more than their boat could handle. That led John to recognize Jesus — and that recognition passed on to Peter sent the impulsive one over the side. They had a fish fry breakfast on the shore of the lake. Then Christ asked Peter: "Simon, son of John, do you love me more than these others do?" When Peter gave an affirmative answer, Christ conferred authority on him by saying: "Feed my lambs." A second time Christ put the same question about love — and a second time responded to Peter's affirmative by a conferring of authority. At the third query which was followed by Peter's most vehement protestation of love, Christ conferred Supreme Authority by telling Peter to "Feed my Sheep." With that bit of revelation before you, you can better appreciate the profoundly true and theologically sound statement of Monsignor Journet: "All its (Authority in the Church) greatness derives from its purpose, which is to be the servant of Love." Then he adds: "When the Pope declares that he is 'the servant of the servants of God' he is telling the truth." And when one knows a little history he can agree with Father Yves Congar when he says: "In the nineteenth century, Romanticist literature, and often history itself, spread the idea that power and the holding of very high office offered an opportunity for greater enjoyment, for complete freedom to do as one liked, and for helping oneself. The Popes, however, of the nineteenth and twentieth centuries, and with them the whole body of Bishops, have stood before the eyes of the world as men for whom power is responsibility and authority, *service*."

If the young men in the clerical ranks, and those others among the laity, who find it so difficult to accept the teachings of the *Magisterium* would only read "His-Story" during this past century, and recognize the "service of love" given by the Pontiffs from Pius IX to Paul VI, they would be much more temperate — and, consequently, much more true — in their evaluation of those teachings. But they are not the ones to whom this book is addressed. Since they are ready to attack the teachings of the very *Magisterium* itself, what would they not do to this effort at clarifying the real issues of the day in the light of Vatican II, and of reassuring sincere Catholics that "all is well?"

But once again allow me to point out to you sincere Catholics that theologians — even the best of them, even the *periti* — do not belong to the official *Magisterium* of the Church Jesus Christ, the Only Son of God, founded. How much less do the so-called "lay-theologians" belong to that august body which is truly the "servant of Love?" So when we want the truth about any doctrine, or the proper understanding of any moral problem, when we want, in short, to know the very Will of God so that we may love Him by bringing our wills into union with His, we do not look to the Rahners, the Schillebeecks, the Küngs, the Härings, not even to the Cardinals Alfrink, Doephner, Koenigs, or any other of that College, not even to all the Bishops in their own Synod — let alone to the Frs. Currans, Kavanaughs, Du Bays, Dranes, Davis and their like, far less to the bold and brave Novaks, Callaghans, Cogleys, but only to the Pontiffs God has given us. — For, in last analysis, the Pope is responsible for the entire teaching authority and the actual exercise of that "service of love" in the Church of Jesus Christ. That is evident from Scripture, from Tradition, from the Councils, from all the teachings of sound theology — and most recently from the clear statement of Vatican II.

"This infallibility with which the Divine Redeemer willed His Church to be endowed in defining a doctrine of faith and morals extends as far as extends the deposit of divine revelation, which must be guarded religiously and expounded faithfully. This is the infallibility which the Roman Pontiff, the head of the College of Bishops, enjoys in virtue of his office, when, as the supreme shepherd and teacher of all the Faithful . . . he proclaims by a definitive act some doctrine of faith or morals." (#25)

Then, because Vatican II was cognizant of the effort of some to resurrect old, old errors, and teach the false idea that the Church Christ founded is a "democracy" of some sort, the assembled Bishops added this: "Therefore, his (the Pope's) definitions, of themselves, and not from the consent of the Church, are justly styled irreformable, for they are pronounced with the assistance of the Holy Spirit, an assistance promised to him in blessed Peter." (ib) Then, as if anticipating the trouble that has been breaking out here and there on certain College Campuses where "advanced thinkers" have taught doctrine obviously differing from the teachings of the *Magisterium*, the Council repeated the truth about the Pope's infallibility, his independence in action, and his total dependence on the *"invigilantia,"* — that careful, constant, omniscient, omnipotent watchfulness — of the

[117]

Holy Spirit, lest the Pontiff use a wrong word in presenting infallible truth. "Therefore," the Council concludes, "they (these definitions of the Pope) need no approval of others, nor do they allow an appeal to any other judgment. For then the Roman Pontiff is not pronouncing judgment as a private person, but rather, as the supreme teacher of the universal Church, as one in whom the charism of infallibility of the Church herself is individually present, he is expounding or defending a doctrine of Catholic faith." (#ib).

What a comfort that is. What a consolation. Small wonder that even Protestant Bishops are now suggesting to their own people that the Pope should be recognized as "chief pastor of men" and the "chief spokesman for the Christian community in the world." In actual fact the Pope has been just such a spokesman for all this century — and never more so than today as Paul VI does again and again what Leo XIII, Pius X, Benedict XV, Pius XI, Pius XII, and John XXIII did before him: plead for common sense in every sphere from that of the individual and the family to that of heads of States and the whole human race. Common sense, another name for "natural law" in one way, could give us peace, justice, honor, and all the virtues needed in our none-too-virtuous world so that we could know happiness and even genuine joy.

Common sense, as used above, is truly connected with what we call "the natural law." That, in its turn, is another name for the "voice of an informed conscience." And that is really the mind and the will of God as made manifest to us by our well-informed consciences. If we follow common sense, then, we actually unite our wills with God's will — and thus manifest love. So whenever we consider authority in its reality we are always led back to God and to love. That is why it can be said that to resent authority, to refuse to accept its dictates, or to conform to its pronouncements is really to sin against love. Vatican II all but pinpointed this truth when it said: "With ready Christian obedience, laymen, as well as all disciples of Christ, should accept whatever their sacred pastors, as representatives of Christ, decree in their role as teachers and rulers of the Church. Let laymen follow the example of Christ, who, by His obedience even at the cost of death, opened to all men the blessed way to the liberty of the children of God." (#37) Need it be said that "greater love than this no man has . . ."?

Now some astute minds — but rather sophomoric and decidedly superficial — may tell you that the operative words in all that has been quoted from Vatican II are "definitions" "definitive act" and "supreme head," etc. implying that only *ex cathedra* pronouncements of the Pope are "official" and require our whole-hearted assent and acceptance. In other words, there are those who look lightly at Encyclicals, and give only passing attention to anything said by a Pope in audience, consistory, or any other medium. These are they who think the Pontiff teaches only when he defines. What a concept of a shepherd! What a mental picture of a real father! What a distortion of the very notion of a teacher!

That is prelude to the statement that the mighty Encyclicals of this past century have been *love-letters* written to you — and that you would be wise to cherish every word as does a fond lover. But let us here and now ask the question some of these others ask: "What is the authority of an Encyclical?" Pius XII answered that query in his *Humani Generis* when he said: "Nor must it be thought that what is expounded in encyclical letters does not of itself demand consent since in writing such letters the Popes do not exercise the supreme power of their teaching authority. For these matters are taught with the ordinary teaching authority of which it is true to say: 'He who listens to you, listens to me.' (Lc. 10:16), and generally what is expounded and inculcated in encyclical letters already, for other reasons, appertains to Catholic doctrine. But if the Supreme Pontiffs in their official documents purposely pass judgment on a matter up to that time under dispute, it is obvious that this matter, according to the mind and will of the same Pontiffs, cannot be any longer considered a question open to discussions among theologians." (#20)

[119]

Vatican II was even more explicit on this matter. "Religious submission of mind and will," it said, "must be shown in a special way to the authentic *magisterium* of the Roman Pontiff, even when he is not speaking *ex cathedra;* that is, it must be shown in such a way that his supreme *magisterium* is acknowledged with reverence, the judgments made by him are sincerely adhered to, according to his manifest mind and will. His mind and will in the matter may be known chiefly either from the character of the documents, from his frequent repetition of the same doctrine, or from his manner of speaking." (#25 Constitution on the Church)

Popes do not write encyclicals as an exercise in literary composition, or for a personal review of theology. They are usually addressed to "Our Venerable brethren — the Patriarchs, Primates, Archbishops, Bishops, and other Ordinaries in Peace and Communion with the Apostolic See" — and through them to each of us. It is said again: they can be looked upon — and with wisdom — as love-letters; and their ultimate aim is always the "interior holiness of the individual."

Were one to simply enumerate the titles of the various Encyclicals from Leo XIII to Paul VI it would be evident that every aspect of an individual's life has been covered in depth and breadth. There are Encyclicals on how to live with and love God; how to live with and love your neighbor; yes, and how to live with and love yourself properly. The conjugal state and society have been covered again and again. The celibate state only recently. Civil Society in its every aspect and appearance from Socialism, Communism, Fascism, Nazism to Christian States. Capital and Labor have been treated in at least three monumental Encyclicals. Education, Science, Sociology, Anthropology, Liberty, Economics, Statesmanship, War and Peace, False Philosophies — and the *Philosophia Perennis;* the Arts — every phase from Painting, Sculpture, Drama and Music down to the Movies and Television. Nothing of any importance has been omitted. So, if you would know the mind and will of God, read the mind and will of Christ's Vicars.

FATHER M. RAYMOND, O.C.S.O.

If you know yourself in your deepest depths you know you are a gnawing hunger and a desert thirst for the face of God and the Voice of God. You crave to come face to face with Divinity. The throbbing longing of your whole being is to know God's Mind and to understand His Will. You can be satisfied this side of Eternity; for Christ has kept His Last Supper Promise. He has not left us orphans. He is with us all days — in the person of the Pope who endeavors to love us with the very love of God and who in letter after letter, in encounter after encounter, speaks to us and tells us what God wills of us and for us. Not every word is uttered with "supreme teaching authority"; that is, not every utterance is an *ex cathedra* definition. But no public pronouncement is without some authority — and authority is the "servant of love." Hence you will never go astray if you follow the teachings of the Roman Pontiffs.

And yet there are those who speak — and with reason — of a "crisis of authority" today. One might gasp at the term and grow affrighted at what that term represents when he realizes that "authority" in any human is a share in the very authority of God — and the Authority of God is but another name for His Love. Further, when one realizes his whole vocation to life is but a call to love, he is bewildered that any thinking man would resist authority. He has a right to be bewildered, and will remain so until he comes to the realization that not all "thinking animals" think. Calm will come when he ponders on the fact that one of the greatest fallacies of all time lies in the oft repeated slogan: "Let your conscience be your guide."

These men who have questioned the Pope and even defied his authority think they are thinking when in actuality they are usually only emoting. When the press often calls such people "philosophers" and at times even names them "theologians", I smile. No philosopher worthy of the name will ever resist authority; for he knows how deep it lies in our beings, how closely it is connected with our origins. As for a theologian defying authority, the very idea is a contradiction in terms.

[121]

The so-called "crisis of authority" is what Pope Paul rightly called it — *a crisis of Faith;* for it takes Faith to accept the Authority of the Church. But, as Cardinal Krol so aptly said: "With a true renewal of Faith there is no reason why the Church of Christ should not go forward through the present storm confidently and courageously. The hand of Peter's successor is firmly on the helm of Peter's bark. The promises still strengthen him: 'Upon this rock I will build my Church: the gates of the netherworld can never hold out against it. I will give you the keys of the Kingdom of Heaven.'

"Confident as we are in Christ's promise and in the strengthening presence of the Holy Spirit, yet we know this promise involves the help of all of us. Our prayers, our loyalty, our obedience, our active support have been guaranteed in Christ's promise. On this 19th centenary of Peter's death we pledge to Peter's successor our full and unstinting effort in the fulfillment of Christ's promise— our willing offering to our Holy Father of complete unity with him in mind and heart. One with Him we shall press steadfastly forward through the darkness of every storm to the glorious sunburst of peace that awaits the bark of Peter at the end of its tumultuous voyage."

We have asked you to do something a little different. From the beginning of this book we have urged you to see Christ walking upon the stormy waters and telling you to "Fear not!" then giving as His reason: "It is I!" That does not call for any vivid imagination, but only for vital Faith; for it is evident to those with eyes to see — Christ walks upon the tumultuous waters of our day in the person of Paul VI. That is why you ought to do as do some Franciscan Friars every Sunday of this "Year of Faith" at the close of their Conventual Mass. After reciting the Creed they add: "I believe that the Pope, the Bishop of Rome, is the Vicar of Jesus Christ on earth; that he is the supreme visible head of the whole Church, and that he teaches infallibly what we must believe and do to be saved. I also believe everything which the Holy, Catholic, Apostolic and Roman Church defines and declares we must believe. I adhere to her with all my heart." Do that and you will have the Truth and be on the Way; for you will be "in Christ Jesus."

Paul VI has told us again and again that "the pressing duty now is that of going to the roots of our religious life, to its inner original principle; that is, to *Faith*." (Gen. Audience June 14, 1967) Nor has he left us in the dark about the nature of Faith. It is the source of our authentic relationship with God. It is the logical criterion and the spiritual energy which must give spiritual and practical direction to our life *Justus ex fide vivit* — the just man lives by Faith.

"Faith," says the Pontiff, "is our first duty before God, before the Church, and before the world. Before God — who speaks and wants us to believe in Him. Before the Church, our teacher — who explains the doctrine of Faith, and assists her children to know it and to translate it into prayer and works. Before the world — which asks at every step: Do you believe? For the world awaits from us what is so often spoken of today: a *witness*."

Paul VI knew well that a clear concept of Faith is required in these days of foggy thinking and alienation from exact definitions. So he told us through an Audience on June 21, 1967 that "Faith, in its true theological meaning, is a gift, a gift from God." Quoting St. Thomas Aquinas, the Pontiff went on to say: "To believe, an inner cause is needed which can come only from God. Faith demands the '*lumen Fidei*' — the light of Faith — which is an inner light which disposes the mind to assent to the truths revealed by God. This light, this virtue, is infused in us at Baptism."

With his knowledge of human nature and its proneness to jump to illogical conclusions, the Pope went on to obviate such a jump. He said: "This gratuity of Faith — its entire dependence upon God — seems to nullify the part man plays. It would seem to insinuate that man resign himself to an inert fatalism, expecting everything from God and contributing nothing himself. But this is not so. Our responsibilities are not taken away . . . our collaboration is not eliminated. God offers; we must accept.

[123]

The Doctor of Grace, St. Augustine teaches that salvation is not reached '*nisi volentibus nobis*' — unless we want it. God's love is first manifest in the vocation to Faith . . . In God, Faith is a call to Love. On our part there ought to be a first, fundamental answer of love . . . Faith demands a free adherence. But, precisely because of this, it demands deep and serious reflection. The use of one's freedom is not an inconsequential game. It defines man in his greatness — and in his destiny."

The Pope then pointed to three obligations consequent on this offer of a gift from God: 1) that of valuing and guarding our Faith as it deserves; 2) that of seeking to know the terms in which the problem of Faith is posed with regard to the truths to be believed and with regard to the spiritual act, the logical, psychological, and moral act that is asked of us in believing; 3) that of praying to have Faith, to conserve it, and to increase it. Pope Paul then quoted Monsignor Romano Guardini: "We ought to fully realize that Faith (subjective Faith) is also life, and as such has its evolution and its history. It is not a firm knowledge established once and for all, no matter what happens in life. It is not a knowledge like the Pythagorean mathematical table, unaffected once it is learned. . . Faith is nourished by the energies of the heart and soul, by judgment and fidelity; in short, by one's whole interior life. . . Faith must endure, and prayer endure with it."

As you see, our Faith can and must grow; for it is living — and growth is a sign of life. But that requires nourishment on our part. Indeed we have our work cut out for us. Pope Paul VI lamented over the trend of our times saying: "We who have the duty to pass on to others the doctrine of our Faith — the doctrine of Salvation — feel great sorrow seeing how little the people of our times care to listen to Our voice. They care so little for religious instruction that at times it seems as if *We are talking to the wind*." But that lamentation did not prevent His Holiness from going on talking. And what he had to say is pertinent to the life of any and every individual. He said: "We will remind you and warn you: Faith needs a teacher. Faith must be taught and studied. If a normal and meaningful relationship is not established between the teacher of the Faith and the disciple, the Faith either does not come alive, or it does not last in the heart and in the life of the disciple. *'Fides ex auditu'* — Faith depends on hearing. Religious teaching is indispensable."

Then this teacher *par excellence* of Faith went on to make a very important distinction between "subjective Faith" and "objective Faith." The first is the "attitude of the spirit to accept religious thoughts, principles, and truths. This is for us the virtue of Faith which we receive for the first time in Baptism." Then the Pontiff went on to explain "objective Faith" by saying: "On the other hand, Faith can mean the religious doctrines, those things in which one has Faith; for example, the articles of the Creed." Perhaps never before was it so necessary to teach, and teach vigorously, the twofold aspect of Faith: subjective or "believing Faith" — and objective or "believed Faith." For even some of our young, enthusiastic, but not too orthodox Newman Chaplains — and others on College Campuses have forgotten or are ignoring what Thomas Aquinas taught so clearly: "Faith is born mainly by way of infusion, and this happens through Baptism. BUT, as far as its determination is concerned, Faith comes through hearing, and so man must be instructed in the Faith by means of the catechism." What many of these young men are doing is encouraging subjectivism with little or no reference to the objective content of our Faith. To read some of them is to conclude that the present day collegians are *essentially* different from all those who went through college before Vatican II.

Pope Paul said: "Two factors concur in Faith. They are both necessary. But they are very different, and act differently. One is the Holy Spirit — that is, the action of the Holy Spirit on the soul — grace with its infused virtues, Faith included. The other is the *magisterium* authorized by Christ and entrusted to the Apostles, to the teachers of the Faith, to the Pope and to the Bishops. . ."

[125]

Could His Holiness have had Dayton, Catholic University, and other such places in mind when he went on to say: "It is easy to find people who say they have Faith, either because they have some good spiritual feelings, or because — as many of our separated brethren — they, by themselves, seek the word of God in the Holy Scriptures with personal interpretation, often free and arbitrary, and ultimately with different and contrasting meanings. This is no longer the '*una Fides*' — the one Faith — willed by Christ and preached by the Apostles. But, unfortunately, it is easy to find learned people, always anxious to proclaim their Catholicism, who nevertheless disregard this indispensable teaching function of the Church, and naively seek to adapt the doctrine of Faith to the mentality of the modern world. They do this, not only by means of a praiseworthy effort to make people accept, and in some way to understand those doctrines, but also by silencing, changing, and even denying those very doctrines according to the tastes and theories of today's popular opinions."

Then for the "apostles of academic freedom" there comes the clinching truth from the lips of him who is Vicar of Truth Incarnate: "Faith is *free* in the *act that* expresses it. Faith is *not free* in the *formulation of the doctrine* that expresses it, when this doctrine has been authoritatively defined."

That is why we can conclude with Paul VI: "Do not think that you have the Faith if you do not adhere to the contents of the Faith, to the Creed, to the symbol of the Faith — that is, to the outlined synthesis of the truths of Faith. Do not think of reviving religious life, or of attracting those who are afar off, by minimizing or deforming the exact teaching of the Church."

In those few sentences you have your reason for relaxing and rejoicing, for you have as Vicar of Christ a man who will teach truth uncompromisingly even though he recognizes the modern mentality in all its antipathy to authority and all its proud subjectivism. He spoke out about this very *"forma mentis"* — this present day manner of using our knowing faculties — and said: "Almost without our knowing it, we have been educated into it

[126]

by our schools. . . In the world of thought today, everything is doubted, and consequently, religion, too. It seems as if the mind of modern man finds no peace except in total negation, in abandoning any kind of certainty, and any kind of Faith. He is like a person with infected eyes who finds no rest except in obscurity, in darkness. . . Religious life may be exposed to tremendous trials in the coming generation if it is not sustained by a strong and genuine Faith. That is why we are exhorting all of you to strengthen it and live by it. Remember the words of St. Paul: we should make our Faith an armor . . . '*Lorica Fidei*' — 'You, brethren,' he says, 'are not in darkness . . . you are the sons of light.' " (I Thess. 5:4-8)

With the surety of a great surgeon His Holiness put his scalpel on the focus of infection when he said: "We would count among the general and principal causes of this present difficulty and possible crisis of Faith, the disassociation of modern thinking, even in some areas of Catholic schools, from the '*philosophia perennis*' — that perennial philosophy — that is, from the natural norm of human rationality — and a rather diffident attitude toward the *magisterium* of the Church. Here, too, the Apostle seems to suggest the right words when he writes to Timothy: 'A time will come when (men) will not put up with sound doctrine. . . For yourself, be vigilant.' " (2 Tim. 4:3-5)

"Be vigilant" by carefully reading what the Pope says. Thus you will come to realize that while you have reason to pray for yourself and others, you have no reason to fear concerning the Faith.

The sophistry contained in the too often heard saying: "Let your conscience be your guide" was to have been the topic with which to close this chapter, but there has come to my desk today a reprint from *The Spectator-Journeyman*, the student newspaper of Seattle University, Seattle, Washington, of a long article by Dr. Martin Larrey, Assistant Professor of History at that University, which substantiates all that has been said about "old errors with new labels" and supports the contention of John XXIII that we are to learn from History. Dr.

Larrey says: "The most curious feature in the new movements in the Church, especially among the intellectuals, is the fact that most, if not all, the ideas so recently propounded as novel, 'relevant,' and essential, are rather tired, old, and shabby. The exaltation of conscience, attacks on the Hierarchy and curial offices of the Church, criticisms of Papal affirmations in Faith and Morals, the frenzied zeal to adapt the dogmatic definitions out of existence — all, in fact, give evidence of an intellectual malaise, all exude the staleness of old heresies.

"As people involved in a profound spiritual ferment, we should be aware of an old religious phenomenon: that reform is always accompanied by heresy. . . That heresy should be present in the contemporary world should not be a source of alarm; rather it would be strange if it were not present. For example, what I would call the neo-Modernist heresy appears vibrant in the present Church, and it is a source of wonder to me that an age which puts a premium on the new and the novel should be mesmerized by the discord of bad theological thought. Barely sixty years ago, in *Pascendi Gregis*, Pius X commented on the 'fever for novelties,' summarily condemned the 'intuitional and subjective approach to religious experience,' and the strong Modernist pleas that the 'ecceliastical government be brought into harmony with men's conscience.' . . .

"But old heresies return in more attractive guises, and the neo-Modernism which has become 'camp' in some theological circles can take a frightening toll in traditional belief if allowed to flourish unchecked."

Then, to enable us to recognize this old heresy even under its new label, this man who has learned so much from History, says: "It (neo-Modernism) does not attack any dogma, but rather attacks the whole concept of Church authority and the nature of dogma itself. It calls for a radical personalization of Faith and continually denigrates the institutional structure of the Church. It is characterized by an historical myopia and arrogance, to wit, that the present judgment stands favorably against the traditional one, that the present situation is so utterly unlike anything before that old solutions are inoperable or that the present age is far advanced over the past and therefore demands new solutions."

Just before reading this reprint there had come to me a copy of Father John J. Kirvan's book on "The Problems of Faith on the American Campus." Father has titled it *The Restless Believers.* If one did not know that Dr. Larrey had written his article months before this book was published, one would believe he had taken it for text for his observations; for everything stated in the paragraph above is found all but italicized in Father Kirvan's book — and obviously Fr. Kirvan is utterly unaware how neo-Modernistic his approach to these problems on Campus is. For example, throughout his book there is wearisome insistence on this "radical personalization of Faith" along with an equally wearying insistence that "the present situation is so utterly unlike anything before that old solutions are inoperable." Father would profit from a pondering of Dr. Larrey's next paragraph: "Paradoxically, it is these modern sentiments that are trite, uninspiring, hackneyed and reactionary. The living tradition of the Faith has seen them come and go, noting that there are few things more quaint and antique than the man who insists that he's a breath away from a 'new dawn'. The neo-Modernists are fond of lecturing the Faithful on 'relevance' to the world, to the individual, to the modern problems etc. etc. Unfortunately, it is a word that has become victimized, and done so by its own equivocal sense; for it means not only 'to bear relation to,' but also, as a result of radical ideologizing, 'to become like' 'to share the values of.' In the former sense the Church has always been relevant; for it is for the world that it has been brought into being. In the latter sense, it has never been, nor ever will be 'relevant.' It has always stood apart from the mainstream of human history, offering a refuge from the riddles of life. In fact, one of its permanent attractions has been precisely that it is not like the world and never became a prisoner to a moment in time."

That the good Doctor was not writing unaware of the Pastoral Constitution on the Church in the Modern World is evidenced by his historically sound and theologically accurate summation: "We Christians correctly look back to those periods in which the Church 'accommodated' itself to the world with a sense of grief. The feudal Church of the tenth century, the Renaissance Church of the fifteenth, or the aristocratic Church of the eighteenth have never inspired us to heroic action; at best, they arouse a certain sense of pity and a strong determination to prevent the same thing from happening again. Consequently, we must not organize the Church in the light of the world, but revolutionize the world in the light of the Church. We can only do this by returning and restoring the living tradition of the Faith. It is, in the last analysis, the tradition which is vibrant, ever new, ever wondrous, ever anticipating the future. It belongs to no time in the Church's history, but is the accumulation of historic development. It is not found in the Scriptures, but rather the Scriptures are found in it. The tradition is the People of God throughout time handing on from generation to generation the practices, teachings, and customs of the Church circumscribed and guided by the Holy See.

"The tradition is a stance of affirmation, an affirmation in the salvific character of Christianity, and the resultant obligation that those who embrace it must penetrate the world with its message and do so not by accepting the world as it is but by elevating it through what St. John Damascene called "the superabundance of grace' . . .

"If we want to restore confidence to the Christian community, we have to undertake a radical reconstruction of the spiritual order by annealing ourselves in the stream of Papal teachings through the last century ever since Pius IX and Leo XIII drafted a charter for modern Roman Catholicism. We must stand, as Unamuno said, for liberty and life against the technocratic and scientific forces which would imperil the human spirit. . .

"We must experiment out of the tradition, developing our lives and our program so as to be teachers to the world rather than learners, and be prepared to withstand criticism. In this highly ideologized age we have become victims to what I would call 'condemnation by clichés.' We wince at the epithets of 'reactionary,' 'hidebound,' 'inflexible,' unconsciously resenting being tied to notions that command neither hearing nor respect. We are made to appear foolish, but this should not alarm us. Christians have always been fools, because we are in this world but do not belong to it. . .

"Our response should be . . ." and this should be "required reading" not only for St. John's, Catholic U. and Dayton, but for every Catholic College and University . . . "to remain steadfast and to double our efforts to make Christianity a positive force in this world, but *not by jettisoning the very things that can save mankind.* Instead of railing against the Papal teachings on birth control, articulate a theology of love; instead of ridiculing the Aristotelian-Thomistic synthesis, *plumb its enormous depths* by continuing the work of the neo-Thomists. Surely, if an eminent scholar like Jeroslav Pelikan can speak high praises of Thomism and commend it to his fellow-Protestants, we should have no inferiority regarding it, nor hanker after the rubble of modern philosophy for an explanation of reality. Instead of following the lead of others in secular affairs, we must make clear the alternative of a new life for men, and invite others to follow.

"The really creative steps in Christianity have had two characteristics: First, they drew their strength from the lived Christianity of the past; and, secondly, they insisted that the world would come close into Christianity on Christian terms. It was so with the flood of Hellenism that almost overran the Church in the fourth century. It was so with the great reforms of the eleventh and twelfth centuries. It was so with the Biblical revolution of the Tridentine Church. It was so with economic materialism of the nineteenth century. And so it must be with the technological secularism of the twentieth century."

And then, as if to substantiate the very thesis of this book, Doctor Larrey concluded with: "As usual, already the Holy See has anticipated the direction of the Church; for in his first encyclical Paul VI enunciated the following guidelines: 'It is not conformity to the spirit of the world, not immunity from the discipline of reasonable asceticism, not indifference to the laxity of modern behavior; it is not emancipation from the authority of prudent and lawful behaviour, not apathy with regard to the contradictory forms of modern thought, that can give vigor to the Church, or make her fit to receive the influence of the gifts of the Holy Spirit, or render her following of Christ more genuine, or give her the anxious yearning of fraternal charity and the ability to communicate her message. These things come from her aptitude to love according to Divine grace, her faithfulness to the Gospel of the Lord, her hierarchical and communal unity."

That shows you the steadiness and the firmness of the hand on the rudder of Peter's bark. That allows me to conclude this chapter as Dr. Larrey concluded his article and the Pope ended that passage in his Encyclical *Ecclesiam Suam:* "The Christian is not soft and cowardly; he is strong and faithful."

Solemn Profession of Monks at Gethsemani

Chapter 6

THE PURSUIT OF PERFECT LOVE
with Greater Freedom

Did I hear you ask: "If all you say about authority being the 'servant of love' is true, and if obedience is naught but an act of love, how do you account for what is going on among Religious and also among the Clergy? Why are so many young priests and nuns 'Copping out'?"

That last phrase is from the "hippies." These youngsters — for the most part they are young chronologically, and for the total part they are very young psychologically — "cop out" of society; that is, they look at society (or think they do) and, finding it absurd, they abdicate their role in society, and as one man said: "they quit the rat race, secede from society, and spend their days contemplating their spiritual innards." Many of the "cop outs" have taken their direction from Dr. Timothy Leary, the Harvard professor of a few years back, who urges his audiences to "take trips" on his LSD, and "cop out". So the term is used about those young nuns and priests who have been turning their backs on all they promised — and many of them vowed! — to secede "not from Christianity," they say, "but from the institutional Church."

The note of horror in many letters that have come to the monastery about the mounting number of those who are leaving the Religious Life and the Clerical ranks, sent me to the official records. Some of the figures are comforting. Some others are surprising. For instance, in 1967 there were in the United States 36,871 Diocesan priests. In 1966 there were only 36,419, and in 1957, ten years back, there were only 30,481. No astounding amount of "copping out" there! The same figures on

Religious Priests lead one to the same conclusion. In 1967 there were 23,021 in the U.S. Last year, 1966, there were only 22,774; and ten years back, in 1957, there were only 19,244. So, despite what the Press might say, there really has not been any shocking number of desertions among the priests of the land. When we look at the totals for the Brotherhood we receive even more consolation. For in 1967 there were 12,539 Brothers in our country. Last year, 1966, there were 12,255 Brothers. But back ten years ago, there were only 9,300 in the ranks of the Brotherhood. A growth of three thousand in ten years assures us that there has been no wholesale "copping out" amongst these wonderful men who teach and nurse and help Christ to grow mystically in our land.

When we turn to the female Religious, however, we are genuinely surprised. There are fourteen thousand more Sisters in the U.S. this year of 1967 than there were in 1957. But the shock comes when we read the totals of this year and those of last year. In 1966 there were 181,421 nuns across the land. This year there are only 176,671. What happened to the other four thousand, seven hundred and fifty?

Before we attempt any answer to that query, let us note that there have been defections among both priests and brothers. The Press assured you in on that fact — and how! Even His Holiness, Pope Paul VI speaks of a "disquieting decline in the ranks of the Clergy" in his truly thrilling Encyclical on Celibacy. He did not hesitate to make mention of the "distressing defections which hurt and sadden the whole Church." The Pope also stressed the fact that there is a "decrease in vocations". So do not think any facts are being blinked. But let it be stressed here and now that, with His Holiness, these lamentable failures are seen for what they are, and will not be covered over with any pseudo-psychiatry or false humanism. Let *Jubilee*, *Commonweal*, and even *America* publish what they deem fit as a paliative. But let us "think with the Church" and speak as does our Supreme Shepherd. A spade is called a spade — and not "some skillfully designed implement for excavating." In section eighty three of his magnificent Encyclical Paul VI wrote: "With fatherly love and affection our heart turns anxiously, and with deep sorrow, to those unfortunate priests, who always remain our dearly beloved brothers and whose *misfortune* we keenly regret: those who, retaining the sacred character conferred by their priestly ordination, have been, or are unfortunately *unfaithful* to the obligations they accepted when they were ordained . . . their sad state . . . its consequences to priests and others . . . and the scandals they inflict on God's People."

With his fatherly heart bleeding His Holiness went on: "If these priests knew how much sorrow, dishonor, and unrest they bring to the holy Church of God; if they reflected on the seriousness and beauty of their obligations, and on the dangers to which they are exposed in this life and in the next, there would be greater care and reflection in their decisions, they would pray more assiduously, and would show greater courage and logic in forestalling the causes of their spiritual and moral collapse."

There is much fatherliness in that paragraph. There is love in every line. There is tender affection in every word. Our Holy Father faces facts, looks them full in the face as he calls them by their correct names. A failure in responsibility is a "failure in responsibility," and a scandal is "a scandal."

But if you want to see what will staunch the flow of blood from his heart read section ninety. "Finally," he says, "and with deep joy we thank Our Lord because many priests who for a time have been unfaithful to their obligations, have, with the grace of the High Priest, found again the path and given joy to all by becoming anew exemplary pastors. With admirable good will they used all the means which were helpful to ensure their return, especially an intense life of prayer, humility, perservering effort sustained by regular reception of the Sacrament of Penance."

And you are involved in this matter personally. The fall of some priest can be prevented by you — or, if you neglect your duty, yours may be the hand that will push him over the brink. That is precisely what the Pope tells you in section ninety-six of this blood stirring Encyclical. "Priestly virtue," he says, "is a treasure that belongs to the whole Church. It is an enrichment and a splendor beyond the ordinary, which redounds to the building up and the profit of the entire People of God. We wish, therefore, to address to all the faithful, our children in Christ, an affectionate and urgent exhortation. We wish that they, too, feel responsible for the virtue of those brothers of theirs who have undertaken the mission of serving them in the priesthood for the salvation of their souls. They should pray and work for priestly vocations; they should help priests wholeheartedly, with filial love and ready collaboration; they should have the firm intention of offering them the consolation of a joyous response to their pastoral labors. They should encourage these, their fathers in Christ, to overcome the difficulties of every sort which they encounter as they fulfill their duties with utter faithfulness, to the edification of all. They should foster, in a spirit of faith and of Christian love, a deep respect and a delicate reserve in their dealings with priests, on account of their condition as men entirely consecrated to Christ and to the Church."

This Encyclical should be studied by every adult Christian. It shows you the heart of Pope Paul VI — and you will find it the Heart of Christ. That heart bleeds because of the defections, but let it be noted that he himself confessed that these make up "a minimal percentage when they are compared with the great number of good, worthy priests." (#85)

That is not "whistling in the dark." Look at our own United States. We have almost sixty thousand priests this very day. How many have defected? "Minimal percentage" is the answer. But, of course, the most minimal — any single defection, is heartrending and truly lamentable.

Why do they do it? One of the most frequently offered explanations is "following my conscience." Have you ever weighed the worth of that saying? Have you ever tried to explain, even to yourself, just what you understand by "conscience" or "the voice of conscience"? Conscience is a word we all use readily enough, but one most of us would find difficult to define. Yet it is, unquestionably, one of the most important faculties we have. It is said that George Washington wrote in his copybook: "Labor to keep alive in your breast that little spark of celestial fire — conscience." There is truth in the maxim — a truth we all recognize since it is common for us to speak of "the voice of conscience" and "the dictates of conscience." We also know what is meant by an "accusing conscience" and most certainly the psychiatric literature of our day has acquainted all with "guilt feelings." So, obviously, conscience has some relation to good and evil. Most Catholics will tell of that dictate which says "Do good and avoid evil" which every man hears within him. It is what is called Natural Law. It is, therefore, like every law a "dictate of reason." When asked whence this dictate, we ultimately answer: "from God." For the Natural Law is the promulgation of His Eternal Law — His Mind and Will made manifest to us by that faculty within us which we call conscience.

It is safe to say that conscience *is* the "Voice of God" within us. But we must immediately add that it is not a "direct voice." No, it is God deep down within us working, working as a Person, calling, inviting, pointing out the right way — but never interfering with our freedom. It is God whispering, if you will, but it is we who make the decision. Error is possible in these decisions, but we can always trace them to their source if we are honest, and it will never be found in the gentle voice of God, but only and always within ourselves. Hence comes the need for an "enlightened" and "informed" and a "rightly formed" conscience — the only kind any man, woman, or child, can allow to be his or her guide!

We hear much about "freedom of conscience," but if one will really think — which means, if you'll bear with the repetition, to think theologically — he will see that conscience binds, much more than it frees. That Voice never says to me "Do what you *like*" — but always "Do what you *ought!*" Therefore, far from freeing me from obligations, it usually tells me how I am anything but free; that I am obliged; that I ought to do such and such. And it is this same Voice that will approve if I do

[139]

what I ought, and sternly rebuke me if I fail to do what I ought — and go ahead and do what I like!

Thomas Aquinas set forth this obligatory nature of conscience in a passage which faces the possibility of conflict between Conscience and Authority — and which leads us to the lesson we are always learning but never seem to learn; a lesson we really need never be taught. In a passage about Truth St. Thomas says: "Therefore conscience is more to be obeyed than authority imposed from outside. For conscience obliges in virtue of Divine Command, whether written down in a Code or instilled by Natural Law. To weigh conscience in the scales against obedience to legal authority is to compare the weight of Divine and human decrees. The first obliges more than the second, and sometimes even against the second." (De Veritate 17,5)

We have read about the application of this principle in the Acts of the Apostles. Chapter Five tells how "the high priest, and all that sided with him . . . seized the apostles and put them in the public prison." The Apostles escaped, thanks to an Angel of the Lord, and went to the Temple and taught the people. "Then the officer went off with his men and brought them . . . and placed them before the Sanhedrin. The high priest questioned them, 'We strictly charged you not to teach in this Name, and here you have filled Jerusalem with your teaching' . . . Peter and the Apostles answered, 'One must obey God rather than men." (Acts 5:17-30)

You can read the sequel and learn how they were "torn with rage and planned to kill them." But Gamaliel told them to use caution saying ". . . keep away from these men, let them alone; for if this plan or movement comes from men, it will be overthrown, but if it comes from God you will not be able to overthrow these men. Otherwise, you may find yourselves fighting even against God." (ib. 5:33-39)

All clear — since the mandate of Peter's conscience was clear. But how about all other men? Are their consciences as clear? Are they acting with as enlightened and as just and as objectively justified and justifiable a conscience? A Charles Davis, for instance, who told the world that "the institutional Church is constantly crushing and damaging people" and that "he could only find Christ and God and lead others to do so, if he were willing to find himself and be true to himself." He acted from "convictions" he said — and that must mean "his conscience."

The London *Observer* carried the full text of Charles Davis' "Special Report" — and countless papers around the globe ran reprints. The kindest evaluation of the *Report* that I saw intimated that Fr. Davis had succumbed to some sort of a "psychic seizure"; for this kind of writing was completely at odds with all he had formerly written. But it is obvious to all that such a "conscience" is not only at odds with the *magisterium* of the Church, but at odds with all that normal people hear from their own *enlightened* and *formed* consciences. Hence, we can understand the wise observation made by Bishop John J. Wright to the effect that "the supreme need" of our day is "the formation of an enlightened conscience."

It is true that from the basic dictate of conscience "Do good and avoid evil" it is *possible* to deduce the Ten Commandments. But in our day of hurried thinking, it is highly *improbable* that many will be able to deduce those Commandments. Like the *possibility* for all men to come to the knowledge of God by use of "unaided human reason," the truth about conscience and its *possibility* must be recognized for what it is: a possibility and not a high probability. Hence, as in the case of "unaided human reason," conscience has been given a guide; and it needs that guide. For Lord Acton was right in his contention that the Reformation turned out to be, in many respects, a movement *against* the freedom of conscience. For it left conscience subject to a new authority — that of the arbitrary initiative of some prince who might differ in religion from all his subjects. Further, it left the individual conscience without a rudder in a very turbulent sea. The "sovereignty of the individual conscience" is a nice phrase — but it has led and it can yet lead to chaos—both moral and social. For the "individual conscience" has not been, and is not now, always on the side of freedom, life, God, or man.

[141]

FATHER M. RAYMOND, O.C.S.O.

Pius XII told us some fifteen years ago that "expressions such as 'the judgment of the Christian conscience' or 'to judge according to the Christian conscience' mean this: that the pattern of the ultimate and personal decision for a moral action must be taken from the word and will of Christ. He is 'the Way, the Truth, and the Life,' not only for all men collectively, but for each single one; the mature man, the child, and the youth." (Radio Broadcast on "Family Day," March 24, 1952)

Obviously then, if we are to have a "Christian conscience" we have to know "the mind and will of Christ." So we are back once again, ultimately, to the *magisterium* of the Church which, alone, can give us authentically and officially the "mind and will of Christ." Father Bernard Häring, C.SS.R., a Council expert, as was Fr. Davis, can be quoted here for the point we are making, and against the stand taken by poor Father Charles Davis. Conscience, Fr. Häring reminds us, is not an oracle which draws truth from its own obscure depths, but, *by its very nature*, seeks illumination and guidance. "God," he says, "the ultimate norm, the truth to which every conscience must conform . . . always instructs conscience *in accordance with its nature;* the natural conscience, through the order of nature; the conscience endowed with the supernatural grace of Faith, through supernatural revelation. Just as it is not alien to natural conscience to draw from the natural revelation expressed in creation . . . so it is also 'according to nature' for the believing conscience, elevated by grace and steeped in humility, to hearken to the word of revelation communicated to us in the Church . . ."

Before giving you Father Häring's conclusion, let me draw your attention to that phrase "steeped in humility." It can well be the answer to the riddle that faces us about these priests and nuns who have "copped out."

Father Häring concluded his exposition: "And so, only one with a totally perverted concept of the real nature and function of conscience, could repudiate the infallible *magisterium* of the Church in the name of conscience. Only a conscience which itself enjoys creative plenitude of infallibility in its own native right could *a priori* reject as contradictory every intervention of objective authority."

It is refreshing to hear a Protestant scholar, Professor C. A. Pierce, in his book, *Conscience in the New Testament*, say: "Dreadful consequences are derivable to society . . . from the use of a plausible word wrested from its proper sense. It has been imagined that, provided men follow the directions of their own 'consciences', they are justified in whatever mode of conduct they may adopt, which (as the term 'conscience' is now too generally understood) is to say that because men are persuaded that a thing is right, it cannot be wrong. When men, therefore, talk of 'liberty of conscience' they would do well to consider whether it is not, as the phrase is now understood, rather a liberty of their own making, than any portion of that liberty with which Christ has made them free."

An earlier Anglican scholar, the saintly John Henry (later Cardinal) Newman, wrote even more forcefully on this subject of the need for some objective criteria for evaluating the "dictates of conscience." He confesses he could not find it in unaided nature, nor in Scripture alone; no, neither could he find it in Tradition alone nor in the voices of the Fathers. At this point in his life — he was still an Anglican, — he admitted that he could not find a rule of conscience in the National Church. So what? So he finally found what he sought in the Universal Catholic Church, endowed with infallibility and teaching through divinely-appointed channels. Therein, he said, authority brings supernatural doctrine to the direction of that conscience which is the herald of the Natural Law. He concluded that the Catholic Church alone provides adequate objective criteria for the evaluation of those dictates of a sincere conscience which the upright man is obliged to follow.

Newman was never taken in by a caricature or counterfeit of "conscience." He would never subscribe, as so many moderns have done, to the "law of liberty" or the "law of love." According to these men this "law of love" is superior to all other laws, and may even contradict them. When asked just what is this "law of liberty" or "law of love" they will tell you it is a sort of divine inspiration received in the depths of one's soul; it is an "intuition of love" which is the ultimate guide for individuals in their moral choices. As you see, this is moral solipsism, subjectivism, and, of course, a form of existentialism; all of which are false. One would think Newman was talking of our day when he wrote: "When men advocate the rights of conscience, they in no sense mean the rights of the Creator, nor the duty to Him, in thought and deed, of the creature; but the right of thinking, speaking, writing and acting according to their judgment or their humor, without any thought of God at all. They do not even pretend to go by any moral rule, but they demand what they think is an Englishman's prerogative, for each to be his own master in all things, and to profess what he pleases, asking no one's leave, and accounting priest or preacher, speaker or writer, unutterably impertinent, who dares to say a word against his going to perdition, if he likes it, in his own way. Conscience has rights, because it has duties; but in this age, with a large portion of the public, it is the very right and freedom of conscience to dispense with conscience, to ignore a Lawgiver and Judge, to be independent of unseen obligations. It becomes a license to take up any or no religion, to take up this or that and let it go again, to go to Church, to go to chapel, to boast of being above all religions and to be an impartial critic of each of them. Conscience is a stern monitor, but in this century it has been superseded by a counterfeit which the eighteen centuries prior to it never heard of, and could not have mistaken for it if they had. *It is the right of self-will.*" (*Difficulties of Anglicans*)

Newman, while still an Anglican, taught clearly that conscience consists in an habitual orientation of the whole man to God; conscience develops in man a profound awareness of the presence of God; conscience implies that a man desires to serve God with a perfect heart; this orientation and desire will be evidenced by consistency in conduct; and, finally, conscience imposes the duty of habitual obedience.

[144]

Obviously, then, conscience and authority not only admit of reconciliation; they demand one another. As Newman put it so well: "The general sense of right and wrong, which is the first element of religion" (and the basic dictate of conscience) "is so delicate, so fitful, so easily puzzled, obscured, perverted, so subtle in its argumentative methods, so impressed by education, so biased by pride and passion, so unsteady in its flight . . . this sense is at once the highest of all teachers, yet the least luminous; and the Church, the Pope, the hierarchy are, in the divine purpose, the supply of an urgent demand." *(Difficulties of Anglicans)*

Newman's entire life, as Anglican and as Catholic, was one in which the tension between conscience and authority was borne with honesty and heroism. It can be doubted that any other man will have to suffer as did Newman from both conscience and authority. Nor, perhaps, will any other man harmonize the two as did this scholarly saint.

In his *Apologia pro Vita Sua* he showed the interplay of both in a passage all who are troubled, as many of our priests have been, would do well to meditate. "Catholic Christendom," says Newman, "is no simple exhibition of religious absolutism, but presents a continuous picture of authority and private judgment alternately advancing and retreating as the ebb and flow of the tide; — it is a vast assemblage of human beings with willful intellects and wild passions, brought together into one by the Beauty and Majesty of a superhuman Power, — into what may be called a large reformatory or training school, not as if into a hospital or into a prison, not in order to be sent to bed, not to be buried alive, but (if I may change my metaphor) brought together as if into some moral factory, for the melting, refining, and moulding, by an incessant, noisy process, of the raw material of human nature, so excellent, so dangerous, so capable of divine purpose."

A present day Anglican Divine sees the Church as having the duty, and the resources for fulfilling that duty, in enlighting and forming consciences by first of all being herself "the best

[145]

possible environment" for the formation of conscience; then of spiritualizing the secular environment in which her children live — for this, too, has its part in shaping consciences; next, of speaking out authoritatively on specific moral questions; and above all, she must not only proclaim the teachings of Christ, but present the very Person of Christ as the pattern to be emulated, making the influence of everything Christ said, and did, and was, penetrate the deepest depths of human intellectual, appetitive, instinctive, and emotional life where conscience stirs.

We must never forget that the "voice of conscience" can be hushed and even silenced. Hence the need to develop — and the Church's obligation to aid in the development — a moral sensitivity so sure and sharp that conscience react not merely negatively to anything and everything that would take us from the perfection of Christian living to which we have been called, but urge us on positively toward greater perfection.

In accord with all the above is Vatican II's *Declaration of Religious Freedom*. There you read: ". . . the highest norm of human life is divine law. . . Man is made to participate in this law . . . every man has the duty, and therefore the right, to seek the truth in matters religious, in order that he may form for himself right and true judgments of conscience with the aid of suitable means . . . man perceives and acknowledges the imperatives of the divine law through the mediation of conscience. In all his activity a man is bound to follow his conscience faithfully, in order that he may come to God, for whom he was created. It follows that he is not to be forced to act in a manner contrary to his conscience." (#3)

That teaching, held by many as "new," can be traced back through Encyclical after Encyclical from John XXIII in his *Pacem in Terris* and *Mater et Magistra*, through Pius XII and Pius XI, right back to Leo XIII in his *Rerum Novarum* and *Immortale Dei*. The foundation upon which this Declaration was set, and the development of doctrine it manifests, merit for it the title "new." "Timely" might be the better word for this magnificent Declaration. But all we want to stress here is that

it teaches man how to enjoy an "enlightened and formed conscience" — and, by following it, to attain to his real dignity.

In this day and age, when often mistaken and excessive defer-
ence is being paid to "individual conscience" (unformed, ill-
formed and even deformed), and when there are excessive rejec-
tions of authority, it is worth our while to pause, as we have
paused, and ponder, as we have tried to ponder, on the truth of
the declaration to "let conscience be your guide" — for the question before us has been answered too often by that maxim.

Back to our question: Why are so many young priests and
nuns "copping out"? First of all, let us note again, with Pope
Paul VI, that only a "minimal percentage" of priests — and even
of nuns — has "copped out." Secondly, let us all admit that we
can no more answer this question adequately than we can the
one about "Why did Judas Iscariot sell Jesus Christ for thirty
pieces of silver?" But, if the reason given be that of "conscience,"
then we must say these people are deluding themselves — or
have been deluded by him who is the "father of lies."

In *An Open Letter to Priests*, Catherine Doherty (the former
Baroness de Hueck) wrote: "As I pray in the night for you,
for the Church, for the People of God, I ask myself over and
over again: Why this impatience? Why this need to change
everything at once? Why this urgency? Whence does it come?"
Then she answers in a manner we can answer the all but un-
answerable question which opened this chapter: "It cannot be
from love, for love is patient, love is understanding, love is
kind. . . So it must be from some other source. Foolish of me,
is it not, to consider the Prince of Darkness in our scientific century? But consider him I do. For I walk in a night of Faith, as
so many of us lay people have to do these days. And Faith can
become utterly dark. I guess its darkness is like the darkness
of the earth into which the seed must fall. But in that darkness
one can hear well, and I seem to hear, symbolically speaking,
the barely audible, slithering movements of a serpent. I may
be a fool, but I confess that I do. And at such moments, fears
hold me tight."

[147]

If Mrs. Doherty is a fool, I am one with her — and have been for years on years. Back in 1928 Pius XI wrote his *Miserentissimus Redemptor*. In it he told mankind that if it did not "turn to prayer and penance, God would let the Devil loose." Mankind, to the best of my knowledge, did not turn to prayer and penance — and the explanation of much that seems inexplicable, lies in that fact!

"Let your conscience be your guide" is a delusion. It is a deception of the Devil. Only an "enlightened conscience," only an "informed and rightly formed conscience" can be your guide — and that will always lead you to God — most often through prayer and penance. Did you notice how Paul VI spoke of those priests who had returned to their duty — and their dignity? He told how they had turned to "all the means which were helpful to ensure their return, especially an intense life of *prayer, humility, persevering* effort sustained by regular reception of the Sacrament of *Penance*."

Prayer and Penance has been the call of Christendom from John the Baptist to Paul VI. Perhaps a neglect of both — or even of only one — can explain much "copping out." Be assured it was not the *"aggiornamento"* of Vatican II.

But, while that is true enough about the priests, is it equally true about the nuns? Before answering that let us add to the above that the Press may have led some young priests into false concepts concerning Vatican II. There is a typically "clerical" witticism going the rounds of Religious to the effect that today "Religious no longer take the three traditional vows, but only promise 'Poverty, Chastity, and *Dialogue*'." Some subjects, misled by what the popular journalists had to say about the establishment of a Synod of Bishops, seem to think that the old "monarchial-hierarchical structure of the Church" is to be done away with, and a "democratic form" introduced. Hence, they no longer obey as did the older generation; they want to "dialogue" and "discuss" with superiors.

Unquestionably, more "democratic" processes *are* being used throughout the Church today, but the Church is not, and can never become, a democracy. Christ founded it as a monarchical-hierarchial Church, and that it will ever remain; for the three-fold power to teach, govern, and sanctify was given to Peter and the Apostles, and through them to their successors: the Pope and the Bishops of the Church. Of course the Pope listens to others — and even discusses with them — as do the Bishops and priests . . . but as far as genuine authority goes — this comes directly from Christ and rests with Pope and Bishops — in no way depending on "the consent of the governed."

"But," you may object, "look at what is happening. Look at the 'new breed'. Aren't they different? Aren't they disobeying their Bishops and Superiors in the name of 'consience'? Haven't they become more and more 'involved' in civil and political matters? Haven't you heard about the full page ad in the New York *Times* demanding a recall of a priest who seems like a 'peacenik' who had been 'exiled' according to the ad because of his public pronouncements on the war in Vietnam? Did you not know that priests have been arrested in civil rights demonstrations in Chicago, Milwaukee, Detroit — and even in your own nearby Louisville? Bishops in Texas and California have felt obliged to discipline some priests for aiding and encouraging agricultural workers who were striking. Then look at our seminarians. Haven't they gotten out of hand? Aren't they dictating to their Rectors and Faculties on what they are to be taught, on how much freedom they are to have, and just how they are to be ruled? Haven't you heard of their picketing and rebelling? Then, as you have been saying, some theologians and scripture scholars have said some mighty strange and upsetting things. Original sin, the Garden of Eden, even the Birth of Christ and those happenings accompanying that Birth have been called into question by these men. At least that is what the Press tells us. Then look at the 'union' — at least that is what it looks like to us — that has been formed in Chicago called the 'Association of Chicago Priests' . . . "

You can stop there. Yes, I have heard about this so-called "new breed." I have even met and talked with some of them.

For the most part they are of the "younger generation." Hence, some of the things they say and do should not too greatly upset you. Youth has always been impatient, impetuous, impulsive — and independent. It has never been known for too much prudence nor for great wisdom. Hence, with them, you have to be patient. They will learn in time. About the "theologians" you mention, I believe I have said enough. They are not the *magisterium* of the Church. You, as a sincere, practicing Catholic, need not pay much attention to them. Let them speculate. Something good may yet come from their efforts. When that good does come, you can be sure the *magisterium* will welcome it, and hand it on to you. As for the "scripture scholars", I say here what I have said about the so-called "theologians": they are not the *magisterium;* you do not have to accept their speculations, theories, interpretations. More may be said about them later. But about the so-called "new breed" I want to say that not all of them are completely wrong; some of them, even, are actually in accord with the spirit and the letter of Vatican II. I suggest that you listen to them as patiently as you can, respect them as persons, and credit them with being sincere — even when obviously in error. Thus you may help them, and, at times, even profit from their ideas, even when those ideas seem "different."

If you want to get them truly "in focus" — and be able to distinguish what is legitimate in their actions, and what is not, you might read both the Decree on Priestly Formation and the one on the Ministry and Life of Priests. Today, those in the active ministry are asked to look for "ways and means to communicate with the modern world." But these two decrees say emphatically that Religion is never to be reduced to "sociology" — nor is "spirituality" mere "psychology."

There is a drive to get the Church into the highly skilled, fast-moving, technological environment. It is a proper drive. But there will be mistakes in its implementation — and many will be made by the young — the so-called "new breed." But both they and we can — and, please God, will — learn from these mistakes. There can be a "Christian secularity" — but there must never be

[150]

a "Christian secularism." In other words, we can, and we must "Christianize" the secular world, but we must never allow the world to "secularize" the Church. Here is where you may see some mistakes. Here already there have been mistakes and that is why Pope Paul VI has had to say: "Some have the illusion that to spread the Gospel of Christ it is necessary to take on the customs of the world, its mentality, its profanity."

That, of course, is an illusion. Nevertheless Vatican II does want us all to become more "involved" in the world — so that we can bring that world to Christ and Christ to that world. That is why there have been experiments — some of which have shocked the older generation. There have been and are inter-church urban projects; there are, once again, worker priests; there are shopping-center chapels, industrial missions, tavern-touring clergy, folk Masses, discussions or dialogue even with atheists, and a thousand church-sponsored coffee-houses across the country. Those experiments should tell even the most impatient that we are on the move, that we are endeavoring to implement the Council Decrees. Of course some of these experiments will fail, some will be found to be a bit extreme, and others not too prudent. Nevertheless they are all moves in the right direction, and we must neither be shocked by them, nor disappointed by them. They are all part of the painful period of transition and transformation. Still, none of them change the Church in her essence. So, in the midst of them all, we can hear His voice; and it is still saying: "Fear not! It is I."

But how about those four thousand seven hundred and fifty nuns? Well, undoubtedly, some of them have been deluded. Further, there is nothing in the Council's decrees, especially the one from which we took the title of this chapter — that on "The Appropriate Renewal of the Religious Life" — that justifies "copping out." Look at its wording. It calls for "Renewal" — not abandonment. And its opening words are *Perfectae carita-tis* — which mean "Complete love." Since we know that "love is a union of ills" and since all Religious Life has as its ultimate the Glory of God, we know that a Religious is one who seeks

[151]

to give Glory to God by a total gift of self out of complete love by professing the evangelical counsels: poverty, chastity and obedience. The Decree did call for "an adjustment (or adaptation) to the changed conditions of the times," and perhaps the failure to distinguish between these two terms has been an occasion, if not a cause, not only of confusion, but of final "copping out."

As Bishop John J. McEleney, S.J. pointed out "one of the basic points for a proper assessment of this conciliar Decree consists precisely in the clear distinction between *adaptation* and *renewal*." Then he pointed out that the first, *adaptation*, has to do with those changes that are necessary because of *external* contemporary needs and outward circumstances of our times. In other words with *externals*, and one might say *accidentals*. Whereas *renewal* points to the interior of the individual. It calls for a renovation of the spirit, the heart, mind, soul of the Religious. It asks for a re-consecration, a re-dedication, a re-animation of that total commitment, that complete love with which the Religious first gave himself or herself to God. That, you see, is something utterly other than a letting down of the hair and a lifting of the hem, utterly other than a change of head-dress or color of habit, utterly other than being allowed to travel without a "prudent companion" or having to ask special permission to write a letter or take a meal outside the convent.

The Council in its Decree made this point clear, and stressed the fact that *adaptation* without *renewal* would spell failure. "Since the religious life is intended above all else," it says almost in its opening lines, "to lead those who embrace it to an imitation of Christ and to union with God through the profession of the evangelical counsels, the fact must be honestly faced that even the most desirable changes made on behalf of contemporary needs will fail of their purpose unless a renewal of spirit gives life to them. Indeed such an interior renewal must always be accorded the leading role even in the promotion of exterior works." (#2e)

Those are the key sentences of this Decree. Some, is seems, have lost the keys!

Perhaps it is due, to some extent, to what is called "feminine psychology," that many nuns have become totally taken up with minutiae and mere externals. For instance, would men get so excited about a mere change of dress? Granted the habit is a holy thing. Granted again it has many sacred traditions attached to it. Granted still further, that we do become attached to it. Nevertheless, to be extreme, could not a nun praise, reverence and serve God even in a mini skirt?

Now understand me. I hold the religious habit in highest regard. I know that it creates a veritable aura about its wearer. And for those extremists who would change what they sneer at as "medieval garb" for something closely akin to an airline hostess' tailored chicness, I have the query: "What would have happened to those nuns who marched at Selma had they been clothed in some of the suggested "habits" of the "new breed," and not in those holy, respected and distinctive robes the same "breed" calls "medieval"? You do not have to guess; you know! And for those who teach, I have this question: Have you ever realized how much the discipline you maintain in your classes has been due not to you, but to that habit you wear? Further, to all who have been respected as they travelled about our country in train, plane, or bus; and to all who have been actually reverenced as they walked the streets of our teeming cities, I pose the query: Do you think men will have the same respect for you as you move in their midst if you dress "like any other girl" that they have now when you dress so unlike all other girls?

My point is not that the habit is not holy and truly distinctive and distinguishing, but that it is not the whole of religious life nor the reality of the religious herself. When we get down to actualities, we can say it is an accidental. Then why get so upset over some minor — or even major — modifications in it?

The next important point to make about nuns and *aggiornamento* is the one made by Cardinal Antoniutti, head of the Congregation of Religious, at the close of the first international assembly of the representatives of the Church's 2,200 women's religious congregations held in Rome in 1967. "Avoid personal, arbitrary, erroneous interpretation of the Council's authentic teaching. To do this it is necessary to be tuned to the authentic transmitter, the Pope, and to his responsible agencies, avoiding those dubious stations which transmit theories, opinions, criteria and proposals which are contrary to the letter and the spirit of the Council."

I fear many of those who have "copped out" failed to heed this kind of advice. I suspect that they tuned in on those "dubious stations" and had no trouble with static. For instance one finds in Sunday Supplements long articles on the "New Nun," and learns that some of them have moved into the ghettos of our large cities to share life with the people, and not teach them how to live. Was that Christ's purpose in coming to earth: to share life with us only — and not to teach us how to live? Maybe Sister was taken in by the Council's word "Witness." But Sister should know that a witness teaches by example. Hence, if she has gone to the ghetto not to teach, but merely to share the life of the poor, she is not Christianizing secular life but being secularized by the life of the world.

Then there is a certain Sister Mary Anne "a delicate, blue-eyed woman in her early thirties" according to the Sunday Supplement's reporter, "who talks to her catechetical classes about the words of Vatican II, such words as 'acceptance', 'understanding', 'love', 'human needs', and 'witness' — and never about those words "religious conversations used to center on: 'sin', 'self-sacrifice', 'penance' and 'moral obligations'." When asked about this Sister is reported to have replied: "Well, really, what is sin? Theologians aren't so sure any more. There are those who think mortal sin is not so much a separate act, but a way of living. Does a good father disown his daughter if she has done something seriously wrong? How serious must it be to be disowned by God? After all, we have drives."

And she is teaching that to her catechetical classes! Note well that this "blue-eyed woman in her early thirties" mentions "theologians" — but makes no mention of the Gospel of Jesus Christ. If she would read that she would find what sin is and just how serious it can be — to be disowned by God. "Go away from me, with your curse upon you, to the eternal fire prepared for the devil and his angels. . . And they will go away to eternal punishment." (Matt. 25:42-46) Let Sister Mary Anne exegete that passage. "After all, we have drives" — yes, Sister, and one of our basic, and really one of our most potent drives, is toward God — and away from what would offend Him — sin.

This reporter tells us that "the modern nun . . . no longer tells herself that virginity is a 'higher state' of life . . ." But Vatican II says: "The holiness of the Church is also fostered in a special way by the observance of the manifold counsels proposed by Our Lord to His disciples. *Outstanding* among them is . . . virginity." (#42 Dogmatic Constitution on Church) Then in the Decree on Priestly Formation, we find the same truth expressed in almost the same words. Section 10 tells how consecrated *virginity* is chosen for its own *greater* dignity and beauty.

By now you must be ready to ask me if you can "Relax" — as has been insisted throughout this book — over the situation in Religious life and among the Clergy. You have heard of dancing nuns and their singing sisters, you have read about the Urban Apostolate of Sisters, you have seen some in their "new" habits, you know some of them marched at Selma, have picketed here, there, and just about everywhere, that they not only visit slums but some live there, you may have heard how some study at Moscow University, others become ski instructors in Austria, and a few have taken charm courses in Dubuque. You also know that over four thousand have left in the past year. How can you "Relax" over such a situation, let alone "Rejoice"?

Well, let us go to *Jubilee*, April, 1967, and read what some stable nuns have had to say about the February issue of the same magazine. In February these editors saw fit to print three articles under the general title *After the Convent*, about the difficulties of ex-nuns. The central article was based on "the experiences of a total of six ex-nuns" . . . At any rate one nun replied:

RELAX!

"What are you, collectively, trying to prove: that Religious Life should be scrapped because six women out of a hundred thousand and more in the U.S.A. have found their particular version of it intolerable? I know, as we all do, that the number of 'ex-nuns' is growing; the total number to date, however, is still a *small minority* compared with those of us who remain." There is the first point for you to grasp. Just as Pope Paul VI told you the defections from the priesthood is still a "minimal percentage," so this Sister finds the defections among her fellows just as small — but still large enough for all of us to lament. But then Sister adds some logic which is more forceful than all that the editors of this magazine seem capable of. She argues: "Easily-obtainable figures show that many more wives, proportionately, are unhappy, separated or divorced from their husbands. Why not interview six, or 60, or 600 of them in a noble attempt to prove that marriage should be scrapped? Or are you trying to present a true picture of religious life in this country today? If so, your approach is very negative, and your sources questionable, to put it mildly. . . Without waiting to be interviewed . . . I can mention a whole galaxy of good things I have found in a long religious life. . . Warm sisterly friendships I could always count on; genuine concern on the part of most superiors for my welfare and that of others; many spiritual advantages; a good education; a challenging apostolate engendering a host of human relationships. Religious life does not claim to be a paradise; it is not 'easy'. But neither is any other life that is worth living. . . If space were not so limited, I could take many other points in the *Jubilee* article for particular comment. I will end this letter with one further reference to a quote from Sister Charles Borromeo CSC. I have not experienced religious life as a 'psychological nightmare' nor have I found in it the 'atmosphere of an oppressive totalitarian society which has been a source of exquisite suffering for women religious'. In other words, I am even happier now in my vocation than I was in my earlier years because I understand much better now the true meaning of my commitment. And I have plenty of company!"

Indeed she has "plenty of company" — some 176,000 of them. What reason to Relax and Rejoice!

And a youngster, only two years and a half in Religion, teaches sense to Sister Charles Borromeo CSC — who is looked upon by the *avant garde* crowd as an "authority." Says Sister John Vincent, SCN: "I was amazed that Sister Charles Borromeo could be so taken in by this article, and would actually give her support to it. She talks about 'improvement in formation' and states that 'a younger woman under the normal strain of intense study is deprived of all adult and creative self-expression and leisure . . . feels boxed-in, snared by a life-pattern that treats human relations in a manner suited to pre-Freudian peasants.' Elsewhere in the article one of the ex-nuns states that 'it is a rough, shocking, even repulsive time before the novice becomes a nun.' If those two statements are true, something must be wrong with me and with many other young girls who are living today in formation and are happy, well-adjusted young women. Study is emphasized . . . but we also have every opportunity for recreation, development of deep, personal relationships, and prayer life, and even have time just to enjoy living . . . I have met *many* sisters who have lived 40 and 50 years in community life — and they certainly do not seem to be dehumanized — but are free, happy *individuals*."

That fact ought to have you "relaxing and rejoicing." And the young nun goes on: "So much is being written in magazines and papers about the ex-nun and the ex-priest . . . but they never mention all the young sisters and priests who are happy and fulfilled in their lives. *Your magazine has shown this same pattern*. Why be so negative? . . . I cannot agree with Sister Charles Borromeo that this is an honest, constructive insight into religious life. . . I think it is distorted and destructive and entirely negative." (Italics are mine.)

Ed Rice and his crew have not yet, to my knowledge, answered the piercing inquiry: "Why be so negative?"

But to give you added reason to "relax and rejoice" let me draw your attention to the emotional element in all the oppo-

[157]

sition to Religious Life as expressed by nuns — especially ex-nuns. One religious exclaimed: "what lies, slander, exaggerated ideas of life in a convent." Another stated: "I found that the first paragraph of '*A Sister Theologian Speaks*' presented at least five of the most diabolical lies that could be written concerning religious life. . . The entire article was simply disgusting for those who understand and know how religious life should be lived, and *is lived:* Faith — love — and sacrifice are needed." When you read such words as "totalitarian" "unwholesome" and "dehumanizing" applied to the whole of religious life, and such as "rough" "shocking" "repulsive" applied to the novitiate, you know you are not reading reason from anyone, but only emotion. Without being the least bit unchivalrous, may I say that women are inclined to be a bit more emotional than men — and that, perhaps, lies behind many "coppings out."

But to be adequate and fair; to be theological in my own thinking, let me say that not all who left have really "copped out" on God. There is such a thing as a "temporary vocation." It is possible that many of those who left religious life had been called to it by God just for a time, so that they might gain certain graces which would enable them to live for God more efficaciously after they had left the convent.

Now let me give you even more reason to "relax and rejoice" regarding the legitimate changes brought about in the Religious Life by Vatican II. Father Joseph F. Gallen, S.J. has commented on the extremes in the Religious Life today — especially among nuns — in this fashion: "A fundamental problem in the Church today, and in Religious Life, is an inflexible traditionalism on the right, and an equally extreme position on the left. . . Both positions are in great part inflexible and blind. Each convinced of the truth of its own tenets or mission, even though both are evidently wrong. Each has regressed into unreality: one into a world of aged persons and past ideas; the other into a daydream of youth and of ideas almost only of the present and future. . . Each extreme is so emotional that it appears almost impervious to a rational argument. One does not read Vatican II; the other has grasped the feeling but not the sense, the emotion but not the intelligence, the drive but not the reasoning of Vatican II — and its 'source' for the Council is frequently only the emotional and excited conversation or discussion, or even mere hearsay, not the documents of Vatican II . . . This period of time may be, and should be, the New Pentecost of the Church, but the Holy Spirit is not merely a consuming Flame, but also the Spirit of Wisdom, Counsel, and Understanding." That is the Spirit we need today — and will need for many days ahead. And we will have HIM if we pray — and do penance; for prayer is powerful, but prayer joined to penance is all-powerful.

Father Gallen has many more sage observations — and these in themselves give us reason to relax. If they are accepted and followed, we will have every reason to rejoice. For instance: "We should listen to youth, take any good idea from the young, realize that their habits of thought, speech and conduct are facts; but we are not to be intimidated nor stampeded by youth. . . . Older religious should make an energetic and constant effort to understand the young of today, who must make an equal effort to comprehend their older brethren. Both are suffering, and neither possesses all knowledge or wisdom." Then again: "The laity should not be put in their place, but given their rightful place — which is not necessarily supreme power. An angry layman is no wiser than an angry priest or religious. Intolerance is the sin of age and of youth; a narrowed vision that of age, and a confused and unreal vision that of youth. . . We should worry at least as much about being *religious* — as about being *relevant*. We want wise, not tired old men; and intelligent, temperate, and progressive, not angry young men." And about those who have "copped out" Father has this to say: "We should investigate the causes of defections and remove those that should be removed. We can and should have sympathy for those who leave, without glamorizing them. Leaving religious life does not, by that very fact, constitute anyone as the standard-bearer of sanctity, truth, and progress — much less the sole standard-bearer."

[159]

Then Father has a set of what can be called aphorisms: "Authority may be service, but it is not subservience . . . give up the tired ideas of the past, but substitute only the sound, not merely the emotional and excited, ideas of the present . . . an excessive number, and minutely detailed laws are to be excluded, but all sons of Adam and daughters of Eve need the guidance and support of necessary and useful laws. . . Why must anything that is done at a *prescribed* time and place be necessarily suspect, and an encroachment on the liberty of the children of God? . . . When did the *obligation* to pray become an obstacle to prayer? . . . When did we Religious reach the thrice-blessed state of universal sanctity — *ruled only by perfect love?* . . . It is an exaggeration to hold that we have fallen into that obstinacy in evil that belongs to the damned, but when did we rise to the impeccability of the blessed?"

When recognized Religious write with so much sanity and real wisdom, you can relax and rejoice. When you find Father going on to say: "Do not accept every idea that is flying from religious house to religious house, from one Order to another, and not even from one convent to another, but *prove the idea* — and never forget to prove also the prophets," you know there is no need for fear. Then Father shows his maturity and true insight when he says: "Let us make sure that the store fronts and apartments are good, long-term apostolic investments, before we knock down the Churches, schools and hospitals. Let us communicate without talking one another into brain fag, and let us always question whether the Church to which the Holy Spirit is always present must always be a Church of exaggerations."

As a final reason for your relaxing and rejoicing let me present to you Sister Mary Rosalyn Zehnder, R.S.M. who says: "Frustrated, unfulfilled, de-personalized, reduced to nonentities, misshapen individuals, part-time persons, irrelevant and so on *ad infinitum*. These choice expressions are among the many being unmercifully hurled at religious sisters or communities of sisters today. The would-be friends, reformers, emancipators, or simply critics . . . are often-times illogical and misdirected if not mali-

FATHER M. RAYMOND, O.C.S.O.

cious in their arguments. From particulars they proceed to universals — and not on the basis of induction. All dissenters to the theory of irrelevancy are discredited as non-realists, traditionalists, or simply passivists. . . Some of the terms that have been loosely and continuously overused need definition. What exactly is *fulfillment?* When does a human being reach this state of *completion* and *authenticity?* . . . It is an accepted fact that a person can reach perfection of being without satisfying every physical drive, provided this urge is sublimated, channeled, and released in a higher and more constructive way. The highest human potential, if actualized, can mean fulfillment of the entire person. Intellection and affectivity are those activities which separate man from the other beings with which he shares a common genus. The intellect seeks truth; the will, love. These objects, however, are found ultimately in their perfection only in God. He is Truth and Love itself. Man, then, to be fulfilled, must seek these ends in God. . . We can discover and proceed along the paths of truth and love to fulfillment only in a human manner — and that way to the Father is shown us in Christ, who is 'The Way, the Truth, and the Life.' If we look at Christ, and judge His life by natural standards, we could very well use the adjectives cited at the beginning of this article to describe His earthly existence. Who was more of a failure than He? Why did He concern Himself with such trivial matters as those of Nazareth for thirty of His limited thirty-three years? Why did He not become more closely allied with the world? Why restrict His apostolate to a chosen few? Why did His followers desert Him at the end? Did He find, in our estimation, *fulfillment?*

"Religious life is *identification with Christ.* It is the total acceptance of this Person, Christ. In an existential framework, it is a free and personal choice, in the here and now, with full responsibilities of the consequences. To follow Christ is to embrace the folly of the Cross. What to the secularistic mind seems ridiculous and nonessential, is recognized by the religious woman to be significant in the achievement of her goals. . . In accepting Christ she is binding herself to the covenant of love and becomes, by

[161]

that very fact, a part of the world — indeed an instrument in the world's redemption. . . The very intimacy of the bond of religious profession makes the religious one with Christ in His mission of salvation. . .

"Religious are restricted in the living of the vows and the rule, but only that they will be free to give themselves to God unequivocally. What after all is religious life — self-fulfillment or identification with Christ? Or is self-fulfillment found precisely in Christ? . . . To follow Christ has, from the earliest times, meant to *give*, and the perfection of that giving lies in poverty — all that one has; in chastity — all that one is; and in obedience — all that one might be. All three counsels imply a personal encounter with the loved One."

As you note, Sister uses all the "in" words — and shows their out-going, or better, out-giving meanings. Now see how she concludes this magnificent article . . . "Only in steadfast fidelity do we attain the fullness of freedom. Freedom is not found in breaking the bonds of obligation, but in fulfilling these obligations in faithful love. For, what *is* free will, if not the power to love, the power to chose to do something because we will to do it in love. Freedom is the power to will to love, and to love with devotion, with dedication, even with fidelity; it is the power to give self permanently in love.

"If, as St. Thomas says, it is the possession of the object of desire which constitutes *happiness*, then truly a dedicated religious has within her power the attainment of the most complete happiness possible on earth in the identification of herself with the object of her desire — Christ Himself, and all others in Christ.

"Christ exemplified the *fullness of personal integrity*. He walked a straight path without deviation or delay. His guide throughout was His Father's Will, and His motive was the *perfection of love*. And He asks the same of His followers. . . This is the perfection of the religious man (and woman) and this the assurance of his (and her) integrity: that he (and she) performs the Will of God — and performs it lovingly."

[162]

That last paragraph tells you why this chapter was titled The Pursuit of Perfect Love — with Greater Freedom. That is what Religious Life is all about — and, hence, you can relax and rejoice despite what you hear and read about those who "cop out." Hundreds of thousands of women and almost a hundred thousand men are identifying themselves with Christ and endeavoring to perform the Will of God, and to perform it *lovingly*.

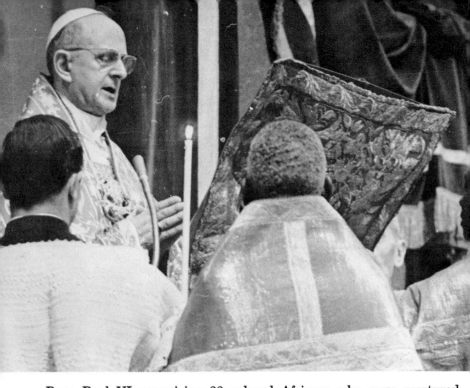

Pope Paul VI canonizing 22 colored Africans who were martyred for their faith.

Chapter 7

"THAT THEY MAY BE ONE . . . " Christ Prayed.

You love God, do you not? At least you long to love Him —
and with all your heart. You call Him — and know Him to be —
your Father, do you not? That being so, is it not quite natural
for you to want Him to be loved, admired, adored, praised by
everyone? What is more, you know Him to be Father of every
human being on earth, a loving Father, a generous Father —
a Father who is to be generously, totally loved — and by everyone. Was it not His only Begotten Son who taught you how to
address Him? Did not Truth Incarnate tell us all: "When you
pray, say as follows: 'Our Father'." Then why not rejoice when
you read of Catholics joining others, and others joining with
Catholics to praise our Father, and to pray that His kingdom
may come?

That series of questions is prompted from the reactions of
many after seeing pictures of Cardinal Cushing praying in a
Protestant Church, reading articles about the same Cardinal
being present, preaching and praying in a Jewish Synagogue, or
hearing about Bishop Bernard J. Flanagan giving a homily in a
Lutheran Church in Worcester, Massachusetts. Many found it
difficult enough to take the news of certain priests holding
"Dialogues" with Protestant Ministers and Jewish Rabbis, but
when our prelates actually prayed with these others, these many
were more than puzzled. Who can blame them when we recall
that it was not so long ago that we all had to hesitate — and
even more than hesitate at times—before being "passively" present at a funeral, a wedding, or something of like nature, in a Protestant Church or a Synagogue? We had heard something about
communicatio in divinis — Some of us even knew something of

the wording of Canon 1258 to the effect that "it was illicit for Catholics to assist actively or to take part in sacred worship of non-Catholics" We also knew that "civil courtesy, duty, or respect," might oblige some of us to be present, but we also knew that presence had to be "merely material" and that there be "no danger of perversion or of scandal." But now . . . Not only "Interfaith" praying — but we have heard of a Presbyterian girl from the United States being given Holy Communion at her Wedding Mass in Assisi, Italy, and even of a United Church of Christ minister being granted permission to officiate at the marriage of his son to a Catholic girl in Oakland, California. Small wonder many ask: "What in the world is going on in the Catholic Church? What is happening to Rome? Are we giving up our Faith?"

That type of questioning comes from many parts of the world. Just recently from Boston came the following: "When I see, hear, and read of the things going on here and abroad, I shudder, feel sorry and even weep for the world. I think the very rocks are crying — and crying out. The young people in so many quarters have no morality at all and say: 'So what? We'll live as we like; for tomorrow will bring the bomb.' Talk about pagan Rome! . . . And to top it all a Catholic magazine tells us 'May Devotions are out of fashion' . . . I think it's about time the Vatican closed the windows and doors the good Pope John opened. Enough is enough. From what I hear and observe priests are now mere figure heads, the people are now the authority in the Church. Soon they will be closing the Churches; for some say 'one religion is as good as another' — and claim that is what Vatican II is teaching. What's all this Ecumenism about — and 'Dialogue' — and 'Interfaith this and that'?"

Admittedly, that is emotional. But it is also quite understandable. That was written in the spring of 1967 — and before summer was near its height, Catholics had taken part in dozens of minor ecumenical activities and a handful of major events. April saw a meeting between representatives of the Catholic Church and the American Baptist Convention in DeWitt, Michigan; a meeting chaired by Bishop Joseph Green of Reno, Nevada. The middle of that same month saw Catholic ecumenical leaders from around the world meeting in Rome for ten days at what was "a plenary meeting of the Vatican's Secretariat for Promoting Christian Unity." That Secretariat is the Church's official body for supervising and guiding relations between Catholics and other Christian Churches. In May of this same spring of 1967, Catholic and Orthodox theologians met in Worcester, Massachusetts, and delegates of the United States Bishops Committee for Eucmenical and Interreligious Affairs met with delegates of the National Council of Churches. Toward the end of that same month Catholics and Episcopalians met in Milwaukee to discuss the question of the Eucharist as Sacrifice.

That kind of thing *is* new. That kind of thing can be traced to Vatican II. Its Decree on Ecumenism, which opens with the resounding words *"Unitatis redintegratio"* — The Restoration of Unity — said that this restoration of unity among all Christians "is one of the chief concerns of the Second Sacred Ecumenical Synod of the Vatican." It then said that "moved by a desire for the restoration of unity among all followers of Christ, it wished to set before all Catholics certain helps, pathways, and methods by which they, too, can respond to this Divine summons and grace."

That last sentence should give any thinking person pause. Why did the Council put in that "too"? Are others at work for this restoration of unity? What did it mean by stating that we would be answering a "Divine summons and grace"? Indeed there were, and there are others working energetically toward unity — others who are not Catholics. For decades the World Council of Churches has been a fact. The aim, ultimately, is unity. For decades, too, Protestant Churches have been grouping on national and also on international lines. There have been mergers. All manifestly aiming, ultimately, at unity. All this activity in the Protestant world came to be called the "ecumenical movement." It was theirs, before it became ours. We had watched with interest. We had prayed with earnestness. But we had not actually joined them in this movement until John XXIII called the Second Vatican Council and announced that it would be a "Council for the Whole Church" and added that he longed to "invite the separated Communities to seek again that unity for which so many souls are longing in these days throughout the world." The world knows the startling steps he took to make that desire a reality. For the first time in the history of the Church, men from Protestant and Orthodox Churches sat in a Catholic Ecumenical Council — and sat across the aisle from Cardinals. Pope John set up, for the first time in the history of the Church, a Secretariat for the Promotion of Christian Unity.

Undeniably, there were many new elements in this Catholic Ecumenical Movement. But the movement itself was not new. One can dare say it began at the Last Supper when Christ Himself prayed to the Father: "That all may be one even as Thou, Father, in Me, and I in Thee; that they also may be one in us, that the world may believe that Thou hast sent Me." (Jno. 17:1) There we have the principle and the ultimate purpose of all Ecumenism and every Ecumenical Movement. Some years later St. Paul was writing to his Ephesians and telling them clearly that the Church was "one body and one Spirit" and that they had been "called in one hope" and that there was but "one Lord, one faith, one baptism" (Eph. 4:4-5) and then to his Galatians he wrote telling them that they had "all been baptized into Christ" that they "had put on Christ" and that they were "all one in Christ Jesus." The Council took all this and wrapped it up in one short, sharp paragraph saying: "This is the sacred mystery of the unity of the Church, in Christ and through Christ, with the Holy Spirit energizing a variety of functions. The highest exemplar and source of this mystery is the unity in the Trinity of Persons of one God — the Father and the Son and the Holy Spirit." (#2)

Further, you have been praying for this annually in that "Unity Octave" which is observed during January 18th-25th each year. In every Mass the first prayer in the Canon asked God to *unite* the Church throughout the world. In point of fact you have been engaged in ecumenism every time you said the "Our Father" — For the petition that His "Kingdom come" is really the object of each and every Ecumenical Movement. So you see, the Movement itself is really as old as the Church; in a certain sense, since the Church was born on Calvary and Christ had taught His disciples the "Our Father" before that, it can be said that Ecumenism antedated the Church. But there can be no question about the new stimulus given the Movement by Vatican II and for some time before the Council there was a healthy ecumenical movement going on among Protestants.

Hence, when you hear or read about "Interfaith Meetings" your heart should rejoice; for you should be hearing the very whir of the wings of Him who descended on the Christ at His Baptism in the Jordan in the form of a Dove. You should feel the heat of Him who fell as Flame on the Disciples that first Pentecost. You should be set thanking God for this latest gift from Heaven; for it is nothing less! In all reality it is a Movement that has been set in motion by Him who was promised by Christ before His Passion when He said: "And I will ask the Father, and He will grant you another Advocate to be with you for all time to come, the Spirit of Truth! . . . I have told you this while I am still lingering in your midst; but the Advocate, the Holy Spirit, whom the Father will send in my name, will teach you everything, and refresh your memory of everything I have told you." (Jno. 14:16-26). That is why Vatican II could state so positively that "Everywhere, large numbers have felt the impulse of this grace, and among our separated brethren also there increases from day to day a movement, *fostered by the grace of the Holy Spirit*, for the restoration of unity among all Christians."

Note the warmth, the gentleness, the irenicism, the honesty in those few lines. Those who are not of our Faith are called "brethren." Their work is enthusiastically approved. Their purpose acclaimed as one with that of this Decree. Finally, it is stated apodictically that they are under the influence of the one Holy Spirit who brooded over every session of the Council, and watched over every Decree, Constitution, and Declaration. From that single sentence you can learn God's mind and will, the world-wide spread of the Holy Spirit's sheltering wings, and come to the thrilling realization that Grace, the very Life of God, has been given to those who though "separated" are yet our "brethren." What would "brotherly-love" prompt in the heart and soul of all who love God and their fellow man but gratitude to God first, and then earnest prayer and love-filled solicitude that more Grace — more of God's Life — be poured out through the one Holy Spirit on them — as well as on us?

Undoubtedly, we have been praying for unity all our Catholic lives, but now there comes a different attitude of mind, a different approach to the matter, a distinctly new orientation. Warm friendliness, delicate and heart-deep concern, love-filled interest in those who share so much of our Faith, but who, as yet, do not have what has been called "the fullness of Revelation," urges all to more prayer for the fulfillment of Christ's Last Supper Prayer, and, in time, will urge many more on to "dialogue" — In correct "dialogue" there will be acute intelligence, real honesty, but above all, there will be "heart" — there will be love. Without this last there may be intelligent discussion and truly honest exchange of views, but there will not be that "dialogue" which the Council mentioned so frequently throughout its Decree on Ecumenism, and indirectly at least in what it had to say to the Laity and to the Clergy.

Can we not all rejoice in what is our common heritage? We have God's gracious and gratuitous Revelation in common. The Bible belongs to all men — but is the treasure of Christians, both Catholic Christians and non-Catholic Christians. That "written word of God" gives more than truth; it can and does give LIFE — the very Life of God which we call Grace. Every validly baptised person has been gifted with the theological and moral virtues, along with the Gifts of the Holy Spirit by the very reception of that life-giving Sacrament. So we have the virtue of Faith in common, along with those of Hope and Charity. Further, the Spirit who has inspired this Ecumenical Movement from the beginning gave to each baptised Christian His "seven-fold grant of Wisdom, Understanding Knowledge, and Counsel, not to mention Fortitude, Piety and Fear of the Lord. If every Catholic Christian and non-Catholic Christian would use those Gifts we would have a much wiser understanding of one another, could counsel ourselves and others with greater knowledge, be stronger in our love, be much more truly pious and have such reverence for each other that we would come to enjoy true "fear of the Lord." Use of the Holy Spirit's baptismal endowment would enable all to engage in very fruitful "dialogue."

Most people are acquainted with the picture, if not with the actual statue, which stands outside Father Flanagan's Boys' Town. It is that of a youngster with another a few years younger than himself on his back. The caption reads: "He ain't heavy; he's my brother." That is the way every real bigger brother feels toward a younger brother. Whatever burden he might be is made light — and made light of — precisely because "he is my brother." Well, what did Pope John — and practically every other pope since the sixteenth century — call non-Catholic Christians? The term is no longer "Protestants," but "separated brothers." Therefore, every Catholic should be happy to have the privilege of helping his "brother" — of carrying him if allowed. As far back as the Council of Florence, which was held in 1439, it was solemnly declared that "all those justified by Faith through Baptism are incorporated in Christ." Granted that the statement was made before Martin Luther's day, nevertheless Vatican II saw fit to cite it in 1964 when speaking of Ecumenism, and went on to draw the inescapable conclusion: "Therefore, they have a right to be honored by the title of Christian, and are properly regarded as brothers in the Lord by the sons of the Catholic Church." (#2)

This same paragraph shows that the Church has learned from History, as Pope John insisted that all should. For it opens the passage with the words: "From her very beginnings there arose in this one and only Church of God certain rifts . . ." Vatican II referred you to St. Paul's Corinthians and Galatians, to St. John

[171]

the Beloved's Gnostics back in the very first century of the Church's existence. Then the Council goes on to say that "in subsequent centuries more widespread disagreements appeared and quite large Communities became separated from full communion with the Catholic Church — developments for which, at times, men on both sides were to blame." That last clause should set every thinking man examining himself and his historical attitude toward those who have separated from the Church in the past. All fault, the Council says, was not always among those who separated. But then the Council goes on to show you the one proper attitude of mind, heart, and whole being today toward those who are not yet in full communion with the Catholic Church. "One cannot impute the sin of separation to those who at present are born into these Communities and are instilled therein with Christ's faith. The Catholic Church accepts them *with respect and affection as brothers.*"

Then, in the next sentence, you are shown why you should love these "separated brothers." You know that you, by the gift of God, have been made a member of Jesus Christ's Mystical Body. You have been blessed by God to live in a time when this enthralling truth has been revivified, thanks to Pope Pius XII and his epoch-making Encyclical on the Mystical Body. From it you learned with what vital intimacy you live with God. St. Augustine spoke of this union of ourselves with Christ as "something sublime, mysterious, and divine." Pius XII went to Scripture and reminded you that God, in His written word, had told you that your union with Him "in Christ Jesus" is likened to "the pure union of man and wife, and is compared with the vital union of branch and vine, and with the cohesion found in our body." Think over the intimacy of those three unions. Could any be closer? and more vital? But then go on thinking of what St. Paul said when he wrote his First Epistle to the Corinthians: ". . . just as the body is a unit, although it has many members, and all the members of the body, many though they are, form but one body, so too is the Christ. . . You are Christ's body and individually its members." (1 Cor. 12:12-27). But even that

[172]

is not all. Pius XII told you that "the unbroken tradition of the Fathers, from the earliest times, teaches that the Divine Redeemer and the society which is His Body form but *one mystical person.*" In this day of "personalism" that truth is well-nigh breath-taking. But even yet we are not through. Pius XII reminded us of that prayer already alluded to. He says: "Our Saviour Himself, in His high-priestly prayer, has gone so far as to liken this union with that marvelous oneness by which the Son is in the Father and the Father in the Son." *(Mystici Corporis* #82) When you add to that the fact that the Holy Spirit is the soul of the Mystical Body, you know why you are so rightly called a "divinized" human being, and come to something close kin to full realization of the dignity of the People of God. Who is there who loves God and his fellow man who would not want each and every human being to know similar "divinization"? That is the ultimate purpose of "dialogue." That is the final end of true Ecumenism.

This "movement," as we have said, is as old as the Catholic Church — and even a tiny bit older. But to show you that it was not born, as some falsely claim, in the 1960's, read what Pius XII said almost a quarter of a century ago. "As you know, Venerable Brothers, from the very beginning of our Pontificate, We have committed to the protection and guidance of Heaven those who do not belong to the visible organization of the Good Shepherd. We desire nothing more ardently than they may have life and have it more abundantly. Calling on the prayers of the whole Church We wish to repeat this solemn declaration in this Encyclical in which We have retold the praises of the 'great and glorious Body of Christ' . . . For even though unsuspectingly they are related to the Mystical Body of the Redeemer in desire and resolution, they still remain deprived of so many precious gifts and helps from Heaven, which one can only enjoy in the Catholic Church. May they then enter into Catholic unity, and united with us in the organic oneness of the Body of Jesus Christ may they hasten to the one Head in the society of glorious love. We

[173]

wait for them with open arms to return not to a stranger's house, *but to their own*, their Father's house." (Ib. #121)

That pen-picture of the Pontiff waiting with open arms to welcome all to the "society of glorious love," the man of ascetic look but in whose breast had a heart as tender and as warm, as far as it was humanly possible, as the heart of Jesus Christ, the Mystical Body's loving Head. Pius XII was what every Pontiff was — ecumenical-minded, ecumenical-hearted. And in the passage above he was drawing the pen-picture of what every Catholic should be: not the angry brother of the Prodigal Son, but that man's forgiving, loving father.

Vatican II urges every Catholic to an identical attitude of mind and heart; to an identical posture of open arms and love. In the very first chapter of its Decree on Ecumenism it says: "The Catholic Church accepts them (non-Catholic Christians) with respect and affection as *brothers*. For men who believe in Christ and have been properly baptised are brought into a *certain, though imperfect*, communion with the Catholic Church. . . Nevertheless, our separated brethren, whether considered as individuals or as Communities and Churches, are not blessed with *that* unity which Jesus Christ wished to bestow on all those whom He has regenerated and vivified into *one body* and newness of life. . ." Then the Council sets forth precisely what "that unity which Christ wished" and yet wishes, was and is . . . "to establish on earth *one Body of Christ* into which all those should be *fully* incorporated who already belong in any way to God's People." (#3) Every word in the passage is important, but the ones I have italicized are, obviously, the most important; for they show us the fullness of fact and truth, even as they stimulate the hearts of all those who love Christ and long for the fulfillment of His Will, for the final acquisition of all that He died for. The fact is that validly baptised non-Catholics can be enriched by you; for you are, in very truth, God's almoner — you are the dispenser of the riches of Heaven. You can dispense those riches through "dialogue."

FATHER M. RAYMOND, O.C.S.O.

The call is not mine, it is that of Vatican II . . . and that of "the times"; which is only another way of saying "God's Will" — for He is the maker of time and the ultimate shaper of events. Realizing this, the assembled Bishops under the headship of the Pope tell you that "Today, in many parts of the world, *under the inspiring grace of the* Holy Spirit, multiple efforts are being expended through prayer, word, and action to attain that fullness of unity which Jesus Christ desires. This Sacred Synod, therefore, exhorts *all the Catholic faithful* to recognize the signs of the times and to participate skillfully in the work of ecumenism." (#4) Then in the opening lines of Chapter Two the same Sacred Synod declares that "Concern for restoring unity pertains to the whole Church, faithful and clergy alike. It extends to everyone, according to the potential of each. . . This very concern already reveals to some extent the bond of brotherhood existing among all Christians, and it leads toward that full and perfect unity which God lovingly desires." (#5)

Too many, perhaps, think that "dialogue" is limited to "competent experts" as the Council stated in section 4. That is not thinking with the mind of the Church, so clearly expressed by the Council. That is why the opening lines of Chapter Two have been cited. "Everyone," the Council states, is included and "everyone" should participate "according to the potential of each."

We most certainly can "rejoice" — but in this area we can never really "relax" in our efforts. We can "rejoice" for many have already taken the Council's exhortation to heart. The Paulists have begun what is called "The Living Room Dialogue." It most certainly is in accord with the Council's aim and spirit, and while we can "rejoice" that there are about "five thousand groups" already engaged in this kind of "dialogue," it is evident that we cannot "relax", for this is rightly called "just a drop in the bucket" since it can be said that "at least seventy-five percent of all Christians do not know a thing about the movement toward Christian unity."

RELAX!

You can no longer be considered among that seventy-five per-cent; for if you have a "living room" — you can "dialogue." I believe it was Bishop Joseph A. Durick, of Nashville, Tennessee, who said: "There is only one voice that I can guarantee will be heard in the world of today — *your* voice speaking to the person next door, to the person you work with in church and civic activities, to the person you play with, to the person with whom you travel." Then he went on to plead: "May I call upon you to heed the battle-cry of Vatican II to each layman, and set in motion regularly your mission of personalism. One layman asked: 'Why do we of the laity fail to bear witness by utterance?' His own answer was: 'Because too many of us see neither what the new nature of human solidarity is, nor how we can help bring about its second spring'." The Bishop then wisely added: "It has been well said: 'If we do not use our eyes to see with, we will use them to weep with'."

That the women of his Diocese whom he was addressing had used their eyes rightly is evidenced by his next words: "Along the lines of promoting human solidarity, may I congratulate you on your excellent implementation of the Church Communities Commission and the Family Affairs Commission. . . In particular, may I commend you on the Ecumenical tuition which prompted you to engage fruitfully in the living room dialogues with women of other faiths. I thank God that Ecumenism has entered the world family scene. . . 1967 is clearly calling us all to a deeper family life together, a life more intensively, faithfully, hopefully, and lovingly lived. And your personalism, your personal friendliness and kindness, will always remain the single most important factor in these interfaith relationships. With your Christian love felt and shown, your grass-roots ecumenism with individuals will continue to be a most fruitful opportunity for ecumenical influence."

That the Bishop had grasped the spirit with which these dialogues should be entered is evident from a glance at the Decree on Ecumenism which states: ". . . such actions are to be carried out by the Catholic faithful with prudence, patience, and the vigilance of their spiritual shepherds." Love is at the bottom, in the middle, and at the top of such dialogues. Catholics are carrying their "brothers" with love — and find it no burden whatsoever.

In fact the benefits to the Catholic can be as great as those to the non-Catholic. First of all there will be a veritable *metanoia* — a complete change of attitude of mind, of heart, and of whole being. No longer will the non-Catholic Christian be looked upon as "other" — but as "one with us," though not fully as yet. Then there will be an awakening of the whole person to matters that are truly "relevant" to each person — a keen and ever-growing interest in the questions that truly matter — those of God, self, others and life. Religion will come to be what it is: the only truly relevant factor in living! Many a Catholic — as well as many a non-Catholic — will begin these "dialogues" with the honest admission that "I haven't asked myself a serious question about my Faith in years." Then these serious questions will quickly follow one another: "What do I really believe? Why do I believe it? What does it mean to me in my everyday life? How does it actually affect my living? Have I been drifting through life, mesmerized by the things of time, committed to making a living rather than to living as a human being should live?" Such questions will set one not only thinking, but reading, and thus, learning — and re-learning. That will quicken in any and every man the realization that the Religion is something we can go on learning and re-learning as long as we live — for God is ultimately unfathomable — and Religion is all about God.

Living Room Dialogue will lead anyone and everyone engaged to know self and Christ better and better, with the consequence that they will live more realistically, because more religiously, and much more Christly. There will be matters which will call for solution by one better informed. This is where "their spiritual shepherds" come in. In these Family or Living Room Dialogues priests are seldom present. But they do visit the groups now and then — after the discussions are ended or temporarily interrupted — to see if their help is needed and to encourage the continuation of the dialogue.

The Council itself pointed to many of the benefits when it said: "In their meetings, which are organized in a religious spirit, each explains the teaching of his Communion in greater depth and brings out clearly its distinctive features. Through such dialogue everyone gains a truer knowledge and a more just appreciation of the teaching and religious life of both Communities. In addition, these Communities cooperate more closely in whatever projects a Christian conscience demands for the common good. They also come together for common prayer, where this is permitted. Finally, all are led to examine their own faithfulness to Christ's will for the Church and, wherever necessary, undertake with vigor the task of renewal and reform."

Granted that the passage above was written primarily for those dialogues between "competent experts from different Churches and Communities," nevertheless all that is said about them is true about every real "dialogue" for "Discussion has ever been the mother of discovery."

After all you have heard and read about making Religion "relevant" to the modern world, very little reflection will be needed to see that from Living Room Dialogues, on a huge scale, there would inevitably flow such a "relevancy," because of the number of people involved and the training they would receive unconsciously and consciously from such "dialogues", that the so-called "modern world" would be made to "sit up and take notice." For who has more pertinent things to say to that world than those members of Christ who know what it is to be "alive to God in Christ Jesus"? They are the ones who have — not only the "Good News" — , but the very *Best* News to announce to that world; namely, that the Son of God became man to enable all the sons of men to become like unto God, and that they can do that fully by becoming members of the Mystical Body of Christ in and through the Church He founded on Peter — the Rock.

[178]

FATHER M. RAYMOND, O.C.S.O.

What is of highest practical importance to Americans is the fact that, owing to the whole history and culture of our country, Ecumenism would appear to have its greatest opportunity here. We are a democratic people. We live in a pluralistic society. We have as a motto *"E pluribus unum"* — "Out of many — One" which can apply not only to our political and civil life, but to our Religious life as well. Further, we "dialogue" quite easily. It seems to be in our blood. Finally, we like results. Therefore, here in America all that the Council hoped for in its Decree on Ecumenism — and all that Christ prayed for in the Cenacle — can be realized more readily, perhaps, than anywhere else in the world.

Is there any escaping the Council's directives? Hardly — when it states so positively that "In ecumenical work, Catholics must assuredly be concerned for their separated brethren, praying for them, keeping them informed about the Church, making the first approaches toward them." How many Catholics in this country have made "the first approaches" toward non-Catholic Christians, inviting them to "dialogue," expressing to them their respect for all that is true in what they hold, showing friendly concern for their religious life?

But even the shyest of individuals cannot escape from the Council's challenge; for, with the wisdom of the ages, the Church spoke through Vatican II and told all that while Living Room Dialogue can be a marvelous implementation of the Council's Decree on Ecumenism, there is even a better way — and without this way even the best "dialogue" may well be fruitless. That better way is by *living as Christ*-ians. This is fundamental. The Council tells you that your "primary duty is to make an honest and careful appraisal of whatever needs to be renewed and achieved in the Catholic household itself, in order that its life may bear witness more loyally and luminously to the teachings and ordinances which have been handed down from Christ through the apostles." (#4)

Then, lest any Catholic shrug his shoulders and think that all the above refers only to the hierarchy or the structured

[179]

Church, the Council became more direct — and even more challenging: "For although the Catholic Church has been endowed with all divinely revealed truth and with all means of grace, her members fail to live by them with all the fervor they should. As a result, the radiance of the Church's face shines less brightly in the eyes of our separated brethren and of the world at large, and the growth of God's kingdom is retarded."

One would think that sufficiently blunt for the most obtuse, but the Council became even more specific. "Every Catholic" it said, "must therefore aim at Christian perfection and, each according to his station, play his part so that the Church, which bears in her own body the humility and dying of Christ, may daily be more purified and renewed, against the day when Christ will present her to Himself in all her glory, without spot or wrinkle" (#4)

That is but another way of saying: "Actions speak louder than words" or "It is not what you say that matters, but what you are." Someone once said: "I'd rather *see* a sermon than hear one." In other words, there is no one who cannot "dialogue"; for perhaps the best form of dialogue is dynamic living of the Gospel, which means being what you are — Christ's member, who not only lives by His life, but who actually lives His life for Him, through Him, in Him, this very day on earth. That is what "witnessing" — a much used, and, perhaps, much abused word — really means. For he, and he only, truly "witnesses" to Christ who actually mirrors forth Jesus to his contemporary world.

But that is not to disparage in any way living "dialogue" — and most assuredly not to downgrade Living Room Dialogues. For it remains as true today as it was in St. Paul's day: "*Fides ex auditu* . . . Faith depends on hearing" Rom. (10:17). It is only to show that there are more ways than one to "speak" — and that no one can avoid the responsibility to "dialogue" — if only by the "witness" of his daily life and hourly living. That such is the mind of the Council can be gained from #7, which reads: "There can be no ecumenism worthy of the name without a change of heart. For it is from newness of attitudes, from self-denial and unstinted love, that yearnings for unity take their rise and grow toward maturity. We should therefore pray to the divine Spirit for the grace to be genuinely self-denying, humble, gentle in the service of others, and to have an attitude of brotherly generosity toward them. The Apostle of the Gentiles says: 'I, therefore, the prisoner in the Lord, exhort you to walk in a manner worthy of the calling with which you were called, with all humility and meekness, with patience, bearing with one another in love, careful to preserve the unity of the Spirit in the bond of peace.' (Eph. 4:1-3)".

The Council went a step further, using St. John the Beloved this time in place of St. Paul, the Apostle of the Gentiles. It said: "St. John has testified: 'If we say that we have not sinned, we make him a liar, and his word is not in us.' (I Jno. 1:10) This holds good for sins against unity. Thus, in humble prayer, we beg pardon of God and of our separated brethren, just as we forgive those who trespass against us."

To keep us from sinning against unity the Council immediately added: "Let all Christ's faithful remember that the more purely they strive to live according to the Gospel, the more they are fostering and even practicing Christian unity. For they can achieve depth and ease in strengthening mutual brotherhood to the degree that they enjoy profound communion with the Father, the Word, and the Spirit." (#7)

And as if that were not enough to hearten us all, the Council added another reminder of the *metanoia* that is so basic to this ecumenical movement. It said: "This change of heart and holiness of life, along with public and private prayer for the unity of Christians, should be regarded *as the soul* of the whole ecumenical movement, and can rightly be called 'spiritual ecumenism'."

Who is there who cannot become part of that "spiritual ecumenism?" Did not Pope Paul himself set us all an example when, four days before the closing of the Council, he joined with Protestant, Catholic, and Orthodox in what can be called a "Bible Service" or "interfaith prayer"? In the Basilica of St. Paul Outside the Walls he assisted, and participated, not as a presiding prelate, but as a member of the group, in a reading of Scripture lessons.

You have heard and read much about "protestantizing" the Catholic Church. People who talk this way point to "Bible Services," "Hymn Singing," the "recitation of Psalms" and the like— and claim this is following the fashion of Protestants in their services. At first glance there seems to be much substance to their charge. But when we recall that the "Our Father" is a common possession of all Christians — and can be said with utmost sincerity by all — together, as well as separately. Then we go on to ask: "Where did the Protestants get their Bible? Was it not from the Catholic Church? What is the Bible but the record of God's revelation of Himself to man so that man could come to know his God and himself more intimately? Further, when we ponder the matter a little more carefully, we realize that the very substance of what these people refer to as a Protestant Service has really come from the Catholic Church; for it was Paul, the Apostle of the Gentiles, who told his Ephesians to ". . . fill yourselves with the Spirit. Recite among yourselves psalms, hymns, and inspired canticles, singing and giving praise to God with all your hearts." That is a "Bible Service" — for the Bible is the very word of God inspired by the Holy Spirit. We borrowed that Service from the Jews. The Protestants borrowed it from us. We are but reclaiming what was — and in a way, has always been — ours.

"In certain special circumstances, such as in prayer services for unity," says the Council, "and during ecumenical gatherings, it is allowable, *and even desirable*, that Catholic should join in prayer with their separated brethren. Such prayers in common are certainly a very effective means of petitioning for the grace of unity, and they are a genuine expression of the ties which even now bind Catholics to their separated brethren. 'For where two or three are gathered together for my sake, there am I in the midst of them' (Mt. 18:20)" (#8)

If Christ Himself is there, what Christian would hesitate about being present? Of course this is not to be done on one's own initiative nor indiscriminately. The Council never fails to caution us. "The practical course to be adopted," it says, "after due regard has been given to all the circumstances of time, place, and personage, is left to the prudent decision of the local Episcopal authority, unless the Bishops' Conference according to its own statutes, or the Holy See, has determined otherwise." (ib)

There have been misunderstandings, misrepresentations, misinterpretations already. Human nature being what it is, there will be more. But that is not the fault of the Council, nor is that to make anyone hesitate. God's Will is clear. Christ could hardly have made it clearer. He prayed that "all may be one." He died for all men. He died that His prayer might be answered. He sent His Spirit as Flame to fire the Apostles first — and down through the ages, their successors. He sent His Spirit into you that "in you, through you, and with you" He, mystically, might keep on casting that fire He said He had come to cast; that He might keep on giving that life which He said He had come to give "abundantly." Ecumenism, then, is only another form of your apostolicity and your apostolate, another way of showing the world that you are His member. So you cannot halt, you cannot hesitate, even when you read such things as a certain prelate, at a convention of Protestant Pastors, expressing his hopes — or dreams — of the future of ecumenism in this fashion: "Will it find Christendom once again united in essentials of belief and worship? The various communions perhaps retaining their identity, all according to the gifts they have received enjoying a proper freedom in their different liturgical rites, and even in their theological elaborations of revealed truth? And perhaps the ring of the Fisherman on the finger of one of the Lutheran or Presbyterian or Methodist tradition, guiding the Holy Ecumenical Church, in collegial union with the shepherds of all communions?"

When Monsignor Bandas answered the one who sent him this quote, he said: "This one leaves me speechless, and I can only repeat the warning of Pope Paul in his Encyclical *Ecclesiam*

Suam — (His Church) August 6, 1964: 'The apostle's art is a risky one. The desire to come together as brothers must not lead to a watering down or subtracting from the truth." We can add that the same Pope has repeated the same truth again and again since that first Encyclical. As recently as May, 1967, in an Ecumenical.Directory, published by the Secretariat for the Reunion of Christians, with the approval of Pope Paul VI, the first lines run: "Ecumenical action must be fully and sincerely Catholic, faithful to the truths which we received from the Apostles and the Church Fathers, in accord with the faith which the Church has always professed, and tending towards that fullness which Our Lord wished His Body to acquire in the course of time."

In a way, that is but a restatement of what the Council said in its Decree; namely, "It is, of course, essential that doctrine be clearly presented in its entirety. Nothing is so foreign to the spirit of ecumenism as a false conciliatory approach (a false irenicism) which harms the purity of Catholic doctrine and obscures its assured genuine meaning" (#11)

No one need doubt the sincerity of that Protestant Prelate or question his "good faith." He has misread the Decree, and misunderstood the ultimate purpose. It looks as if he has failed to grasp just what Jesus meant when he prayed at the Last Supper that "they may be one." It was not for a "détenté" — not for any form of co-existence — but for union, for unity.

But such a misunderstanding as that of the prelate would not shock Catholics as much as would the report of an "interfaith concelebrated Mass" which recently came this way. On May 26, 1967, in a certain Religious House, it is said that a Jesuit stood beside two Protestant ministers and "concelebrated" "Mass." I put those words in quotes to alert you to the impossibility of anyone who has not received Holy Orders actually celebrating Mass. These three clergymen did not wear vestments of any sort. Goblets of wine and a loaf of bread were "consecrated" — Again the quotes are called for. Then the "congregation," composed of nuns, ministers and students were given a share in this bread and wine.

This, of course, may have been merely a "dress rehearsal," as it were, of what these "advanced thinkers" hope for in the future. Hence, only an experiment, a bit of a stage play as a preview of what they dream of as possible in the future. But even if that was all it was, it shocks; for the Decree on Ecumenism is quite explicit about the difference between "prayers in common" and "common worship." The first is not only allowable in certain circumstances; it is desirable. The second is "not to be regarded as a means to be used indiscriminately. . . Such worship depends chiefly on two principles: it should signify the unity of the Church; it should provide a sharing in the means of grace. The fact that it should signify unity generally rules out common worship." That was the Decree itself. The New Directory is even more explicit, saying: "Participation of non-Catholics in our Sacraments of Eucharist, Penance, and Anointing of the Sick is forbidden — because of lack of unity in faith, worship and life."

Such bold experimentation as the "Mass" referred to above is one of the surest ways of off-setting all that the Council worked for, prayed for, and hoped for. You saw the same thing happen in the case of "updating" the Liturgy. Even as "progressive" a Prelate as the late Cardinal Ritter had to come out with a strong prohibition against this kind of dangerous and unauthorized experimentation in his own Diocese of St. Louis, and his prohibition was soon followed by guidelines from the official Commission.

You may read in the Press statements by some "Catholic Theologian" to the effect that "for the sake of Christian charity and ecumenism, it is permissible for a Catholic party in a mixed marriage to participate in a Protestant religious service each Sunday," or you may hear how some "Confessor" told a Catholic that "since we have unity now, it is permissible to go to a Protestant Church on Sunday instead of to a Catholic Church," or read how some "Chaplain" said that "If you cannot assist at Mass on a Sunday, but can go to a Protestant Church, by all

[185]

means go. You will there hear the Word of God — and, after all, that is the essential thing." Such "Theologians" "Confessors" and "Chaplains" are seldom identified by name in the news. But even if they were, and even if they enjoyed the highest repute, they would have been wrong according to the Directory published in May, 1967. Paragraph 59 of that Directory states: "Catholics may occasionally attend a Protestant service for a *just* cause: for example, because of one's public office or because of courtesy and friendship (funerals, marriages): though courteous *'guests'* of that community they, nevertheless, may take no part in anything that contradicts the Catholic faith."

It is worth while noting that this latest Directory gives us all reason to "relax" concerning the reception of certain Sacraments by non-Catholics. The Press made headlines out of two exceptional cases (the two mentioned previously: a non-Catholic girl receiving Holy Communion during her Wedding Mass at Assisi, and the non-Catholic minister being witness to the marriage of his son to a Catholic girl in Oakland, California), but the reporters very seldom elucidated the actuality. That Presbyterian girl in Assisi had been validly Baptised and believed with her whole heart in the Real Presence of Christ in the Eucharist — she was a Catholic in everything but name and external union with the Church. That minister was merely acting as witness, he did not administer the Sacrament; for it is the parties to the matrimonial contract who actually administer the Sacrament to one another. However, the latest Directory is most explicit about all such matters. It first states that "in cases of necessity — danger of death, persecution, imprisonment — a non-Catholic may receive our Sacraments (Eucharist, Penance, Anointing of the Sick) provided —" and this the most important part of this grant — "he spontaneously asks for them, embraces and receives them with the *faith of a Catholic*, and is rightly disposed." Then as regards Mass, Matrimony and Baptism, the Directory states: "A non-Catholic may not exercise the role of lector or preach at our celebration of the Holy Eucharist. A Catholic may not exercise these functions at the celebration of

[186]

the Lord's Supper and at the principal services of non-Catholics. A non-Catholic may not serve as sponsor at a Catholic Baptism; he may serve only as 'witness'. The same principle governs the Catholic in regards to a Protestant Baptism. Our separated brethren may serve as witnesses at Catholic marriages, and Catholics may serve as witnesses in Protestant marriages — subject to the rules of the Diocese."

So there is every reason to "relax" — and even to "rejoice" over the Decree and the Directory; for not only is there no "watering down of Doctrine" but there is every effort made to break down barriers — prejudice, misunderstanding, distance. One of the tenderest and kindest relaxations, if you want to call it such, which came from this Movement, is the latest legislation on Funerals and Burial. Those who are partners in a mixed marriage — and all their children and relatives — must rejoice greatly over the fact that now ". . . when requested by the family of the deceased, priests may be permitted to conduct funeral services and to lead prayers at wakes for those not of the Church. It is for the local Bishop to determine what rites are to be used on these occasions. In such circumstances burial in Catholic cemeteries may be permitted to those not of our communion, especially spouses and relatives of Catholics. On the occasions of burials in Catholic cemeteries of those who are not Catholics, it is also recommended that clergymen of other churches be permitted to conduct graveside services."

The cautious, the conservative, along with the alarmist, have feared indifferentism becoming something of a vogue because of this marvelous Movement and the Council's Decree. But they can relax totally. If there is any "indifferentism" bred, it will not be from the Council's Decree, let alone from the Directive; though there might be a touch of it brought into being by some of the so-called "new breed." First of all, look at some of the lines in the Decree. In section four it tells just what it understands by the "ecumenical movement" and "dialogue"; the "movement" means "those activities and enterprises which, according to the various needs of the Church and opportune occasions, are started

[187]

and organized for the *fostering of unity* among Christians." Then the "dialogue" it calls for is that between "competent experts from different Churches and Communities." It is "organized in a religious spirit"; it is conducted not only with civility but with real charity and mutual respect; in it each of these capable men "explains the teaching of his Communion in greater depth and brings out clearly its distinctive features." (#4) Surely there is no indication there that any sort of "compromise" is called for; nor is there any evidence that "indifferentism" is to mark the meetings or be characteristic of the "dialogue." Just the opposite!

Then read again that passage already cited about "The manner and order in which Catholic belief is expressed should in no way become an obstacle to dialogue with our brethren. It is, of course, *essential* that doctrine be *clearly* presented in its *entirety.* Nothing is so foreign to the spirit of ecumenism as a false conciliatory approach which harms the *purity* of Catholic doctrine and obscures its *assured genuine* meaning." (#11) In this same paragraph Catholic Theologians are told that "while *standing fast* by the teaching of the Church . . ." they ". . . should act with *love for truth,* with charity and with humility." (ib) Then for Scripture Scholars there is a paragraph which they can consider their own: ". . . when Christians separated from us affirm the divine authority of the Sacred Books, they think differently from us — different ones in different ways — about the relationship between the Scriptures and the Church. In the Church, according to Catholic belief, an *authentic teaching office* plays a special role in the explanation and proclamation of the written word of God." (#21)

Finally, there is a note for all — a note of caution and a note of enthusiastic concern and bright hope. In its closing number (#24) the Council says: ". . . we confidently look to the future. This most sacred Synod urges the faithful to abstain from any *superficiality* or *imprudent zeal,* for these can cause harm to true progress toward unity. Their ecumenical activity must not be other than *fully and sincerely Catholic,* that is, loyal to the truth we have received from the Apostles and the Fathers, and in harmony with the faith which the Catholic Church has always professed, and at the same time tending toward that fullness with which Our Lord wants His Body to be endowed in the course of time."

With that before you, who can worry about "Indifferentism" — and who cannot "rejoice" to be alive, by God's directive Will, at such a time, and, by God's manifest design, to be part in this building up of the Mystical Body of Jesus Christ?

But before we leave this point on "indifference" and its associate idea of "compromise," let it be said that to water down in any way the Doctrine of the Church, or to avoid the points where we disagree, or to give a non-commital answer when a question is posed on matters that are controversial, is not only to defeat the purpose of "dialogue," it is to do a distinct disservice to those with whom we are "dialoguing" and, in a very real sense, to play traitor to Christ. Let it be remembered that what has attracted thousands upon thousands to the Catholic Church has been *authority* and *certainty*. What has always been admired is the Church's spirit of no compromise — the spirit of the martyrs — and that word really means "witness." The world today, with all its neo-paganism, salutes intransigence where ultimates are concerned — and where is there anything more ultimate than truth — especially the truth about God, man, and the relations between both? Modern man, despite what some so-called theologians say, has not abandoned faith in eternal life as a snare and a delusion. Let that man find relief and reassurance in the fact that traditional Christianity is still intact, and will be kept intact, in the Catholic Church. Make any false irenic approach to this same modern man, let him discern in you the slightest inclination to compromise, let him find you watering down Christ's doctrine, and he will turn from you with a sneer, or at best, a sadness and a great disappointment. He is searching — and he is searching for what you have! Give it to him with love.

Do not stress only the points we have in common. That is not "dialogue"; that is dishonesty. Recognize the points of difference.

That is what is to be discussed with honesty and openness. The purpose is not to convert or convince by this "dialogue" — but only to acquaint him with the truths you hold — and *why* you hold them. It is to help him understand your stand. It was Dr. Robert AcAfee Brown, an outstanding Ecumenist in the Protestant fold, who said there is no point in trying to make believe that the differences do not matter. "They do," he says, "else they would not have persisted for four hundred years." The Council itself recognized there differences and named some by name. "We are aware indeed that there exist considerable divergences from the *doctrine* of the Catholic Church concerning Christ Himself, the Word of God made Flesh, the work of Redemption, and consequently, concerning the mystery and ministry of the Church, and the role of Mary in the plan of Salvation." (#20)

That is being open and honest. Nor was *doctrine* the only point mentioned. In the very next paragraph the Council took up *Scripture:* "While the Christians who are separated from us hold the divine authority of the Sacred Books, they differ from us — some in one way, some in another — regarding the relationship between Scripture and the Church. For, according to the Catholic belief, the authentic teaching authority of the Church has a special place in the interpretation and preaching of the word of God." (#21)

That is the purpose of "dialogue" — to show the differences as well as the likenesses. Read the Decree and you will find the Council being keenly aware of the areas wherein we differ. They can be reduced to Doctrine, Scripture, Sacramental life, Moral teaching, Worship, and Authority. Perhaps this last will be the stumbling block for most. Catholics believe firmly that Christ built His Church on Peter; that He gave this Fisherman the Keys to the Kingdom, supreme authority. We also believe that this supreme authority has been transmitted to Peter's successors — the Popes — in unbroken line from Peter to Paul VI. We believe that Christ gave authority to the other Apostles along with, and under, Peter — and through them to their successors, the Bishops. These, with the Bishop of Rome, His Holiness the Pope, have power to teach authoritatively, to govern authoritatively, to serve — or sanctify — authoritatively. Non-Catholic Christians hold none of this. They claim their one duty is to obey God alone — with no intermediary.

With such basic differences, what hope is there for unity? The Council seems to have had plenty; not in "dialogue" alone, but rather in Divinity. It opened its first chapter of this Decree with "What has revealed the love of God among us is that the only begotten Son of God has been sent by the Father into the world, so that, being made man, the Son by His redemption of the entire human race give new life to it and unify it." It ended its Decree with ". . . we confidently look to the future. . . This Synod declares its realization that the holy task of reconciling all Christians in the unity of the one and only Church of Christ transcends human energies and abilities. It therefore places its hope entirely in the prayer of Christ for the Church, in the love of the Father for us, and in the power of the Holy Spirit. 'And hope does not disappoint, because the charity of God is poured forth in our hearts by the Holy Spirit who has been given to us.' (Rom. 5:5)."

We could add to that the other encouraging query: "If God be with us who can be against us?" (Rom. 8:31) and leave this chapter stand. But we want to add something the Council itself added. We not only can pray together, we can *work* together. "Since in our times," the Council says, "cooperation in social matters is very widely practiced, all men without exception are summoned to united effort. Those who believe in God have a stronger summons, but the strongest claims are laid on Christians, since they have been sealed with the name of Christ. Cooperation among all Christians vividly expresses that bond which already unites them, and it sets in clearer relief the features of Christ the Servant. Such cooperation, which has already begun in many countries, should be ever increasingly developed, particularly in regions where a social and technical evolution is taking place." (#12)

That sounds like a call for "social justice" or even for "civil rights"; it sounds more especially like a summons to aid the "emerging nations." But actually it is from the Decree on Ecumenism. And the Council showed how it faces the Modern World, and is up to the minute on all developments, by stressing the immediate results of such cooperation — and the areas in which it can most fruitfully be employed. It said: "It should contribute to a just appreciation of the dignity of the human person, the promotion of the blessings of peace, the application of the Gospel principles to social life, and the advancement of the arts and sciences in a Christian spirit. Christians should also work together in the use of every possible means to relieve the afflictions of our times, such as famine and natural disasters, illiteracy and poverty, lack of housing, and unequal distribution of wealth. Through such cooperation, all believers in Christ are able to learn how easily they can understand each other better and esteem each other more, and how the road to the unity of Christians may be made smooth." (ib.)

That road is rough. Yet look how Pope Paul has walked it in so many directions already: to the Holy Land, to India, to the United Nations, and lately to Constantinople. Like Our Lord Jesus, the Pope can say: "I have set you an example, so that what I have done . . . you, too, should do." (Jno. 13:15) As he set out for his meeting with the Orthodox Patriarch, Paul said he was "smoothing the way toward the reestablishment of a perfect communion" between the two Churches. After the meeting Patriarch Athenagoras I said: "We are approaching the goal of unity." That separation is older by centuries than the one begun in the sixteenth century by Luther. So if the separation between Catholics and Orthodox can be closed, why despair of closing the one between Catholics and Protestants?

It will be done "In God's own time" — and with Him a thousand years are as a day. But this is your day — and this is your hour. Pay no attention to pessimists. Let the high optimism of both the Council and the Pope beat in your heart; for God's arm is not shortened — and that arm is Omnipotence.

Some of that pessimism is expressed by John Cogley. After telling of the thrill he felt as he saw the more than 2,000 Bishops stream out of St. Peter's the day the Council closed, and after telling of the light in their eyes — and in his own — a light kindled by hope, he goes on "It is becoming increasingly clear, however, that the spirit of the Council and the Pentecostal hope that lighted up so many eyes that day are already dying. They are being transmuted into discouragement, disillusion, disappointment, and in some cases, sheer despair. . ." Mr. Cogley, like many another writer, allowed his fondness for alliteration to carry him just a wee bit too far. That series of "d's" did not end with "despair," but led him on to say: "Father Davis (note the other D, a capital this time!) has given up. Other, less significant Catholics, have become embittered. Today the Church seems to be going through a neurotic phase . . ." That is enough of that. But you see why one might justly wonder if it is not Mr. Cogley who is suffering from a neurosis.

Turn from that to something much more substantial. Frank Sheed is always much more stimulating; for Frank thinks theologically. Yes, he really thinks — and thinks reality and realistically. Signing off a series of articles on the Church in our day of "*aggiornamento*" he wrote: "We are at the end of our journey. We have seen that it is the same Church — we have examined some of the differences this sameness embraces! But what lies ahead? Looking at the world to be won, the task seems hopeless. Looking at ourselves, it seems ridiculous. We are so obviously inadequate. But watch that word 'obvious'.

"When I was in Rome during the Council, I found myself saying some lines from W. S. Gilbert.

> Bishops in their shovel hats
> Were plentiful as tabby cats —
> In point of fact too many.

"But then I heard two thousand of those Bishops singing the *Credo* in St. Peter's. In that moment, nothing seemed impossible. Mere emotionalism? Watch out for that word, too.

[193]

"Back to 'obvious'. Certain things seem beyond question. In regard to the world outside, growing more rapidly than the Church is, we hardly seem to expect to convert it — we are concentrating our effort on primitive peoples, we seem almost to have given up the civilized.

"Are we even holding our own? . . .

"There are those — the famous Jesuit Karl Rahner is among them — who expect the Church to be everywhere reduced to small groups, with the world no more aware of them than of some of the microscopic sects today. . . For myself, I make no guess. But there is a certain attitude toward the Church thus reduced which I find hard to understand — the feeling that it really doesn't matter whether the Church is large or small; that there indeed may be more spirituality — more gain to the world therefore — in a Church of obscurity.

"This strikes me as more spiritualising than spiritual, as though the order of secondary causes were of no importance. I long for more and more people, people by the hundred millions to live the Catholic life in the Church. And this is not worship of bigness: it is just that I cannot sleep comfortably with the thought that millions are starved of food Christ wants them to have, food of truth, food of sacrament. That, I imagine, was why He told His Apostles to preach the Gospel to every creature. How would the atomised Church the pessimists dream of fulfill that commission?

"Pessimism has a way of taking itself for realism. But realism says: 'You never know.' . . . I conclude our long march with a quotation from Christopher Dawson: 'To the observer of the first century A.D. the efforts of the Government to solve the economic crisis by a policy of free credit to producers may have seemed infinitely more important than the doings of an obscure handful of fanatics in an upper room in Jerusalem.'

"That observer was wrong. He did not know that the Holy Spirit was in the upper room. When the Church is in question, never omit from your calculations the incalculability of the Holy Spirit."

[194]

Frank Sheed ends almost as did the Council — with St. Paul's reminder that "the charity of God is poured forth in our hearts by the Holy Spirit who has been given to us." (Rom. 5:5) Yes, that same Holy Spirit who was in that Upper Room in Jerusalem when the Church was very, very young, and had many, many less human resources than have we.

So the only spirit worthy of a Catholic is "Forward! With high hopes and love-filled hearts."

We have spoken only of "Dialogue" with non-Catholic Christians, but neither we nor the Council ever limited Ecumenism or "Dialogue" to them. You can dialogue with Mussulman and Mohammedan, with Buddhist and Brahman, with Confucionist and even with Atheist. But there is no one with whom you should be able to hold dialogue with more easily, more often, and with more love than with those who first bore the name "The People of God" — the Jews. For Whom do we love as much as the Son of the Virgin-Mother, the Virgin-Mother herself, and her spouse, the virgin Joseph. Jesus Christ was a Jew. Mary Immaculate was a Jewess. Joseph of Nazareth was a Jewish carpenter. Then look at the early Church. Peter, Paul, James and John, Andrew and all the rest of the Apostles were Jews. The seventy-two disciples were of the same race and people. How we should love every Jew and Jewess! For Pius XI was very exact when he said we are "spiritual Semites." How could it be otherwise when we worship "the God of Abraham, Isaac, and Jacob." How could it be otherwise when in the greatest Act of Love we perform — the Mass — and in its most solemn part — the Canon — we recall "the gifts of Thy just servant Abel, and the sacrifice of our patriarch Abraham, and that which Thy high priest Melchisedech offered to Thee. . ." Is there not some law of reciprocity? *"Salus ex Judaeis* — Salvation comes from the Jews" (Jno. 4:22) Can we not return the gift "through Him, with Him, and in Him" who was a Jew — Jesus Christ, Our Lord?

"The Word of God is Living"

Chapter 8

THE BURNING BUSH — MUST NOT BURN US,
BUT ONLY INFLAME

Moses was curious. So you must be too. "Moses looked; there was a bush blazing but it was not being burnt up. 'I must go and look at this strange sight,' Moses said, 'and see why the bush is not burnt.' Now Yahweh saw him go forward to look, and God called to him from the middle of the bush. 'Moses, Moses!' he said. 'Here I am,' he answered. 'Come no nearer,' he said. 'Take off your shoes, for the place on which you stand is holy ground. I am the God of your father,' he said, 'the God of Abraham, the God of Isaac and the God of Jacob.' " (Ex. 3:2-5)

Who is the human who does not want to come in close contact with God? Who is the human who does not want to hear God speaking to him personally — and in Person? You, certainly are not that man, else you would never be reading this book. Well, you can hear God speaking to you — personally, and in Person. You can come into close, very close contact with God — and you need not remove your shoes, but only some preconceptions. God not only talks to you, He awaits your response — even as He did that of Moses that day in "Horeb, the mountain of God." You are to hold dialogue with God Himself. You are to do it through the Scriptures. You can hear Him speak in the Bible. You are to reply by the way you live. That this dialogue has not been going on since your earliest days may be due to your lack of curiosity about "a flame of fire, coming from the middle of a bush" — that Flame of Fire is God; that burning bush is the Bible. Put off your preconceptions as Moses put off his shoes, and you will hear Yahweh telling you He is

[197]

"the God of your father, the God of Abraham, the God of Isaac and the God of Jacob."

That is reality. The Preface to the Dogmatic Constitution on Divine Revelation reads: "Hearing the word of God with reverence and proclaiming it confidently, this most sacred Synod takes its direction from these words of St. John: 'We announce to you the eternal life which was with the Father, and has appeared to us. What we have seen and heard we announce to you, in order that you may also have fellowship with us, and that our fellowship may be with the Father, and with His Son, Jesus Christ.' (1 Jno. 1:2, 3) Therefore, following in the footsteps of the Councils of Trent and of the First Vatican, this present Council wishes to set forth authentic teaching about divine revelation and about how it is handed on, so that by hearing the message of salvation the whole world may believe; by believing, it may hope; and by hoping, it may love."

Every word is important, but there are none more important than that "fellowship with the Father, and with His Son, Jesus Christ." After all, that is the essence of Heaven — and St. John tells us we can have it on earth! Other very important words are "authentic teaching" and "following in the footsteps of the Councils of Trent and of the First Vatican." There are those, you know, who seem to sneer at Trent and laugh off the First Vatican. You would be led to believe that these people think the world began October 11, 1962 or even December 8, 1965; that the previous twenty Ecumenical Councils of the Church were not only "updated" by Vatican II, but out-moded! The more than two thousand Council Fathers of Vatican II had no such notion, nor did John XXIII who called it, nor Paul VI who closed it. This Document, like practically every other that came from the Council, tells you of the continuity of doctrine from Christ to our own day. Christ "is the same today as He was yesterday and as He will be forever" (Heb. 13:8) — So is His Church in all its essentials — and one of those essentials is its doctrine on Revelation.

FATHER M. RAYMOND, O.C.S.O.

It was a Protestant scholar, Professor Frederick C. Grant, official observer at the Council and professor emeritus of biblical theology at Union Theological Seminary, New York City, who said: "The theological basis (of this Constitution) is certainly sound. . . This has always been the teaching of the Church . . . and is not an echo of modern biblical theology with its emphasis on the covenant idea — or upon *Heilgeschichte* — as if they were new and recent discoveries. Rather, the discovery is the other way about. In this respect Neo-Orthodoxy is really *Vetusta Orthodoxia*." (All the learned man is saying with those foreign words is what you have heard almost from the beginning of this book; namely, that what many of the "new breed" are hailing as "new" merely reveals their ignorance of the past.)

". . . Both Trent and Vatican I used the language of *one* source with two modes of transmission (for God's Revelation), written and oral. The quotations from Vatican I form a very fine summary of the first chapter of this Constitution. The Article rules out the erroneous idea that God is the Great Unknown, not only to all men in general but even to Christians, for it safeguards the sound principle that God has revealed Himself to all men, in nature, in history, and may be known by the light of reason. This has always been one of the most stable and dependable principles in Catholic Theology, and its modern repudiation in some areas of Protestantism has been a major tragedy, whose full consequences are now becoming apparent among those who speak lightly of the 'death of God' and of 'Religionless Christianity.'"

Indeed God is not the Great Unknown, or if He be to some forlorn individuals of the human race, it is not God's fault. For, as this same Professor has said, "The Christian faith, as many of us believe, reflects the climax of a divine revelation which began long before human history and has been available to all men everywhere. (Jno. 1:9; Acts 14:17) This revelation was available not only to the descendants of Abraham but to all men — Greeks, Romans, Arabs, Scythians, Persians, Indians,

[199]

Chinese, and to nations on the far outskirts of the habitable earth."

You have known that all along, one can presume. But, of late, there have been rumors, reports, and sensational reporting that could have shaken you in your confidence and in your convictions. Like every good Christian, you have always held that God is a personal God — a Three-Personed God — and that He has spoken to man. Now you are being told something else you always knew; namely, that God has begun a dialogue with you — that you are to listen — and respond. His word is *revelation;* your response is *faith* — your fidelity in carrying out the mission He gives you as truly as He gave one to Moses from Horeb's Burning Bush.

The Council taught this in the first chapter of the Constitution saying: "Through this revelation, therefore, the invisible God, out of the abundance of His love, speaks to men as friends, and lives among them, so that He might invite and take them into fellowship with Himself." That is telling you what life is all about — you are to come to know God and live in intimate fellowship with Him — in Time as well as in Eternity. The climax of this paragraph comes in the last sentence: "By this revelation, then, the deepest truth about God and the salvation of man is made clear to us in Christ, who is the Mediator and at the same time the fullness of all revelation." (#2)

"Jesus Christ, therefore, the Word made flesh, sent as 'a man to men', 'speaks the words of God', and completes the work of salvation which His Father gave Him to do. . . He confirmed with divine testimony what revelation proclaimed: that God is with us to free us from the darkness of sin and death, and to raise us up to eternal life." (#4)

Are you beginning to hear that Voice from the Burning Bush? Are you beginning to understand what His Name means — Yahweh — I Am who I Am — and He is always with us? Having heard it, you are to give "The obedience of faith" — "an obedience" says the Council" by which a man entrusts his whole self freely to God, offering 'the full submission of intellect and will to God who reveals' and freely assenting to the truth revealed by Him." THE Person has called to you personally — and He would have you respond by a personal engagement, a real self-committment to Him, made with full freedom — and out of loving gratitude." (Cf. #5)

The whole point is that, as the Council says, "in the sacred books, the Father who is in Heaven meets His children with great love and speaks with them." So if you want to hear your God speaking to you directly and in Person, read Sacred Scripture! And the result? — "the force and power in the word of God is so great that it remains the support and energy of the Church, the strength of faith for her sons, the food of the soul, the pure and perennial source of spiritual life. Consequently, these words are perfectly applicable to sacred Scripture: 'For the word of God is living and efficient' (Heb. 4:12) and is 'able to build up and give the inheritance among all the sanctified.' (Acts 20:32)" (#21)

The most important question in the world today is not how we can attain peace; not how we can settle the differences between the Communistic World and the Free World; not how we can keep the millions in India and like places from starving; not how we can aid the emerging nations to real nationhood — but only "What think you of Jesus Christ?" Let that query be answered as Peter answered it at Caesarea Philippi: 'You are the Christ, the Son of the living God." Then your reply must be lived. That is the "obedience of Faith" the Council has talked about; that is the total committment your contemporaries so often refer to; that is what will enable you to enjoy the "life that is living."

As you have been told: Vatican II had you in mind throughout its four sessions, and in all its proclamations. But, perhaps, never more so than when it said: "This sacred Synod earnestly and specifically urges all the Christian faithful . . . to learn by frequent reading of the divine Scriptures the 'excelling knowledge of Jesus Christ' (Phil. 3:8). 'For ignorance of the Scriptures is ignorance of Christ.' Therefore, they should gladly

[201]

put themselves in touch with the sacred text itself. . . And let them remember that prayer should accompany the reading of Sacred Scripture, so that God and man may talk together; for 'we speak to Him when we pray; we hear Him when we read the divine sayings' (#25).

The lack of that "excelling knowledge of Jesus Christ" can explain much that is wrong with the world, and the emptiness in many an individual's life. It may even explain the confusion in some minds over the actions of Vatican II and the consequent "*aggiornamento*" of the Church. What does Jesus Himself say in Matthew but: "I tell you solemnly, when *all is made new* . . ." (Mt. 19:28) Granted that Christ is talking to Peter and referring directly to the messianic renewal to be revealed when the world ends — but spiritually that renewal has already begun, and has been going on since Jesus rose from the dead. Does not St. Paul, speaking to his Romans, tell you, "From the beginning till now the entire creation, as we know, has been groaning in one great act of giving birth; and not only creation, but all of us who possess the first fruits of the Spirit. . ." (Rom. 8:22) "*Aggiornamento*" has been going on, really, since Mary first said "*Fiat mihi* . . ." and was overshadowed by the Holy Spirit.

Read Scripture, says the Council — but read it *prayerfully*. It is not a novel — though you will be surprised at how many novel things you will discover therein. It is not a romance — but if you listen to God and respond as you should, you will learn that life is naught but a Divine Romance, with God as your Lover, and you as His beloved. It is not an essay, a biography, nor a bit of news — and yet, when you read as you should, you will be hearing the "Good News" — or as we have said before, the very *best* news.

You must not "read it as you run." Rather you should take it up as Sir Arnold Lunn, in one of his excellent books, suggested. He made the supposition of the Gospel falling into the hands of a people who had never heard of Jesus, and had them taking it up and reading it for the first time. Imagine the impact it would make on them! Try it yourself some day. Read the words

[202]

and the doings of Jesus *as if for the first time*. They will strike you as utterly unbelievable: that God should *so love* the world — and that means *you* — as to send His only begotten Son; have that Son "empty Himself" as St. Paul said, and become like unto us in all things, sin alone excepted, and yet to be "made sin for us." Read Scripture as what it is: revelation: God speaking to you just as really as He spoke to Moses out of that Burning Bush, and, practically speaking, for the same purpose: to let you know who He is, and to let you know what mission it is He has for *you*. You, as you must know "are one sent by God." There is no other ultimate explanation of your existence. God never does anything without a Divinely wise purpose. Reading Scripture as Vatican II tells you to read — *meditatively* — will let you discover that Divinely wise purpose for *your* life; for you will enter into dialogue with God.

There is only one prudent way of reading the Revelation of God — and that is as the Trappist-Cistercians do. Their *"lectio divina,"* to which they devote hours each day, is the reading of Scripture in what I like to call a "ruminative manner" — They do it slowly — chewing over the words so as to assimilate the message, make it personal, part of their lives, pertinent for this very day and this only hour they have with any certainty (for who can promise himself his next heartbeat or breath?). Thus do they — and you can do the same — come in to contact, intimate, personal, dialogical contact with God. Thus do they hear Him speak — and they respond. Since this "ruminative manner" assures proper digestion and assimilation, you can see that the heart is as much, if not more, engaged than the head. For the purpose of all such reading of Scripture is knowledge of course — that "excelling knowledge of Jesus Christ," spoken of by St. Paul and the Council, but only that such knowledge lead on to love. St. Thomas Aquinas was all but stressing the obvious when he said: "Nothing (really no one) can be loved, unless it (he or she) is previously known." And this was really the theme of a very popular song not too long ago: "Growing to know you — Growing to love you." That is the theme song for

all who read Scripture "ruminatively" — and that "you" referred to in the song is the Christ of the Scriptures.

Any man can read Scripture with profit. No man can exhaust
the meaning of Scripture. For the word of God is both simple
and sublime. The child of tender years can understand enough
of the revelation to have his childish heart set aflame. The most
learned of men can never fathom to its deepest depths what
God in His love has seen fit to open out to us of Himself — and
the meaning of our existence. So no one need ever hesitate about
doing what Augustine did when he heard the children at play
singing: "take up and read." You know the result of his reading
of Scripture. He became a Saint. And you . . .? "What God wills
is *your* sanctification" (1 Thes. 4:3) That is the one great work
of life on earth; for time was given us to attain Eternity with
God; we are on earth to get to Heaven. But — only *saints* are
allowed in Heaven!

Perhaps many have been intimidated by some of the things
that the Press has seen fit to print. Perhaps you have read how
some "Scripture scholars" — that is how they are identified frequently by our Press — have taught that there never was a
Garden of Eden; that our First Parents — may have been multiple! — that Adam and Eve never enjoyed the "preternatural
gifts" Theologians have claimed that they possessed before
the Fall; even that there was no Fall — no Original Sin. All
such extravagances have been put in print by our sensation-loving Press. Not too long ago you could have read that the "Gospels of the Infancy" — of Christ — are "legendary and unhis-
torical." There are those — and here we are not speaking of
capable Scripture scholars, but of some newly ordained priests,
seminarians, nuns, and college students — who confidently state
that there never was a "star" that led the Magi; that the whole
story as found in St. Matthew, chapter two, about the Magi, is
"plainly legendary," that Herod, if he had ever summoned the
chief priests and the Scribes, and learned from them that
Jesus was to be born at Bethlehem, would never have been so
naive as to send the Magi off to "make careful inquiries about

the child, and, when you have found him, report to me," without shadowing them, keeping them under strictest surveillance. Some of them have told the youngsters in their Catechetical classes that the Archangel Gabriel who appeared both to Zachary, the father of John the Baptist, and Mary, the Mother of Jesus, was "not a spiritual being — but only a symbol." Mary and Zachary only had "profound spiritual experiences." Recently I saw an article about Heaven and Hell in one of our very popular news magazines. It quoted "certain Scripture scholars," as usual, and told how they no longer believed the Scriptures told of a real Heaven and a real Hell. All that sort of thing could scare any man — and might make him hesitate about taking up the Scriptures to read them. But, I beg you, never forget Barnum. He was right: "There's one born every minute!"

A real Scripture scholar is a very rare bird. For as Father Barnabas Ahern C.P. — a real Scripture scholar — has said: "The contemporary Scripture movement began with the discovery of the world of the Bible. Excavation at biblical sites, the discovery of whole libraries of Near Eastern Literature, the deciphering of ancient languages and law codes — all this opened the Bible wide to light which revealed meanings hitherto unknown." Stop there and study that last sentence and you will see what is required of a true Biblical scholar: all he needs to know *before* he begins to exegete — that is, give a critical and competent explanation of some portion of Scripture — is something about archeological discoveries, the sociological milieu in which the sacred writer lived and moved, much about the Semitic versions of the Bible, especially the Hebrew, Syriac, and Arabic versions, not to mention the Septuagint version of the Old Testament. That calls for quite a knowledge of Oriental languages, philology, semantics, sociology and history. Along with that, if he is to be orthodox, Philosophy and Theology. How many such men have we?

True it is that Pius XII, in his *Divino Afflante Spiritu*, gave official approval of a distinctively modern approach to the Bible; granted again that he explicitly said: "Let the interpreter, then, with all care and without neglecting any light derived from recent research, endeavor to determine the peculiar character and circumstances of the sacred writer, the age in which he lived, the sources, written and oral, to which he had recourse and the forms of expression he employed;" nevertheless, in the same Letter he said: "The Commentators . . . mindful of the fact that here there is question of a divinely inspired text, the care and interpretation of which have been confided to the Church by God Himself, should no less diligently take into account the explanations and declarations of the teaching authority of the Church. . ." (#24) Further, Vatican II has stated unqualifiedly that "The task of authentically interpreting the word of God, whether written or handed on, has been entrusted *exclusively* to the living teaching office of the Church (in other words the *Magisterium)* whose authority is exercised in the name of Jesus Christ." (#10)

Now to be just and truly adequate, let us say that Vatican II immediately added: "This teaching office is not above the word of God, but serves it, teaching only what has been handed on, listening to it devoutly, guarding it scrupulously, and explaining it faithfully by divine commission, and with the help of the Holy Spirit." (#ib) Then let it be noted what Pius XII said in *Divino Afflante Spiritu:* "Let all the other sons of the Church bear in mind that the efforts of these resolute laborers in the vineyard of the Lord should be judged not only with equity and justice, but also with the greatest charity; all moreover should abhor that intemperate zeal which imagines that whatever is new should for that very reason be opposed or suspected. Let them bear in mind above all that in the rules and laws promulgated by the Church there is question of doctrine regarding faith and morals; and that in the immense matter contained in the Sacred Books — legislative, historical, sapiential and prophetical — there are but few texts whose sense has been defined by the authority of the Church, nor are those more numerous about which the teaching of the Holy Fathers is unanimous." (#47)

Pius XII — in line with all that had been taught from Leo XIII down through Pius X, Benedict XV, and Pius XI —

wished the real scholars to enjoy true liberty, yet he did add a qualifying and clarifying phrase after that "true liberty" which runs: "which adheres faithfully to the teaching of the Church." That is the "liberty" which as Pius XII said, "upheld and sustained in every way the confidence of all, is the condition and source of all lasting fruit and of all solid progress in Catholic doctrine." Then he added a quote from Leo XIII: "Unless harmony of mind be maintained and principles safeguarded, no progress can be expected in this matter from the varied studies of many."

So, in all truth, we have nothing to fear, but everything to expect from the true Scriptural scholars; for behind them is the *Magisterium*, and over that is the Holy Spirit. Yet it was one of the best, and most respected, among such scholars, Cardinal Bea, who told us what we do have to fear, and from what we can expect confusion: "*popular* writings on Biblical subjects." And that characterizations seems to fit many of the Press reports perfectly.

So the first practical conclusion from all this is that you, whoever you are, and whatever your educational background, need never hesitate to "take up the Sacred books and read." Secondly, you can trust the truly competent Scripture scholars, but you must ever and always read Press reports about them with some mistrust. Perhaps Father Barnabas Ahern C.P. has given us the best attitude of mind in regard to all this. He says: "The existentialism of Kierkegaard, Heidigger, and Sartre, as a philosophic system is on the wane. Its spirit, however, is still active. For one reason or another, people of our day are practical existentialists, keenly sensitive to the feel of experience in the here and now . . . Men of our times are intuitive, not reflective, with a sharp sense of what lies deep beneath the mere surface and beyond the facade. Feeling and realism: these are the focal points of contemporary thought and life. This . . . is penetrating more and more into the spirit of the Church. Today our Catholic people are seeking true values and brook no substitute. . . The burning heat of criticism dissolves the tinsel of pretence and the facade of make-believe. Nothing is too time-honored to escape the fire of passion for the real. . . This spirit can lead to unwarranted iconoclasm. The devouring flame of passion for the real can destroy not only the rind, but the fruit, not only the shell, but the meat which it encases. In Scripture studies scholars have had to save the Bible from the devastating fire of 'demythologizing.' Under the influence of the existential philosophy of Heidigger, men like Rudolph Bultmann and Karl Schnidt in Germany and F. C. Grant in our own country, have so demythologized the Gospels that they have left only the shadow of a merely human Jesus and the meaningless memory of a life without content or challenge."

Why is it that our leading news magazines, which have had so many references to "demythologizing" the Bible, never have any words similar to those of this brilliant scholar and truly objectively honest man?

Father Barnabas goes on to say: "The search for the real, on the other hand, if only it cherishes respect for what is truly real, truly unchanging, truly the teaching of the Church, is bound to bring out what is richest in the Church's life. For the Holy Spirit is breathing in the *Zeitgeist* of our times, giving the power of His grace to our human search. It is His action as much as the spirit of the times which has forced our Catholics to measure up to tested standards of excellence. Facing squarely the compelling requirements of vital needs in our times, the Church in America has prepared a thorough going plan for Sister formation and has launched signal advances in the fields of education, social work, and hospital administration. The spiritual life of our people and the apostolic work of the Church are becoming more and more an expression of a passionate search for true and lasting benefits. . . Men seek nourishment no longer in crumbs which fall from the table, but in the very food which God has provided in word and worship."

After all you have heard and read from the "new breed" who are always, it seems, denigrating the Church, is it not refreshing

[208]

to read so much that is complimentary and truly *factual* — especially when it comes from an able man?

Before coming to a treatment of what has shocked many; namely, the new catechetics, let me give you one more reason to "relax and rejoice" as I give you Father Barnabas' clear distinction between modern and modernist. He says the spirit alive in the Church today is modern, through and through; it is not modernist. For he points out the fact that the contemporary Catholic Theologian is a man of Faith — one who accepts all of God's revelation. The modernist, on the other hand, is an unbeliever. He sees nothing divine in the deposit of faith. For him those truths have not been revealed by God; they are nothing but the human mind projecting its inward drives outwardly in what it calls dogmatic truths. That is a very important distinction; for there are those who take everything modern to be modernism. You can distinguish the two quite clearly so long as you hold fast to the Church, "the ground and pillar of truth." That means that you are solidly anchored in dutiful and loving obedience to the Church, dependent on her teachings, love her institutions, frequent her Sacraments, participate ever more intelligently and ardently in her Liturgy, and maintain, and even enhance your respect and reverence for her *Magisterium*. Do that and you can always relax, and will ever rejoice!

There has been a new catechetical method introduced. Just because it is new is no reason to suspect it, far less reject it. But there is every reason to examine it. Under an influence which came from Europe, especially from the Eichstatt Conference and from men like Hoflnger, Goldbrunner and Danielou, not to omit the *Lumen Vitae* in Belgium, teachers of sacred doctrine in colleges and high schools, as well as leaders in the CCD work, have been driving for a new presentation of the Faith. The new Catechisms, then, will present the truths of Faith and the demand of morality in what is called the "Kerygmatic" fashion.

Already the texts which will be used in many of the Catholic schools are under attack. Thirteen thousand Catholic parents have signed petitions asking that the books be withdrawn from

Chicago's archdiocesan schools. The charge is that they "attempt to disparage authority — both parental and civil — and that they abound in references aimed at slighting traditional values." That may, or may not, be true. But the point is that we all have to be on our guard, and exercise our right and our obligation to guard our children from what Fathern Ahern saw fit to call "iconoclasm."

Auxiliary Bishop John J. Ward of Los Angeles and Monsignor John K. Clarke of the same city, saw fit to issue admonitions to 1,100 lay catechists of the CCD saying that "the religious formation of children should not be sacrificed for the sake of senseless experimentation, and that teachers of religion should adhere to fundamentals and not become involved in conveying mere opinions." The Bishop scored those experimental theories in education which seem to ignore the fact that there is such a thing as Original Sin which darkens the intellect and weakens the will. He begged for a "return to common sense which recognizes that children need urging, and prodding and forming." The Monsignor, who is Archdiocesan Director of the CCD, said: "The CCD is not concerned with opinions. We must allow for the development of dogma, but we are not interested in teaching opinions. Do not be scandalized by opinions; for they are like hypotheses in relation to established fact. But you simply cannot afford to experiment, because you must convey fundamentals."

There is real ground for such admonitions; for the old *Baltimore Catechism* has come in for much scorn these days. And yet it was nothing less than an abbreviated edition of the *Catechism of the Council of Trent*, a scholarly work which contained the official teaching of that great Council. Vatican II abrogated nothing — rather it positively restated and stressed many — of Trent's teachings. But the trend today is to do away with the question and answer method. Pedagogically, one can question the wisdom of this new approach. Too little insistence is given to memory — and what teacher, worthy of the name, does not know the paramount importance of training the memory and the almost complete dependence of the intellect on that priceless faculty for real education? But the new method is here. Your duty is not to be shocked, but to be watchful. If the texts your children bring home from school have no questions or answers, if the so-called art in it is "modern," that is, childish and even ugly, if there is no mention of the Ten Commandments, nothing about Angels or Devil, nothing about Purgatory, Heaven or Hell, if the Mass is presented as a Meal and not as a Sacrifice, if there is no distinction made between venial and mortal sin, if the very ideas of sin is down-graded, if frequent Confession is not inculcated, if Papal Authority is neglected, moral absolutes questioned, Original Sin obscured, miracles reduced to natural happenings, Sacred Scripture distorted, your child has one of the "new catechetical books" but, while based on the "Kerygmatic" method, it is not Kerygmatical; and while using a Biblical approach, it is far from true Biblical Theology. You have every obligation to protest the use of such a text — and you have even a more pressing obligation to supply for all that is wanting in your child's religious education. Catholic common sense will tell you that without the doctrine of Original Sin Christ's coming to earth, taking a human nature, suffering that Passion, undergoing that Death on the Cross, and then rising from the Tomb, makes no sense. If He is Saviour, He must have saved you and your children from something. It was not from suffering; for all of you have known, and will yet know suffering. It was not from sickness; for once again you and yours have been, and will yet be sick. It was not from death; for you and yours will one day die. Then from what did He save us? Only from Eternal Death — from Hell — from everlasting separation from Him, His Father, and His Holy Spirit. He saved us for Heaven! Catholic common sense will also tell you that your child needs to know about his "wounded human nature," his inclination to evil, his enemy who will tempt him, and his freedom to say "No" — either to God or the Devil. He has to know what sin is — and to realize that not all refusals of obedience to God are of equal demerit and detestation.

But do not panic. Refuse to "get all shook up." Competent

[211]

authority will care for all such aberrations before long. The Dutch Catechism, spoken about earlier, is already under close scrutiny at Rome — and has not yet been given an *Imprimatur*. Never forget that "the mills of God grind slowly, but they grind exceedingly fine" — and *right*. So relax — and "refuse to get all shook up." The use of that phrase set some bell ringing in my memory. It is recognized now for what it is. Herbert Hart, a convert and a journalist, wrote an article not too long after his conversion, but long enough after Vatican II, to have point for all of us. Mr. Hart said the one thing that kept him out of the Church for so long was Papal authority and infallibility. That, he thought, "was for the birds." Yet, today, amidst all the "frustrations and confusion experienced by many since Vatican II," it is wholehearted belief in that same Papal authority and especially in that Papal infallibility that has saved his equilibrium. He says it is that — and that precisely — which has him "refusing to get all shook up" when something new is introduced in the Liturgy; when he can eat meat on Friday — without sin; when he sees the priest at Mass facing the people, and hears him using the vernacular; when he meets those idiosyncratic people who are "more Catholic than the Pope"; or when he hears some cleric or layman offer some nostrum which guarantees "instant Heaven." Herb shows rare insight when he says that "it may surprise many Catholics to find that the Documents of Vatican II are nothing more than an appeal for a return to the basic teachings of Christianity; "for, when stripped to the bone, these 16 official texts are simply an exhortation to love God and neighbor. They form a blue-print for positive action. The accent is on *love*." But never forget what we have already stressed: we cannot love those we do not know. Hence, our need to read, and re-read, Scripture.

Hart ended his "confession" of why he "refuses to get all shook up" with something like a *Credo*. He said: "If I did not believe that Vatican II was called by Pope John XXIII at the inspiration of the Holy Spirit; if I did not believe that Pope Paul VI was the visible head of the Catholic Church, and if I did not believe the promise of Our Lord that He would be with His Church 'even to the end of the world,' I would be the first to say: 'Move over, give me room to start shaking with the rest of you.' However, I cannot believe that the blood of martyrs has been shed in vain; I cannot buy the put-on that God is dead simply because there are many who would like to go to the funeral. It is not the first time that hate has tried to kill love and lost the battle, and because I believe that God is Love, I refuse to get all shook up."

And you — do you believe all that Hart believes? Cardinal Leger of Montreal, at the close of Vatican II said: "The minds of Catholics are bound to be shaken up." In one sense that is true, but not in the sense that Mr. Hart was using "shook up" in his article. There is a good sense in which we all should be shaken up by the Council. We should reassess every gift and grace we have from God, probe the mysteries of our Faith more deeply, rediscover the wealth that has been lavished on us "in Christ Jesus," restudy every article of the Creed, re-examine our attitudes toward Code and Cult, and see if we have a hard and fast grasp on God — as hard and as fast as He has on us. That kind of a shaking up is good for each of us. But the kind that Herb Hart was talking about is good for none of us — and need never be known by any of us — especially because of that Burning Bush which is the Bible. It need never burn us, but it should ever inflame us. That it will do if you will but distinguish between opinion and established truth, between hypothesis, theory and fact.

Just as there were extremists in the Liturgical Movement, so there are extremists in Biblical renewal. Some of them say that to express religious truths in any but Biblical language is to be condemned. They scorn the theological explanations and developments of doctrine through which real Christian thinkers throughout the ages have endeavored to fathom the depths of God's revelation to man and to clarify the message from Him and the response man should give. In some circles the very name "theologian" is one of those bad words like "proof" and "logic" and "reason," and "Scholasticism."

Here we must beg you to be stubborn. Refuse to be driven by these extremists. Stand fast — as St. Paul told Timothy to stand. Never allow yourself to be intimidated, far less *condemned by clichés*. That is a technique becoming distressingly common. It is undignified in the user, and an insult to the dignity of the one they are using them on. The "woods are full of them." Watch out, for it is a none too subtle form of real "brainwashing." They use such words as "conceptualizing" and use it in a derogatory sense. But can they themselves think without concepts? They will loftily look down on you and almost sneer as they say "philosophizing" — But let me ask you in the name of all that is good and holy: what is degrading in a human being, who has been made by God to be a rational animal, what is wrong, I ask, in using that rationality to reason rightly, to philosophize inasmuch as he uses his intellect to search for the causes of things — and most especially for that First and Final Cause, who is God? Another favorite of these extremists is *"categorizing"* — They will try to make you feel ashamed of your thought-processes and your clear thinking by scornfully saying: "But that is *categorizing*" — and you are supposed to curl up and die as far as further thinking along those lines is concerned. But ask them what is wrong with thinking and speaking in clear-cut and well-defined categories? What is wrong, in other words, with thinking clearly? Can anyone think rightly in any other way, or express his thought intelligibly without using categories — genus, species; living, non-living; substance, accidents; and so on down every limb of that ancient and respected "Porphyrian Tree"? If these youngsters — for most of them are young — succeed in cutting down that "tree," the intellectual world will be so deforested that it will become a desert. Cut that tree down and you have really felled the one sheltering growth in our world of human communications.

Another word they will use with disparagement is "logic" which they too often connect with "scholasticism." When asked recently what was wrong with Scholasticism, a prominent Professor of Philosophy and the History of Philosophy with obvious embarrassment, smiled sheepishly and replied: "Nothing. But the present-day student does not want it. He prefers Phenomenology and Existentialism." Could any reply more completely condemn so-called Educators? Since when have students been the ones to dictate to faculties, form their own curriculum, and tell teachers what they are to teach? Pope Paul VI, like many of his predecessors, has referred again and again to the "*philosophia perennis*" — that is, Scholasticism. And one need be no prophet to say that when Phenomenology and Existentialism have long been discarded, real thinkers will still be using the logic, the common sense, the natural, existential and essential *philosophia perennis*. So don't be stampeded into change. Stand fast, try the "spirits" — use your intellect as God made it to be used: *logically* — as have, and as yet do, the true "Scholastics."

Of course you will be condemned as "medieval" by these same "modernists" — but look again at that substantial and truly historical book "The Thirteenth The Greatest of Centuries" — that thirteenth century happens to be among those that mark the middle ages, it was truly "medieval." But can our vaunted Twentieth point to such art and artists, such thought and thinkers, such poetry and poets, such writings and writers? But why endeavor to disprove what has never been proved, especially when the cliché-mouthers often wear badges that read: "Trust no one over 30." Stand fast. Refuse to be stampeded — by mere clichés.

They have no respect for anything they can call "ancient," "old," or "old-fashioned." But how *new* do they find the alphabet, the multiplication table, or the law of gravity? This abandoning of tradition has always impressed me as fatal. Any botanist will tell you that if you cut roots, your tree or plant will die. Tradition can be looked upon as roots. Many novelities of the day can be regarded as leaves on the limbs of trees. Cut roots and watch those leaves wither, turn yellow, die and fall off despite how shiny, green, vital and vivid they appear at the

[215]

moment. Charles Dickens once said something about the man who has confidence in "untried friends." It has sharp point for many of the extremists today. He said such a man "has hope — the hope of happy *inexperience*." And one of our English poets has a couplet which runs:

> Be not the first by whom the new, is tried,
> Nor yet the last to lay the old aside.

But be sure it is worn out, is the added addendum to that.

But the most devastating of the clichés — devastating for the weak — is that about the *"ghetto."* When this cliché came to the ears, recently, of Pope Paul VI, he cried out against it. Coupled with this term frequently is "provincial" or "parochial." Tell me who is there who does not come from, or belong to, some province or parish? So being "provincial" and "parochial," in one sense, is inevitable. Like the proverbial old lady who "accepted the universe" and was told by the long-suffering priest: "By God, Mam, you'd better" — all of us had better accept being both "provincial" and "parochial" — and it might be well to remember where "charity" begins! But, of course, these "cosmopolitan" cliché-mouthers are down-grading us as narrow and ignorant. No one likes to be considered such; so too many capitulate. But some of us have a fondness for the root meanings of words. Take the word "ghetto." It is derived from the Italian. Historically, and originally it signified that quarter of the city to which the Jews were restricted for residence. Later it meant any quarter of a city or town where many Jews lived. To be "ghetto-minded," as the cliché-mouthers accuse some of us, must mean, basically to be "Jewish-minded" — and for any Christian, but especially for Catholic-Christians, what greater compliment could be given? Christ was a Jew. Our Lady-Mother was a Jewess — "the glory of her people" — and ours! Pius XI said we are all "spiritual Semites." And what a beautiful "ghetto-mind" John XXIII showed when he greeted a group of Jews with open arms and the salutation: "I am Joseph your brother."

Of course these new modernists do not use it in that ennobling sense. They use it not only to convey distaste, but something more like disgust. And yet, accepting it as they use it — narrow, restricted, small — one can yet ask: Can a man be truly orthodox, truly Catholic-minded, unless he has a "ghetto-mind?" Truth is one of the most intolerant things in the universe. Absolute truth is most narrow, truly restricted. Two and two make four; only four, nothing but four, and will never make anything else but four. It stays in that "ghetto." So can we Catholics stay in the "ghetto" of the true, as restrictive against the false; the good as narrow, in opposition to the evil; and the beautiful which may seem small, in comparison to all that is ugly.

These men are now saying: "Change or you will perish!" They even use what was used in the earliest chapter of this book to stampede you into the changes they want. They insist, as we have, that "Change is the law of life." But we have seen what they seem to close their eyes to; namely that a tree changes but only so long as it holds on to its roots. Your body changes but only so long as it adheres to the fundamental skeleton God gave it. The Church changes but always retains the fundamental structure Christ gave it — the rock is still Peter — the bark is still his. Perennial and ever contemporary is the nature of Catholicism. We change, but never for the mere sake of change. The truth is we grow — but growth of the "mustard seed" demands roots in the soil, if it is to become the "tree" Christ spoke of in His parable. So it is not against change we take our stand, but only against those changes which are rootless. "Do not cling to things that have proved valuable in other ages," is the latest cry, "for we are in and of a new age."

John XXIII told us we should learn from history. There is the lesson of the Irish and the Jews. These two refused to change. They were told that if they did not, they would perish. But their refusal to be stampeded into change; their standing fast by the inner truths, the fundamental truths that gave them meaningfulness, have brought these two peoples through centuries of crises, condemnations, that have seen those who yielded to

[217]

threats pass from the scene. The Irish and the Jews have re-found a lost nationalism, in the best sense of that word, by stand-ing fast by the Faith that was theirs, being true to the God who had revealed Himself to them, and now seem sure to outlive those who told them to "Change or you will perish." It is well to recall Christ's saying about "he who perseveres to the end shall be saved." The cry: "Change or perish" is an idle threat, for it is a stupid alternative.

Paul VI faced up to the cliché about being in a "ghetto" in this fashion: "It is true that the Church is an institution suffi-cient to herself, whose sources of life, spirtual energies and guide-lines for action come from within . . . But the Church is not a "ghetto" — She is not a closed society. . . She is not *of* the world, but she is *in* the world, and *for* the world." The Pope is denying the false supposition of the cliché-mongers. He continues: "We would err if we thought of resolving the problem (of understand-ing and communication between the Church and the world) by debasing the Church, diluting her doctrinal and moral demands, and bringing the thinking and customs of the Church into line with those of the world. We would err if we attempted . . . to rejuvenate the Church by a dose of worldliness and by taking an attitude of indulgent and ephemeral historicism. The Church would lose herself — and she would not save the world."

In other words, Paul VI is saying "Stand fast — and you will be saved." He is reversing the cry of the "Progressives": "Change or you will perish." And he had a very penetrating remark to make toward the end of this audience: "Mind the fact that the world does not ask for an accommodating Church." Maybe the "children of light" can learn from those who "sit in darkness." What modern man really seeks today is not "change" but "stabil-ity" — and where will he find greater stability than on that "rock" which is "Peter" — and the foundation of the Catholic Church?

When you are condemned by some of those who are advocat-ing a "new approach" to everything, but most especially to our understanding of the Bible, when your children come home from their classes in religious instruction with "Sister said . . ." this and that in the Bible . . . is "not true," see the Sister and ask her "Is this established fact, or is it merely an opinion?" If merely an "opinion" recall what Bishop Ward and Monsignor Clarke had to say about "mere opinions" — and you go on holding to and teaching your youngsters the fundamentals.

What Pope Pius XII said about the fewness of texts in the Bible that have been definitely established by the *Magisterium,* and a like fewness about which there was unanimity among the Fathers of the Church, can be said about Scripture Scholars today. No one of them of real repute will ever put forth *his* opinion as *final.* And if he is honest, he will tell you how few points there are on which there is unanimity among the experts.

Never forget two things: "Authority is the weakest of all arguments" — when that "authority" is merely human. Secondly, "Authority is worth as much as the *reason* behind it." So never be frightened by big names. Listen to *what* they say, but then ask *why* they say it. The one "Authority" you never really need ask that question of, is the Authority of the Church, the *Magisterium;* for when you hear that, you hear God.

Which brings us back to the Burning Bush — the Bible. You can read yours without any knowledge of Latin, Greek, Hebrew, or Arabic. You can read it in English and hear God speaking to you. You can readily understand His message — and learn your mission. What is more, if you read it prayerfully — some little part of it every day, or at least every week — you will gradually recover what this modern age has lost: *a sense of the sacred.*

You know everything has been made by God. Hence everything — and that means everything — should be for us what the *Shekina* was to the original People of God; a sign that God is with us; that His name is *Yahweh* — and *Emmanuel.* Daily reading of the Bible will enable you to see God everywhere and have you saying with Gilbert K. Chesterton: "There was a Man who dwelt in the East centuries ago, and now I cannot look at a sheep or a sparrow, a lily or a wheatfield, a raven or a sunset, a vineyard or a mountain, *without thinking of Him.*"

[219]

Persistent prayerful reading of the Sacred Books will inevitably develop a true God-consciousness and real Christ-consciousness in you — and that means heaven on earth. That is Reality.

The world of the West is growing more and more unconscious of God and has lost its sense of the sacred. Since that is so, we can take the cliché of the threateners and use it wisely: *Change—* we of the West must change in this matter of God-consciousness and our sense of the sacred — or *we will perish*. The reading of the Bible will help you to change. It will save you. It will make all nature more lovable and all life much more livable. An example: You have looked upon rocks, seen rain, and studied roses; you have gazed at stars, admired both snow and the ever-moving sea. But have you ever looked at any of these, or all of them, and seen what the three favorite Apostles saw after the Transfiguration: "Only Jesus"? An Irish patriot and poet did. Joseph Mary Plunkett wrote:

> I see His Blood upon the rose
>   And in the stars, the glory of His eyes.
> His Body gleams amid eternal snows;
>   His tears fall from the skies.
>
> I see His face in every flower.
>   The thunder and the singing of the birds
> Are but His voice. And, carven by His power,
>   Rocks are His written words.
>
> All pathways by His feet are worn.
>   His strong Heart stirs the ever-beating sea.
> His crown of thorns is twined with every thorn.
>   His Cross is every tree.

That is Christ-consciousness; and it can be yours if you will take the means: prayerful, persistent Bible reading. Think how you will look on "the hairs of your head" — if you read the Gospels slowly, "ruminatively." Think how you can come to think on your own infinite worth as you see "two sparrows." Even grass can tell you much about your immortality — the ordinary "grass of the field." . . . You see what the Council had in mind when it exhorted you to read the Sacred Books.

No one, after Vatican II, can look upon Bible reading as a "Protestant devotion." Now all must see it for what it is: a Dialogue with God. Truly the Bible is a "Burning Bush" — GOD is in the midst of it, and He will always inflame but never burn. Become as "curious" as Moses — go and "look at this strange sight — and see why the bush is blazing, but is not being burnt up." Make Bible reading one of your precious "private devotions."

Chapter 9

THAT WE MAY BE MADE WORTHY
OF THE PROMISES

Most of you will recognize the heading of this chapter as a clause in a very important prayer. It is prefaced by the plea: "Pray for us, O Holy *Mother of God* . . ." It is concluded by ". . . *of Christ.*" Who will not hold that the "promise" we all look forward to as the one we most want fulfilled in our personal regard is that made by Christ when He told of His Second Coming: "He will place the sheep on his right hand. . . Then the King will say to those on His right hand: 'Come, you whom my Father has blessed, take for your heritage the kingdom prepared for you since the foundation of the world . . ."? (Mt. 25:33,34) For what is the ultimate purpose of earthly life save that we attain to the everlasting life of Heaven?

The title came to me recently as I knelt singing: "We fly to your patronage, O holy Mother of God. . ." during a Conventual Concelebrated Mass. I had been thinking of you and the danger of confusion in the modern world — and especially that confusion generated by some impulsive enthusiasts after the promulgation of the Dogmatic Constitution on the Church by Vatican II. I refer to their downgrading of devotion to Our Lady-Mother.

Perhaps the Versicle: "Pray for us, O Holy Mother of God" held special meaning at the time because I had just come from assisting at the Byzantine Liturgy concelebrated by two priests of the Oriental Rite. That Liturgy (which is their much more telling term for the execution of Christ's command to "Do this as my memorial," then the one we use: "Mass") had made a profound impression on me. On reflection I found that there was one recurrent phrase that kept running through my mind as I listened with all my being to this magnificent Act of Worship — of Love — of complete involvement of the People of God with God in His Saving Act of Love. It kept repeating itself: "How old the new!" For here before me was everything the younger generation are hailing as "brand new."

Today's youth believe they have "discovered" the need for "dialogue" with God. The Byzantine Missal calls their Liturgy "The most holy conversation between God in His Mercy and His Eternal Glory, and Man in his frailty and his present pain." A conversation is dialogue, is it not? This Byzantine "dialogue" goes back to before the death of the Emperor Theodosius, who learned whether he was "worthy of the promises of Christ" in the year 395. At his death Christendom was divided into two great political spheres: Byzantium, or the Greek Empire, and Rome, or the Latin Empire. This division really brought into being the two Rites I had witnessed and assisted in that morning: Oriental — or Byzantine, and Occidental — or Roman. Thanks to Vatican II and its Liturgical renewal, we of the West — or Roman Rite — are recapturing what was ours when the Church was much younger than it is today: the idea that Mass or the Liturgy is a "dialogue with God."

Youth today is totally given to what it calls "love" — especially in the matter of Religion. As I assisted at the Byzantine Liturgy I could not escape recalling what the Greek Church insists upon — even in the very Prologue to their Liturgy: The ways of God are unchanging: they are one continuous Act of Love. Not as if love flowed from God: for *Love is God* and *God is Love*.

Then, to show that the Liturgy follows the unfolding of Revelation, this same Prologue insists that . . .

1) There is *God-Love* in the creation of man: in the making of a being to whom the All-Perfect could give Himself, since man was not made for the benefit of God, whose delight cannot be increased, but for the multiplication of love. (And I add: for the multilocation of Love who is God; for God is in all men by His Power, Presence, and Knowledge.)

2) There is *God-Love* in the promise of the Redemption: in the tender care lavished upon the seed of Abraham. (And again I add: We are of that seed; for we are of the Chosen People of God — we are "spiritual Semites").

3) There is *God-Love* in the privileges of the Chosen People, so clearly manifested in the miracles of the Exodus, and commemorated in the liturgy of the Passover. (And who can miss the typology between the Passover and the Paschal Mystery, which is our Mass?)

4) There is *God-Love* in the songs of the kings, in the anxious warnings of the prophets, in the hopes of a whole people for a salvation yet to come. (We hear those songs, those warnings, those hopes in every Mass from Introit to Post-Communion!)

5) There is supreme *God-Love* in the Sacrifice of the Lamb upon the Cross, under which we live unto this very day. (The Sacrifice of the Mass is the re-presentation of that Sacrifice of the Lamb upon the Cross).

Then the Prologue to this liturgy of the oriental rite ends with: There will be *God-Love* at all times, now and always and forever and ever. Amen.

How old the new. "Love" does "make the world go around" — for the "going around" of the "world" depends entirely on God — and He is Love.

Many of the young enthusiasts stress "active participation of the laity" as something discovered during the "*aggiornamento*." They should assist at the Liturgy as offered in the Byzantine Rite. It is true that Pius X insisted that "the active participation in the most holy mysteries and in the solemn prayer of the Church is the first and indispensable source of the true Christian spirit." It is true that the Liturgical Movement begun at least a century ago emphasized the part the people were to play in the offering of the Sacrifice of the Mass. It is even more true that today, thanks to Vatican II, there is greater actual participation than we have had for years. But, as I assisted at the Byzantine Liturgy and heard the Deacon "dialogue" with the Concelebrants, pray with them, answer their prayers, and even

[225]

complete their prayers; as I heard him, representing in our tiny chapel the congregation as it would conduct itself in a large Church of the Oriental Rite, from the Office of Prime, which precedes the Liturgy itself, to the Final Dismissal or the Apolysis, I realized that they have always had what we are now only recapturing — Mass as a "dialogue" not only between God and Priest, but even more articulately among God and Priest and People.

How old the new! The young are disturbing some of the older members of the People of God by their enthusiasm for "Guitar Masses" "Hootenanny Masses," and, in general for singing during Mass. Many of the old are finding even more reverent congregational singing somewhat disturbing. But in the Byzantine Rite there is no such thing, strictly speaking, as a Low Mass, far less a "Silent Mass." The Liturgy is sung — by priest and people. Very few, and very brief are the pauses where there is no song. Truly it can be said that the Oriental Rite needs no such exhortation as we of the West; namely, "Do not pray during Mass: PRAY THE MASS." That is what they do as they sing — and they are almost continuously singing. "He prays twice who sings."

But what impressed me most of all, and what brought me to this chapter, was the insistence in the Byzantine Liturgy of devotion to Our Lady-Mother. It insists that "the greatest concern of the Byzantine Liturgy is to foster in the minds of the faithful and in their hearts, a great devotion to Christ Himself *and to His Blessed Mother* . . ." Since the Divine Liturgy is the supreme act of the Christian cult, Mary has to have in it a place worthy of her presence at the foot of the Cross. The Byzantine Church has always granted this place to the *Theotokos:* glory, honor, and prerogatives come to her because of this very dignity. There is a multiplicity of Marian representations in all Byzantine Churches, in their apse, on their iconastasis, on their walls. Clouds of incense envelope the ikons of the *Theotokos.* The flickering candles that light them are a testimony of devotion, of tender and filial love rising toward the Mother. The prayers of the Divine Liturgy contain all the Marian Theology: her divine motherhood, her perpetual virginity, her holiness, her queenship, her mediation.

What a relief, what a consolation, what a thrill — especially in these days — was this manifestation of appreciation of her part in our redemption, and its holy expression!

Of course there were practices in the Rite that struck one as "different." Their sign of the cross. They cross themselves from right to left; not as we do from left to right. They hold their hands differently, too. And what a magnificent symbol they make of that: they insist that this sign is an act of faith in the three basic dogmas of our holy religion. They join their thumbs to the index and middle fingers of their hands, while the third and little fingers are bent so as to touch the palm of their hands. The thumb joined to the index and middle fingers signifies the Dogma of the *Trinity:* One God in three Divine Persons. The two fingers that are bent to touch the palm of the hand signify that in Jesus Christ there are two natures: human and Divine — united through the *Incarnation* in the one Person — the Holy Trinity's Second Person, the Word. By making the sign on themselves they invoke their faith in the *Redemption:* Christ suffering and dying on the Cross to redeem us. They touch their head to consecrate their minds to God; they touch their breasts to consecrate their hearts with all their affections to God; they touch their right shoulder to consecrate all their good actions, then their left shoulders to ask forgiveness for their sins. They point to the fact that in Holy Scripture the right always represents the good, and the left, the evil. That is why they touch their right shoulders first. They can also tell you that up until the thirteen century we of the West crossed ourselves the same way. Their sign of the cross is made at every mention of the Trinity in their Liturgy, and thus becomes afresh an Act of Faith and a total consecration of self to God.

The next difference did not strike this Trappist as so very different. I mean the *metanies* — with palm turned up, the worshipper lowers his hand almost to the floor, while making a deep

[227]

bow of the whole body as if making a humble offering of his whole being to God in a gesture of magnificent surrender and adoration. These *metanies* did not strike me as truly strange for we Trappist make almost the same "profound bow" in place of the customary genuflection of the West.

Perhaps because we Trappist-Cistercians have such a devotion to Our Lady-Mother, and because we have heard that there is a decline in that devotion outside our monasteries, the continual calling on Mary during this Byzantine Liturgy impressed me so deeply. During the Office of Prime which preceded the Liturgy they sang: "What shall we say to thee, O Full of Grace? — A Heaven — for Thou hast given rise to the Sun of Justice; a Paradise — for Thou hast brought forth the Flower of Immortality; a Virgin — for Thou hast remained undefiled; a Mother — a pure Mother holding in her holy arms a Son who is the God of all. To Him intercede for the salvation of our souls." Then in the Prayers before the Holy Doors they called upon her as "Source of Mercy" . . . begged her to make them "worthy of pity" — pleaded with her to "look down upon a sinful people" and to "show her power as always."

During the Preparation of the Offering, the Celebrant, taking a part of the bread in his hands, prays: "In honor and memory of our most blessed and glorious Lady, the Mother of God and ever-virgin, Mary, through whose intercession do Thou, O Lord, receive this sacrifice on Thy heavenly altar. At Thy right hand did stand the Queen, in a robe of gold, wrought with many colors." Then throughout the Litany of Peace, or Great Synapty, Mary is mentioned again and again by both priest and people, and before the Hymn of the Incarnation which is sung by the people. On throughout this glorious Liturgy, before the Creed and after the Consecration, Mary is hailed with love by priest and then again by the people, then before Communion "the pure and ever-virgin" is again mentioned with filial trust and devotion. Finally at the Dismissal or Apolysis, Mary, "His immaculate and all-pure Mother" is remembered and as the priest ends the Liturgy, just before he kisses the altar, he prays: "O Theotokos, the ever-blessed, the entirely spotless, more honorable than the Cherubim, and infinitely more glorious than the Seraphim: we exalt thee who didst bear without corruption God the Word, thee verily the Mother of God."

With that before you, perhaps you can understand why I went from that Liturgy toward my Conventual Concelebrated Mass with the thought: The real fullness of Catholic worship cannot be appreciated without taking in the East and the West as one great whole: the Mystical Body doing on earth in perfect harmony what Christ is doing in Heaven: glorifying the Father through that Celestial Sacrifice which is Himself: "ever living to make intercession for us" — The Whole Christ — as St. Augustine named Him and all of us. I recalled what Benedict XV had said: "The Church of Jesus Christ is neither Latin, nor Greek, nor Slav — but Catholic (universal); therefore, she makes no difference between her children; the Greeks, Latins, and Slavs, and members of all other nations are equal in the eyes of the Apostolic See." And of course, in the eyes of God and of His Blessed Mother.

As I sang the *Sub Tuum*, then heard that antiphon: "Pray for us, O Holy Mother of God" then replied: "That we may be made worthy of the promises of Christ," you can readily understand why I reassure you that She is still our Mother — the Virgin "Most Venerable" and that we are to remember ever the words of Gilbert K. Chesterton: "A woman was His walking home" and are to do as he did: cry to her *"Foederis Arca, Ora pro nobis."* Despite what some may say, she is still "House of God" and in truth our "Gate of Heaven."

I recall an article in a prominent Catholic magazine in the fall of 1965, which told of what the author called a "piety void" in the lives of many of our contemporary Catholics. He pointed to the fact — and it is a fact — that "many popular, so-called pious devotions had been downgraded in recent years." Then he listed some of them: "The rosary, visits to the Blessed Sacrament, devotional confessions, novenas, missions, even retreats." He added that though the new Liturgy had been readily enough ac-

[229]

cepted, it had not become "sufficiently meaningful or satisfying to fill the void left by pious devotions. As a result, many Catholics feel a loss in their lives and they are not happy about it."

Indeed they are not. How could they be? The "iconoclasts," spoken of indirectly by Father Barnabas Ahern in the last chapter, have been hard at work in this field of personal piety, popular devotions, traditional and well-loved practices. With great sophistication these young people, many of them young priests, seminarians, nuns and Catholic College students, downgrade and decry anything that is not "communal," "Biblical," "Liturgical." Sorry to say they have been quite successful in certain areas, and by their success have created for many what *is* a "piety void." More than one of the faithful has complained that since the new liturgy came in, something very personal seems to have gone out of their lives: their sense of personal intimacy with God in prayer and worship. They feel that they are "lost in the crowd" at Mass these days of communal worship, congregational singing, lectors, commentators, and music directors. They find collective worship very impersonal. And that is tragic.

What an irony it would be if the Council, which sought renewal through *personal* active participation and real involvement of the whole person, should lead to something very like an impersonal if not anti-personal worship.

Another irony is that these very people who decry the "routine religion" of the past, the "regimentation" that went on in parish services, and the stifling of the "individual" and neglect of the "person" as a person in the days that are gone, are now insisting on a regimentation of their own in communal worship, are developing routine by their drive for "involvement" and their repeated use of the same prayers and hymns.

But the ugliest irony of all is that these "iconoclasts" use Vatican II as their justification. Have they read the Documents? Why, even in the Constitution on the Liturgy we read: "The spiritual life, however, *is not confined* to participation in the liturgy. The Christian is assuredly called to pray with his brethren, but *he must also* enter into his chamber to *pray to the*

Father in secret." (#12) Then almost immediately we read the statement: "Popular devotions of the Christian people are warmly commended. . . Such is especially the case with devotions called for by the Apostolic See." (#13) Do these "iconoclasts" know that the Holy See, from the beginning of the present century to this very day, has sounded forth almost year after year a call for devotion to Our Lady-Mother, and has especially recommended the recitation of her Rosary? Leo XIII gave us eleven — yes, eleven separate Encyclicals on Our Lady — and always mentioned the Rosary. St. Pius X gave us a gem in his *Ad Diem Illum* — and states something these young men who are so eager for an *"aggiornamento"* should ponder. He says: "upon her, as upon a foundation — the noblest after Christ — rises the edifices of the Faith of all centuries." They might also weigh well the closing passage of this very important Encyclical and thus learn that they, and their generation, are not the only ones who faced crises. St. Pius X said: "True we are passing through disastrous times, when we may well make our own the lament of the Prophet: 'There is no truth, and there is no mercy, and there is no knowledge of God in the land. Cursing, and lying, and killing, and theft, and adultery have overflowed.' (Osee 4:1-2) Yet, in the midst of this deluge of evil, the Virgin Most Clement rises before our eyes like a rainbow, as the arbiter of peace between God and man."

Steadily, throughout this century, has the attention of the faithful been directed toward Mary, Mother of God and Mother of men. In the midst of World War I Benedict XV wrote a letter on Mary as "Queen of Peace" and said "We urge that in this terrible hour, the trusting petitions of her most afflicted children be directed to her." Ten years later his successor, Pius XI was saying: "If the Church falls on difficult times; if faith wanes and charity grows cold; if morals, private and public, deteriorate; if any danger threaten the Catholic cause or civil society, let us have recourse to her (Mary) begging help from heaven." *(Lux Veritatis)* Then in 1937 he sounded the same call in his *Ingravescentibus Malis:* ". . . for the increasingly grave evils of our times

[231]

there is no remedy but in the return of mankind to Christ" — then he shows us the way of return: *Mary*. Pius XII gave us the identical warning and way out of danger in his *Menti Nostrae*. Now comes Paul VI with his *Signum Magnum* in which he recalls his own proclamation of "the august Mother of God as the spiritual Mother of the Church" and also the Consecration of mankind to Mary and to her Immaculate Heart made by Pius XII in 1942. He exhorted all the faithful to "renew personally their consecration to the Immaculate Heart of the Mother of the Church" — thus combining his own proclamation with the Consecration made by Pius XII. In this same Encyclical Paul VI said: "It is the duty of all the faithful to pay as tribute to the most faithful handmaid of the Lord a veneration of praise, of gratitude, and of love." The entire second part of this magnificent Letter was devoted to "Devout imitation by the Faithful of the Virtues of Mary" — and yet there are those who dare to say Vatican II "downgraded devotion to Our Lady." How warped can the human mind become?

Vatican II in its Dogmatic Constitution on the Church, in sections 50 and 51, gave the traditional doctrine on the cult of the Blessed Virgin and on veneration of the saints. How could it do otherwise when our Creed tells us that we "believe in Jesus Christ . . . who was born of the Virgin Mary . . ." and further on states "And I believe in the Holy Catholic Church, the Communion of Saints." And yet these brash youngsters will endeavor to stampede people into believing that this Council downgraded all that as archaic. Have they ever read Chapter Eight of this Dogmatic Constitution? It is devoted entirely to "The Role of the Blessed Virgin Mary, Mother of God, in the Mystery of Christ and the Church." The Fourth Section in this authentic teaching tells of "Devotion to the Blessed Virgin in the Church" and states: "As it has *always* existed in the Church, this cult is altogether special" (#66) Then it goes on to say: "This most holy Synod deliberately teaches this Catholic doctrine." How foreign to the *"aggiornamento"* they are who dare to downgrade devotion to Our Lady-Mother! Perhaps it is worthwhile to quote

[232]

the final paragraph to reassure all and to show the "iconoclasts" how far removed they are from "the spirit of Vatican II." The Council ended its Document with: "Let the entire body of the faithful pour forth persevering prayer to the Mother of God and the Mother of men. Let them implore that she who aided the beginnings of the Church by her prayers may now, exalted as she is in heaven above all the saints and angels, intercede with Her Son in the fellowship of all the saints. May she do so until all the peoples of the human family, whether they are honored with the name of Christian or whether they still do not know their Saviour, are happily gathered together in peace and harmony into the one People of God, for the glory of the Most Holy and Undivided Trinity." (#69)

In contrast to the "iconoclasts" within the Church I can offer as reason to "Relax and Rejoice" the tribute lately paid Mary by a Lutheran theologian, Dr. Jeroslav Pelikan, now teaching at Yale University. "Honoring Mary," he says, "is a way of emphasizing, not of obscuring, the centrality of Christ alone. She is called Mother of God not only by the ancient Church, but by the Reformation creeds and confessions, because that is a way of asserting that the holy Child of this holy Mother is nothing less than the Son of God, the Second Person of the Blessed Trinity. Where He is thus honored, she must be acknowledged as Mother of God; and where she is rejected as Mother of God, there the centrality of Christ is not enhanced, but threatened.

"The present attitude toward Mary held by most Protestants is far from the spirit and intent of Luther's Reformation. She represents principles of truly evangelical and, in the fullest sense, Catholic Christianity.

"The faith and trust of the Blessed Virgin in the grace of God can help us to fight the temptation — to rely upon ourselves, our piety, our morality, our right doctrine — rather than solely and utterly upon the action of God.

"An increase of Protestant respect for the Blessed Virgin would also make its contribution to the healing of the wounds in the body of Christ."

[233]

RELAX!

One often wonders if the so-called young enthusiasts have missed the whole point of Vatican II and the *"aggiornamento."* Its stress is on *"interior renewal"* — all the *external* changes and developments are but means to this end, and woe to the individual who makes the awful mistake of confusing the two and taking the means for the end. People will never become holy by mere external devotion; no matter how well or how often they recite the liturgical formulas and sing in Church, unless there is true interior renewal; unless there is real heart and soul in their externals, all will be in vain. What the Council called for was what the Fathers set forth in their *Message to Humanity* issued on October 20, 1962, nine days after the Council opened: "In this assembly, under the guidance of the Holy Spirit, we wish to inquire how we ought to *renew ourselves*, so that we may be found increasingly faithful to the gospel of Christ."

Paul VI, as late as August 9, 1967, showed how the real purpose of *"aggiornamento"* was being missed by many when he said: "People are attempting to attribute to the Council every sort of new idea, especially in the manner of visualizing the Faith, and presenting it to the contemporary world, often calling into question fundamental doctrines of Catholicism, declaring matters of opinion to be truths defined by the Church, and claiming for freedom of conscience and the inspiration of the Holy Spirit a personal and arbitrary judgment concerning important, and at times, constitutional principles of thought and ecclesiastical discipline. A certain critical fervor seeks to justify this spiritual inquietude and to impute a hope for Christian renewal to the intentional stirring up of an impatient uneasiness regarding the traditional fashion of Catholic life and regarding the authoritative forms which recommend and promote it." Then after declining to examine the various visible forms these innovations are assuming, he turned to his audience and spoke to them "a simple word about the attitudes which should be assumed in face of such sprouting opinions. . ." Some he said seemed to think that they should separate themselves from "tradition, authority, philosophy, culture, canon law, institutions, and even certain dogmas, certain forms of interior life and worship" that have belonged to the Church. Do you recognize your "iconoclasts" in that word-picture? The Pope told these that if they separated themselves from all these they ran the danger of "losing the Faith with its security, its power, its peace."

To all others who would help the Church in its renewal he recommended: *"Awakening* and *Fidelity."*

To awaken you to fidelity to devotion to Our Lady-Mother — and her Rosary, let us look at the teacher John XXIII recommended: History . . .

Ours is not the first generation or century that has had to face a menace from the East or from Russia. In the early thirteenth century, without technology of any sort, without tanks, atomic artillery or jet planes, without any blundering on the part of those in the West such as we have seen, Genghis Khan with his powerful Tartars on their shaggy, swift horses, swept from northern China clean across Europe to where the Iron Curtain rests today. In the sixteenth century Suleiman the Magnificent with his terrorizing Turks did practically the same thing. In the following century the Turks were again hammering on the last strongholds of civilization in Europe. But what happened to all these swift conquerors? Khan passed away. Don Juan of Austria, in a well nigh "miraculous" victory in 1571 put an end to Suleiman and his conquests. And John Sobieski of Poland ended the Turkish threat by a similar victory before Vienna in 1683. With each of these triumphs Mary was connected. History will tell anyone who cares to look that it was her Rosary, along with Simon de Montfort, that stopped the spread of false doctrine in the late thirteenth century. And what does Fatima tell us but that "in the end her Immaculate Heart will triumph" — But on the condition that we pray her Rosary.

It was refreshing and a real cause to "relax and rejoice" to read the concluding words of Fr. Charles Sheedy C.S.C.'s address on *The New Morality.* After giving much that sounded like the avant garde, he returned to basics and said: "Think of being a Catholic in all the old ways. Don't think the Church is going soft or going Protestant. The new morality will actually be harder, not easier, because it will be less covered by detailed rules, less open to minimalism, more requiring of generosity and extra action. Love the Blessed Mother, say her Rosary, go to Confession and Holy Communion frequently, be a Catholic and be known as a Catholic, in the parish, in the neighborhood, and in the office. And do all these things with the large, forgiving and humble heart which is the gift of the Holy Spirit."

In these days when "all the old ways" are being attacked, it gives us ground for hope and optimism, and optimism that was well grounded and well expressed by another Holy Cross Father, John L. Reedy, editor of *Ave Maria*. "We base our optimism," he said, "on the recognition of a deepening understanding of what it really means to be a Christian in a world whose values are no longer Christian. We are optimistic because we can see more and more signs of true holiness under the fireworks of controversy and shrill statements and confusion. We are optimistic because we simply cannot avoid seeing this process of renewal as being the work of the Spirit, whose guidance was promised to the Church, even to the consummation of the world."

That Spirit is Spouse of Mary Immaculate. He will never allow His Bride to be dishonored. So relax — and really rejoice in the fact that Mary *is* our Mother. Then take the words of Paul VI to heart. As he neared the end of his *Signum Magnum* he turned to the Bishops of the world and said: "Venerable brothers, the persuasion that the thought of the Church regarding the veneration of praise, gratitude and love due to the most Blessed Virgin is in full accord with the doctrine of the holy Gospel, as it was more precisely understood and explained by the tradition of the East as well as of the West, stirs in our spirit the hope that this pastoral exhortation of Ours for an *ever more fervid and more fruitful Marian piety* will be received with generous acceptance not only by the faithful entrusted to your care, but also by those who, while not enjoying full communion with the Catholic Church, nevertheless, together with us, admire and venerate the handmaid of the Lord, the Virgin Mary, Mother of the Son of God."

We must, of course, listen to His Holiness rather than to the avant garde. He has the grace of his office. I know not what grace the avant gardists may have, but I am sure it is not that of the Chair of Peter. They can be the recipients of special light from the Holy Spirit so long as they are on earth. But we can be positive that the Holy Spirit will never contradict Himself — giving one charism to the Pope and a directly opposite one to the avant garde. So in this matter of Marian piety, take Paul VI's words to heart. He prays for an "ever more fervid and fruitful" devotion to Our Lady.

As said above: She *is* our Mother. That is a fact neither Pope, Council, avant garde, nor even God Himself can now change. So follow your nature — give heed to that "drive," "instinct," "inclination" — call it what you will — of a child to love its mother. Hold fast to that fact that she *is* your mother and you will never be led astray by sophisticated, but often sophistical, clichés used as a form of "brainwashing" by enthusiasts for change; nor will you ever be intimidated by big names in Theology or Scriptural Studies who may speculate in ways that, at best, can be called only fanciful.

Public practices of devotion to Our Lady-Mother may decline; in fact, they already must have — for only this spring I heard that at Boston College, where, in the not too distant past, May was always marked by special devotions to Our Lady, this year, in place of a "Procession" in her honor, or some similar external manifestation of praise, there was held what was called a "love-in" on the lawns. From what I have heard such things can be innocent enough, but surely no one will say they are better than such a thing as special meeting of the Sodality of Our Lady, or a May Procession in her honor, or even a Crowning of her statue. So, as I say, public manifestations of devotion to Mary may decline even more. But your private, personal love for her who *is* your Mother is to become, in the words of Paul VI, "ever more fervid and fruitful."

[237]

Which brings us to a consideration of a phrase used by Fr. Sheedy, C.S.C. in that talk of his about the "new morality" being "*harder*, not easier." Strictly speaking, that is not true; for again, strictly speaking, there is no such thing, nor can there be such a thing as a genuine *new* morality. There is, and there must be a new attitude, a new frame of mind, a new orientation toward the "ever ancient, ever new" morality. It is that of personal responsibility for the fulfillment of our duties toward God, self and neighbor. Take but one example: *Friday* — the *law* of abstinence has been taken away, but not the *duty* of showing God the Father we are grateful for what He and His Son "who was conceived by the Holy Spirit, born of the Virgin Mary," did for us by "suffering under Pontius Pilate" — being crucified, dying, and then rising again from the dead. We have not been freed from offering God some sign of our appreciation by some real "abstinence" — some real self-denial, some real penance. The "guideline" has gone; but the road we must travel is still before us.

Perhaps an example from everyday living will clarify the "new" attitude that is, and will later, perhaps, be more and more demanded of us. We have traffic lights in practically all our cities and towns. We have yellow lines on most of our highways. We have double lines on curves and other places where it is dangerous to pass. We all know these things are for our good — to save our lives ultimately speaking, and, more immediately speaking, to enable us to drive more safely and more speedily, really; for if there were no traffic signals, no traffic lights, no traffic laws, imagine the chaos. Imagine the slaughter! All these lights and lines and laws are for the common good, and for our own personal good. Thus they are ultimately for the good of the State and Country. Suppose for a moment that all traffic lights, traffic lines, and traffic laws were done away with. Would that give us the liberty to drive on the left side of the road, to pass on blind curves, to drive through intersections with utter disregard for self and others? Not among civilized people. Not among truly rational animals. Never among intelligent, and responsible individuals. The operative words are civilized, rational, and especially *respon-*

sible. We are free persons; therefore, we are responsible agents. The adult person would never drive without care for self and for others whether there be laws, lines, or lights or not. So, too, with regard to true morality. Definite laws are like traffic lines, traffic lights, and traffic legislation. Remove them and we still remain bound to be responsible, rational, civilized and Christian people. So if some "lights" are turned off, some "lines" rubbed out, some laws abrogated, I am still not free to do as I like, but only, as I am now with all the laws, lines, and lights still known and visible: free to do what I *ought.* But just as it is easier now to drive correctly with all these guidelines apparent, so it will be "harder" — in the sense that I will have to be more adult, more rational, and more responsible, as it were, in the time of the so-called "new morality." I am a creature, therefore, positive law or no positive law, I am obliged to worship my Creator — to love my God.

Let every precept of the Church be scratched out, let every man-made law in Religion be abrogated, I am still bound by the "law of Christ" to love — God, myself and my neighbor. Let every rule and custom among Religious be done away with, every Religious would still be bound by that fundamental directive of Jesus Christ to "take up his cross daily, and follow Him." But, without the "guidelines" of the customs and the Rules, it would be "harder" for each individual to become what he is — a follower of Christ, for it would require much more maturity than most of the human race ever attain.

But it is this sense of responsibility, this maturity, this adulthood that is the ultimate aim and the real purpose of the *"aggiornamento"* of Vatican II. Renewal will be had when we recognize and discharge our real responsibilities — and do it, as it were, on our own, out of love. Thus will we "be made worthy of the promises of Christ."

But we would be fools not to plead daily: "Pray for us, O Holy Mother of God. . ." that we attain to this sense of responsibility and to the discharge of all the real responsibilities that are ours. For she *is* our Mother. Hence, the shortened form of

[239]

the prayer so universally used before the "downgrading" by some — the *Memorare*, which has been attributed to my father, St. Bernard — can be used with judiciousness in these days of change: "Mother, help us! You can't say you can't; for you are His Mother. You won't say you won't; for your are our Mother. So you will, won't you?"

She will, I promise; for she has been rightfully called "*Omnipotentia Supplex*"; which really means she can't be refused by God. Further, she should be called upon in this manner; for, as Pope after Pope has recalled: St. Bernard was right when he said: "Such is the Will of God that we should receive everything through Mary." If you think that strange or exaggerated, just pause long enough to reflect on what you have actually received through your own mother. Has it not been, at least radically, just about everything?

Mother Mary, who is "Virgin Most Prudent," "Mother of Fair Love," and "Our Lady of Good Counsel" will get all you need in the way of prudence, counsel and love, to implement Vatican II as God wishes you to. You will be neither "progressive," nor "conservative." You will be "Catholic." You will be neither "extreme right wing" nor "extreme left wing" — but only and always prudently "Catholic." You will be in the middle where wisdom tells us virtue always stands. You will never say: "Only the Bible" nor "No need of the Bible" but "Both the Bible and the Living *Magisterium* which authentically interprets the Bible." You will never say "No Theology, but only the living Word of God as found in Scripture" nor "Theology alone suffices for me." You will be a Catholic of Vatican II and say: "Biblical Theology with sound tradition". So with prayer and worship. It will never be "Only communal worship and Liturgical prayer," or "Only private prayer and individual worship." You will show yourself one striving for the renewal sought by "*aggiornamento*" by manifesting love for the Liturgy *and* for private devotions. The same attitude regarding what some, I think very mistakenly, term "legalism" and its opposite extreme "the one law of love" — without any positive legislation whatsoever. You, knowing human nature, recognize the need for positive legislation. But knowing, again, your elevated state of being one who has a "super-nature," thanks to God's grace; you are free from anything like what is rightly called legalism. Being a Catholic of the time of Vatican II you will be an alert, responsible, mature, adult, balanced person — who will neither idolize tradition nor change — but holding fast to what is right and good of the past, will adapt to the needs of the present under the able direction of the authentic and authoritative teaching body of the Church, and stretch forward to the future in which you will have, as far as in you lies, the face of Christ shining out upon all men from within your real self as *Christ*-ian. You will realize ever anew that *you* are His *member* — and that *she* is your *Mother*.

It is that last realization that will urge anyone and everyone on to true renewal; for we know something about the daily renewal in our physical bodies, and can see the necessity for daily renewal in Christ's Mystical Body; further, since we find our hearts ever on our lips saying: "Show thyself a Mother," we hear in our keenly God-conscious and Christ-conscious souls her maternal reply: "Show yourselves my children."

Six times in less than a hundred years lately, Our Lady-Mother has appeared: at Paris, Lourdes, La Salette, Pontmain, Fatima, Beauraing — and we can quite safely add the seventh, Banneaux. Yet she has had one message for us, her children. It was, and is, identical with that of the Gospel and the latest Council. It was a call for *metanoia* — a change of heart, mind, will, orientation of whole being toward GOD by prayer and penance. That is the *"aggiornamento"* or which we — and the entire world — will daily, and even hourly, ever stand in need. We can have it through Mary and thus become "worthy of the Promises of Christ." We will have it through Mary if we pray:

> Maid who wed Infinity,
> Clay that shaped Divinity,
> Lady of the Trinity
> *Life is filled with fears.*

RELAX!

Golden Wheat that made the Host,
Mortal Woman loved the most
By Father, Son, and Holy Ghost,
    Life is wet with tears.

Flame of Wisdom, Holy Shrine,
Chalice of the Bread and Wine,
Vineyard that produced The Vine,
    Death speeds like a dart.

Immaculate Virginity,
God-filled Feminity
Lady of the Trinity,
    *Keep me in your Heart!**

That she will do gladly, because she *is* our Mother and we *are* His members.

* (From MARTIN, by Eddie Doherty, New York, 1951—With permission of the Author)

[242]

Three views of Irish Trappist abbey in ruins. It was destroyed by Cromwell about the year 1550.

The Irish people, for a WEEK OF CENTURIES, suffered persecution. For 700 years they lost homes, churches, monasteries, and their lives, too — but never lost their faith. American Catholics, in this late time, should not lose their faith.

DON'T STEP OUT OF THE BOAT!

We opened this book by looking at Peter's boat rolling in a turbulent sea — long, long ago on the Lake of Tiberias. We saw sturdy fishermen, capable in any sea, really frightened. Then, over the tumbling waves, we saw One walking, and above the violent winds we heard His voice: "Take heart! It is I . . . Do not be afraid." (Mt. 14:27) We had hardly adverted to the parallel between that boat that night and "Peter's Bark" — the Holy, Roman, Catholic Church — wallowing in the winds of change that have stirred up such a vicious sea, when we heard Peter calling: "Master, if it is you, tell me to come to you over the waters." We heard Jesus say: "Come!" and we watched bold Peter actually walk on water — until he "lost his nerve."

We close this book by telling you "Don't step out of the boat . . ." for the angry sea in which Peter's Bark is riding will not completely subside for some years to come. One would be dishonest if he did not tell you something similar to what G. K. Chesterton had Our Lady say to King Alfred in his celebrated poem *The White Horse:*

I tell you naught for your comfort, yea, naught for your desire
Save that the sky grows darker yet and the sea rises higher.

To implement Vatican II fully will not only take time; it will take all the Faith and fidelity of all the People of God. That Faith will be tried; that fidelity, challenged. For as the winds of change keep blowing, many voices will be heard above the waters — not all of them will have the same tone — or truth! So "don't step out of the boat" unless you clearly hear Christ Himself calling you — as He did Peter. It can be doubted that He will call many. It can be doubted whether He will call any.

[245]

But it cannot be doubted that He is saying to all of us what He said to those in Peter's boat that night: "Take heart! It is I. . . Do not be afraid!"

If you stay in the boat — as wisdom tells you you should — you will hear another Voice — and see Someone else above the waters. As there is once again some "darkness over the deep," just as there was at the "first creation," so, too, if we peer through the darkness of our day not with our eyes of flesh, but with our eyes of Faith, we will see "brooding" over our waters the same Spirit who "hovered over the water" when "the earth was a formless void and there was darkness over the deep." It is now, as it was then, "God's Spirit" — the Holy Spirit.

As you look out from Peter's Bark today and with the clear vision that comes from lively Faith, see the Christ walking upon the waters, if you listen, as you should with those ears attuned to the Voice of God, you will hear what was heard at the Jordan after John the Baptist had poured water over the Christ "This is my Son, the Beloved . . ." It is the Voice of the Father — He is talking to you! Listen closely — and hear clearly — for there are many other voices above the storm and in it . . . You will hear some say: "Never has the Church been so creative" — and others cry: "Never have things been so chaotic." One voice will claim we are "passing through another Pentecost — the Flame of the Holy Spirit is falling upon us all." Another will lament that there are those today who are actually "tampering with the very Soul of the Church" — and you know the same Holy Spirit who fell as Flame is actually the Church's vivifying Soul. There are those who anxiously, when not angrily, say there are too many "irresponsible, irrepressible extremists" making "scandalous statements" for the sensation-loving Press. While others, like the late Monsignor Conway, will tell you that "The Spirit of Christ is rampant in a world that needs that Spirit badly." Bishop John Wright will tell you that there is "both excitement and bewilderment." Paul VI will echo the Christ and say: "Blessed is he who is not scandalized." You will be amongst those "blessed" — for you will heed our directive:

"Don't step out of the boat . . ." You will be amongst those "blessed" — for, while recognizing the certain degree of truth in every statement, you will distinguish above them all and among them all that Voice which has all truth; you will heed the Voice Peter, James, and John heard at the Transfiguration — "This is my Son, the Beloved; he enjoys my favor. *Listen to him.*" It is the Voice of the Father telling us to heed, in these dark and troublous times when "the skies may grow darker still and the seas rise higher," the one Voice worthy of all attention — the Voice of Christ. How can we distinguish it above the whistling winds and the many haughty cries and calls? It is quite simple. Christ said: "Anyone who listens to you, listens to me" (Lc. 10:16) That was addressed not to sound speculative theologians, not to learned Scripture scholars, but only to those disciples He was then sending out to teach — and, by consequence, to those whom He has empowered to teach us today — the *Magisterium*. That is the Voice of Christ talking to us quite tranquilly above the turbulence of the times and saying precisely what Christ said that night of the storm at sea: "Do not be afraid."

You will hear things that can trouble one. False freedom and foolish pride will assail the very one Christ called to teach His truth with His authority. That will seem to some like scuttling the ship of the Church. It would be, if it were effective. But it will ever be nothing but false and foolish. Individual opinions will be offered as substitutes for sound Sacred Theology. Subjective feelings will be followed instead of the objective Moral Law. Persons without qualification or training will be heard pronouncing, yes, even "pontificating" on the most difficult, intricate, and delicate matters in Moral and Dogmatic Theology — and will be furnishing fodder for the ever hungry sensation-seeking Press. The Home and the sanctity of Marriage; the School and its right to educate religiously; the Church itself with all its God-given prerogatives, will be openly, haughtily, and fiercely attacked even by those who come from good Catholic homes, have been thoroughly educated from kindergarten to University

[247]

degree in Catholic schools, and have long been nourished by Holy Mother Church. It was so in the beginning — Judas was "one of the Twelve." It will be so until the end — "it must needs be that scandals come," said the Christ. But you will never be scandalized, for you will remain among those who stay in the bark of Peter and both see the Christ above the waters and hear HIS Voice above the storm.

We all know a new world is springing up all around us. We also know that it is pregnant with countless new and amazing possibilities — and one of the most important is the winning of that world to and for Christ. That possibility can be made actual not by any "new Christ" — but only by many *renewed* Christians.

Today "newness" is all around us in almost an infinite variety of forms. We have new Math, new Physics, new Psychology, new Philosophy, new Astronomy, not to speak of the new Art and Music. Hence, there is no call for excitement or even of surprise that there are those who are crying for a "new Church," a "new Christ," a "new Religion" to save this whole new world. Of course it is absurd to ask for such newness, but that is the one element that is not "new" in the cries of many — for absurdity has never been wanting among humans.

Two further quotes from Gilbert K. Chesterton are in place here. Since so many of these voices are crying for an "open mind," it is well to tell them what the astute Chesterton told the same kind of clamorers of his time: "The purpose of an open mind is identical with that of an open mouth: to close over something solid." We of the *"aggiornamento,"* who listen to the Church and look to Christ, have that kind of mind and we use it as one should his open mouth. We clamp down with vigor on the sound, solid, substantial doctrine given us by the *Magisterium.* That we "chew," "swallow," "digest," "assimilate" — and thus make *live.* The second quote may be even more apropos. Chesterton said "Christianity has never been tried and found wanting. It has been tried and found hard." That could be the trouble with some of those who are crying for a "new Christ". . .

FATHER M. RAYMOND, O.C.S.O.

If there is no need for a "new Christ" — there is demand for *renewed* Christians. For we — and the Church herself — recognize that it is not the Church of Christ that has been tried and found lacking in what will fulfill the needs of our times. It is rather that we have never thoroughly tried — tried to be all the Church of Christ asks and enables us to be. Our commitment has never been complete; our involvement never entire; between our good resolutions and our full execution of the same, the gap has been embarrassingly wide. Our "putting off the old man" has never been stripping to the bone; our "putting on Christ" has always left something to be desired. The point is that we need no new Religion and most certainly no new Christ, but what we do need is the "new man" — who came forth in the "new creation" — as he came to know a "new life." We need the fullness of the Paschal Mystery lived in our own bodies and souls as we walk the ways of the world today. We have all that newness from Baptism; hence, we have in ourselves, but not of ourselves, everything our new day calls for — Amidst all the changes that are, and yet will be, the call of the times is really for the Changeless Christ — So we can relax amidst all the tensions of our very tense times, and rejoice amidst all the glooms and fears of these frightening days, because we are in that bark which can never founder, the one launched by Him who not only walks on waters, but whose voice commands both winds and waves . . . the Changeless Jesus Christ, who is ever immutable amidst all mutations.

Have you noted the changelessness in all the changes of Vatican II? The Constitution on the Church calls us now "The People of God" and names us "The Pilgrim Church." That is what can be called changelessness amidst change. For before we were called the "society" — that perfect society founded by Christ. Since a society is made up of people — and Christ is God, you see the changelessness in the change. Before we were "wayfarers" — making our way through the world to our heavenly home. Now we are the "Pilgrim Church" — But what is a pilgrim save one who is on his way — and ultimately on his way home?

Now we are "the Mystery of Christ." Before we were His Mystical Body. Before there were two fonts which blended to make the one river of Revelation. Today there is one Revelation that comes from the two fonts of Scripture and Tradition. At the birth of this Century we heard again and again about the Liturgy being the indispensible source of Christian life, what does Vatican II tell us as this Century nears its demise? And so one might course through the sixteen Documents that came from the Council and find amidst all the changes very definite changelessness; for the Church is Christ, is the Whole Christ, and He, as Paul told us, is "yesterday, today, and the same forever."

That oneness of ours in the Changeless Christ should end all this futile separation fostered by those who are fond of labels: The New Breed and the Old Guard; The Now Generation — and The Command Generation; The Progressives and The Conservatives; The Non-conformists and The Conformists; The Followers of Love — and The Followers of Law; Vatican II Catholics and The Catholics of Trent; Those who are free with the freedom of the children of God — and Those who obey like slaves. As we have been saying: "We are all in the same boat" — the bark of Peter — and in this time of "*aggiornamento*" none of us should "rock the boat" — let alone abandon ship!

Is it the part of wisdom, let alone of love, to stress differences, rather than to emphasize similarities? There are "senior citizens" — even in the Church, and there are also "bright young men." But, basically, how different are they? Haven't they, in the Church, the one same Lord, one same Faith, one same Baptism? Are they not members of the one same Body? Are they not riding the waters on the world in the one same bark?

A lawyer friend of mine, Edward B. Hanify, of Belmont, Massachusetts, did a masterly bit of work toward bringing light to this darkened area between the generations, as he addressed the graduates of a Jesuit institution in the east. After giving all the various actual differences between the generation that was graduating and the generation of the parents of those graduates, he turned and said: "We are much more alike than we are different. Our unity should go to essential matters, our differences to accidental and non-essentials. Love — filial and paternal — is the solvent of all differences. We have so much to do together — and such a little time in which to do it — and so very much in common, that we must cease concentrating on our alleged separatism and analyse together our common problems."

That is very excellent advice for the supposedly separate "generations" in the Church. We have so much to do together — and such a little time in which to do it! "There is nothing startling or shocking," this man continued "about the phenomenon of unrest or discontent or desire for change among young people. Let me read you an account of a certain era in history. The author says: 'It was a time of experiment. Never was there a time when the young were so young, or the old, so old. There were strange pale youths with abundant hair. The rising generation felt as if it were stepping out of the stages of convention and custom into a wider freedom full of tremendous possibilities. An imp of disquiet was abroad scattering words of interrogation like confetti of fire among cherished principles and customs. The young men enjoyed the fun as they rushed about smashing up the intellectual and moral furniture of their parents."

My friend then asked: "Was that written about the nineteen forties — or the nineteen twenties? No — it is a description of the younger generation of the eighteen nineties. There is nothing new about 'imps of disquiet,' or 'smashing up parental intellectual and moral furniture,' or even 'strange pale youths with abundant hair.' Somehow the good furniture eventually escapes destruction, even if the junk gets scrapped; the long hair gets shorn, and the race goes on — no worse because of the enthusiasm and idealism of youth which has forced an examination of the conscience and the premises of the age."

Next there was an examination of the assertion that never had any two similar generations had such diverse experiences in their formative years, hence the impossibility of similar intellectual or emotional — perhaps even of ethical and religious — reactions to problems of the present. You have heard that. I have heard it.

[251]

RELAX!

Who hasn't heard it? But now listen to Mr. Hanify: "You have been nurtured in the era of the atom and the missile; the exploration of space, the explosion of knowledge, and the updating of the Church. Hence, it will be argued that there is a tremendous gulf between you and your fathers. But, I ask you: were we of the older generation on a leave of absence from mankind when all this took place? Many of us were in uniform when the first bomb was exploded at Alamorgordo on July 17, 1945. Our own youth was hardly spent in a sea of tranquillity. My first impression of war is the sound of church bells ringing out the Armistice of 1918 and the parade of returning 'doughboys.' We ran from the school yard in wonder when the first airplane we ever saw flew overhead. The radio with its earphones and the first family Oldsmobile with its isinglass were strange new phenomena. Then there was the Depression with its bread lines — and the gathering storm in Europe and Asia. So, we have had, in addition to the *new* experiences taking place in your lifetimes, quite a few *new* experiences of our own when we were in grade school, high school, and college. It is well then for your generation to keep in mind that the novelties of this disturbed century have affected your fathers' and mothers' lives as well as your own. These great and dramatic changes in human life should not create a chasm between our generations. We each have been, in varying degrees, a generation of violent changes. The experience should unite — not separate us."

What was true of the fathers and sons at that graduation can be said with equal truth about the priests who have been the spiritual fathers to the younger generation among clergy and laity today. We have been through the theological and scriptural barrages of the past and present century. We have battled "modern morals and mores" both in our day and in yours. These facts should unite, not separate us.

As my friend said: "We are children of the twentieth century — with a few decades of living between us, and the great heritage of our membership in the People of God to unify us. The worst mistake we can make is in dealing with each other as isolated armies fighting by night on a darkened plain — and blaming each other for the ills of the world. Young people frequently look at the older generation and then at Vietnam, the Middle East, and the Ghetto, and say: 'What a mess you have left us!' Those of us who lived through the disruption of the Depression and World War II were tempted to feel the same about the generation which preceded us — until we recalled that they had valiantly fought and died 'to make the world safe for Democracy'. They, in turn, doubtless resented the whole series of international power plays taking place before their time which sowed the seeds for the First World War. The process of blaming prior generations for the current state of the world finally gets us back to Adam and Eve and Original Sin. There is not much sense or profit in blaming our first parents for that primordial estrangement from their Creator. But there are awesome, yet essential, truths affecting human destiny in the account of mankind's original Fall, truths which every generation must recognize and which should unify us in awareness of our common peril and our common hope as we march together toward eternity. There is the Original Sin itself, man's initial revolt against his Maker. There is its inheritance of the weakened will and the darkened intellect. There is Satan on one hand to aid and abet the human anti-God revolution as he had fomented and led the anti-God revolution of the Angels in aeons of time before. . . Satan incarnate, immortal hate, whom our sophisticated age would like to ignore, as he prowls incognito through the iniquities of our time. Then there is Calvary — consummated promise of Redemption — eternal Love.

"Can any difference of years, or experience, separate the generations which ponder life's terrible choices between good and evil in the light of these realities? If we grasp their significance, the process of useless 'buck passing' between the generations stops. We of different generations are then triumphantly united on essentials, aware of our common dangers, yet confident that religious Faith gives us the invincible means for ultimate victory."

[253]

Do you see the appositeness of all this for the People of God? We who are a little older should show a little more wisdom than youth, and by patience with their enthusiasms, and humble, loving kindness toward them, as we point out excesses, we should unite in the common awareness of the dangers to the Mystical Body of Christ — as well as be ever more united in that confidence of ultimate victory for Christ.

My friend's peroration can serve as close to this endeavor to get us all to be what Christ prayed that we be: *one!* — and especially *one in Him!* Mr. Hanify claimed that the predilection of each generation for its own words should be nothing more than a very minor abrasive and not produce a yawning chasm between the generations. Very wisely he said: "If you like the term 'self-expression' and we like the term 'discipline,' let us both remember that all the great human achievements in self-expression were achieved through self-discipline. If you like the term 'love,' and we like the term 'obedience,' let us both remember that Christ said: 'If you love me, keep my Commandments.' If you like the term 'freedom' and we like the term 'authority,' let us both remember that true freedom is liberty to do what one *ought* — not what one pleases — and 'oughtness' implies authority. In the lexicon of thoughtful men, self-expression is not hostile to self-discipline, love is not the enemy, but the source of obedience, and authority is the friend, not the foe, of freedom. On these essentials, again we are united!

"As I conclude, may I suggest that you are going to have at least one exciting experience which your fathers and mothers will not share — at least in the same numbers or with the same vitality. You are going to see the twentieth century close and witness the birth of a new century. There has generally been a remarkable quickening of life, and a burst of explosive developments, as a century closes. The fifteenth century closed with the Renewal of Learning and Columbus' discovery of the New World. The sixteenth century closed with the destruction of the Armada, and the appearance of Shakespeare, Ben Johnson, Spencer, Marlowe and Bacon. The eighteenth rang down its curtain with the

French Revolution and the First Consulate of Napoleon. So you are truly a unique generation — the generation which will be in full maturity when the twentieth century ends. That means that you will be the 'Command Generation' of the Twenty-First Century. As you assume that responsible role, many of us from 'the hid battlements of eternity' will be watching and cheering you on. You may even imagine that you hear us proudly saying: 'Our boys are in charge.' "

Changing what has to be changed in that address, but seeing also the parallel between spiritual parents and those who physically generated the youth of today, you can understand why I say: *Let us all stay in the one boat* — the bark of Peter. Don't go "over the side" — either to the right or to the left. Don't try walking on water! But look over the waters — with the eyes of Faith — and listen to the Voice above the winds. He who walks above the waves will be praying: "Now Father, it is time for you to glorify me. . . I have made your name known to the men you took from the world to give me. . . I pray for them: I am not praying for the world. . . I am not in the world any longer, but they are in the world. . . Holy Father, keep those you have given me true to your name so that they may be one. . . May they all be one, Father, may they be one in us . . ."

Isn't that reason enough to relax and rejoice?